Gordon R. Willey and American Archaeology

Gordon R. Willey and American Archaeology

Contemporary Perspectives

Edited by Jeremy A. Sabloff
and William L. Fash

University of Oklahoma Press : Norman

Library of Congress Cataloging-in-Publication Data

Gordon R. Willey and American archaeology : contemporary perspectives / edited by Jeremy A. Sabloff and William L. Fash.
     p.   cm.
   Includes index.
   ISBN-13: 978-0-8061-3805-3 (hardcover : alk. paper)
   ISBN-10: 0-8061-3805-X (hardcover : alk. paper)
   1. Archaeology—America.   2. Indians—Antiquities.   3. Willey, Gordon Randolph, 1913–   4. Indianists—Biography.   5. Archaeologists—America—Biography.   6. America—Antiquities.   I. Sabloff, Jeremy A.   II. Fash, William Leonard.
   E61.G76 2007
   973.072'02—dc22

                                                                    2006027684

The paper in this book meets the guidelines for permanence and durability of the Committee on Production Guidelines for Book Longevity of the Council on Library Resources, Inc. ∞

1 2 3 4 5 6 7 8 9 10

Contents

List of Illustrations   vii

List of Tables   x

Acknowledgments   xi

Introduction, *William L. Fash*   3

1   Gordon R. Willey and the Archaeology
of the Florida Gulf Coast, *Jerald T. Milanich*   15

2   Peru: Willey's Formative Years, *Michael E. Moseley*   26

3   Legacies of Gordon Willey's
Belize Valley Research, *Wendy Ashmore*   41

4   Willey and Phillips, *Richard M. Leventhal
and Deborah Erdman Cornavaca*   61

5   Great Art Styles and the Rise of Complex Societies,
Joyce Marcus   72

6   The Intermediate Area and Gordon Willey,
     Jeffrey Quilter   105

7   Serendipity at Seibal, *Gair Tourtellot
     and Norman Hammond*   126

8   The Classic Maya "Collapse" and Its Causes,
     Prudence M. Rice   141

9   A Crossroads of Conquerors, *David A. Freidel,
     Hector L. Escobedo, and Stanley P. Guenter*   187

10   Culture Heroes and Feathered Serpents,
     Patricia A. McAnany   209

     Conclusion, *Jeremy A. Sabloff*   233

     List of Contributors   237

     Index   241

Illustrations

Figures

I.1. Gordon Willey at the Smithsonian Institution, 1946   5

I.2. Willey, second from left, with mentor Byron
      Cummings, circa 1934   7

I.3. Studio portrait of Willey, 1972   13

1.1. Willey, fourth from left, at the Ocmulgee site, 1936   17

1.2. Wood-paneled station wagon that Willey
      and Richard Woodbury used in the field, 1940   19

1.3. Chart from Willey and Woodbury's 1942 article
      on northwest Florida   20

3.1. Willey in an excavation at Barton Ramie   42

3.2. Reconnaissance map of prehistoric Maya settlements
      in the Belize Valley   44

3.3.   Map of Barton Ramie site   45

3.4.   Willey, Richard Leventhal, and Wendy Ashmore
        at Copán, 1976   52

5.1.   Mexican motifs representing Earth and
        the four world directions   77

5.2.   Mexican art depicting man's relationship with fierce
        animals and supernatural forces   78

5.3.   Gulf Coast Mexican art depicting men wearing
        headdresses and helmets   79

5.4.   Pre-Chavín art featuring warriors, trophy heads,
        and butchered remains of victims   82

5.5.   Raptorial birds in Chavín art   87

5.6.   Chavín art featuring fierce animals and warriors   88

5.7.   Chavín art featuring caymans   89

5.8.   Tenoned heads, facade of the New Temple,
        Chavín de Huántar, Peru   90

5.9.   The crocodile in chiefly art   92

5.10.   Fierce animals and warriors from Panama and Colombia   94

5.11.   Ancestors and warriors featured in Maori art   95

5.12.   Maori pendants   97

7.1.   Seibal Stela 1   129

7.2.   Willey, second from left, at Seibal, 1968   130

7.3.   Seibal Structure A-3 after restoration in 1968   131

7.4.   Jadeite celts and blue jade "stiletto" bloodletter
        from Seibal   132

7.5.   Willey at Seibal, 1965   137

9.1.   Map of western Petén and the Usumacinta region
        showing location of Waka'   188

9.2.   Reassembled fragments of Stela 15   194

9.3.   Stela 16   198

9.4.   Detail of Stela 16   201

9.5.   Detail of Stela 15   202

9.6.   Examples of Teotihuacan-style fire darts from Copán   202

10.1.   Highland culture hero Ce Acatl Topiltzin Quetzalcoatl   219

10.2.   Excavated portion of a circular shrine at
        the Samuel Oshon site, lower Sibun Valley, Belize   221

10.3.   Conch shells found at the Augustine Obispo site,
        lower Sibun Valley, Belize   222

10.4.   Bird and coyote/jaguar cartouches from Pakal Na,
        Sibun Valley, Belize   224

Tables

8.1.   "Warfare"-related Maya words   157

8.2.   "Warfare"-related events in the southern Maya Lowlands   158

8.3.   Classic-period "warfare"-related events by type
       and Gregorian month   161

8.4.   "War"-related events by type and Maya "month"   162

8.5.   K'atun endings at fifty-nine-year intervals and on
       maximum elongation of Venus as evening star   170

10.1. Frequency of the term "ideology" in anthropology
       and archaeology journals, 1966–2002   213

Acknowledgments

The editors gratefully acknowledge a number of people who were instrumental in making the publication of this book possible. This volume started its life during the 2003 annual meeting of the Society for American Archaeology, in Milwaukee, Wisconsin, at the Sponsored Session of the Archaeology Division of the American Anthropological Association. We thank both organizations for their support in making the session possible (and well attended!). Our gratitude and thanks also go to all of our contributors, who rose to the occasion—on several occasions! They did this first with high-quality, timely contributions at the session, then with quick turnarounds of their initial papers for review, and lastly with the final versions, illustrations, and supplementary data needed by the University of Oklahoma Press. At OU Press we would particularly like to thank Alessandra Jacobi Tamulevich and Jo Ann Reece, as well as the editorial division. All the contributors benefited from the comments of two anonymous reviewers, to whom we are all grateful. We would like to extend special thanks to Linda Ordogh, assistant to the director at the Peabody Museum, for her many hours of careful reformatting, collating, cross-checking, and assembling of the many essays in the volume. William

Fash would also like to thank her for editorial input on the introduction to the volume.

We also acknowledge with deep appreciation the many ways in which Gordon Willey shaped our professional lives and those of countless others in the field of archaeology. The royalties for this volume will go to the endowment for the Gordon R. Willey Award of the Archaeology Division of the American Anthropological Association. We believe this to be a fitting destination because Willey served as the association's president and because the award is given to archaeologists whose writing and research enhance our profession.

JEREMY A. SABLOFF

WILLIAM L. FASH

Gordon R. Willey and American Archaeology

Introduction

William L. Fash

In this volume we invite the reader to reflect on the scholarly life and contributions of Gordon Randolph Willey, a gentleman and a scholar for the ages. We hope that this book will impart a sense of what made Gordon Willey such an outstanding figure in our profession, illuminating how his personality and intellect left their mark on American archaeology. Many readers will remember their first meeting with Gordon and the sense of awe and trepidation that almost imperceptibly turned to lively conversation and intellectual exchange. His gift for bringing out the best in colleagues and students alike was an integral part of why he was such an esteemed leader in his field. His passing gives us an occasion to consider the depth and breadth of his professional contributions.

In this section I will introduce the book's chapters, each of which examines a different aspect of Willey's broad-based and prolific contributions to American archaeology. When Jerry Sabloff and I discussed assembling a book of essays to honor and gauge the impact of Gordon Willey's contributions to the field of American archaeology, there were many paths open to us. Jerry suggested that we assess Willey's legacy by selecting certain of his key publications and soliciting assessments of them from pivotal players in the relevant arenas. We selected ten of Willey's published works that cross-cut geographic regions and areas of inquiry and that, to our way of thinking, reflect our mentor's contributions to field archaeology, innovations in method and theory, the history of the discipline, and archaeological synthesis. The chapters (and the introduction) provide an evaluation of these works, in chronological order from his earliest work to some of his latest. In this way we hope to give the reader a sense of the cumulative nature both of Willey's contributions to American archaeology and of the larger field in which they played a leading role. Those interested in a more biographical treatment may enjoy reading some of the appreciations that have appeared since his parting. Willey's own views about his life are laid out in his autobiographical chapter in *The Pastmasters: Eleven Modern Pioneers of Archaeology* and interwoven throughout his *Portraits in American Archaeology* (1988).

As all Americanist archaeologists know, Gordon Willey had impeccable credentials as a field archaeologist because of his substantive and theoretical contributions to the prehistory of North, Central, and South America. He was particularly devoted to studies of ceramics and other artifacts and interested in what such studies could tell us about what he called "space-time systematics." James Ford was a powerful force in Willey's early professional development, framing what was easily one of the most interesting chapters in Willey's long and productive life. Ford was one of the few archaeologists that Gordon referred to as a genius, the possessor of a tremendously creative and inquisitive mind. It was with Ford that Willey immersed himself in the study of prehistoric pottery and in the insights that such study could provide into "the big picture" (another of Willey's favorite expressions) of cultural change and exchange, through time and space, in the southeastern United States. Jerald Milanich masterfully explores the depth and breadth of Willey's contributions to the archaeology of the Florida Gulf Coast while providing the reader with a keen appreciation of the young archaeologist's formidable skills.

Willey and Ford were both considered important innovators in archaeological method and theory and ceramic analysis, and they enhanced their reputation with their subsequent work in South America. When Willey was in graduate school at Columbia, under the tutelage of Duncan Strong, his research and teaching allowed him to look at space-time systematics on a continental scale. Willey was to pursue and expand this interest during his postdoctoral work with Julian Steward in compiling the monumental *Hand-*

Figure I.1. Gordon Willey at the Smithsonian Institution, with an aerial photograph of the Virú Valley in the background, 1946. Courtesy of the Peabody Museum.

book of South American Indians (see fig. I.1). Michael Moseley's chapter gives us profound insight into the importance of Willey's research in coastal Peru to both his own development and that of the field of Andean archaeology. Willey's innovative plunge into settlement pattern studies in the Virú Valley allowed him to pursue his interest in examining ancient landscapes through both space and time in ways that had not previously been possible. With characteristic modesty, Willey occasionally attributed this contribution more to Julian Steward's thinking and the tenacity of James Ford in the field than to his own efforts. But this new way of seeing the larger picture dovetailed nicely with Willey's fascination with looking at change on a regional level. He later wrote that his work in Peru also taught him how unwieldy and difficult multidisciplinary, multi-institutional research projects could be.

Wendy Ashmore explores how Willey's next great foray, into the Maya field, forever transformed the archaeology of Mesoamerica through his application of the settlement pattern approach to the Belize Valley of the southern Maya Lowlands. Upon his arrival at Harvard's Peabody Museum, in 1950, Willey initially planned to slowly dig his way up from Panama to the Maya area in order to place the accomplishments of the Classic Maya in a broader cultural and geographical frame of reference. He loved recounting how Alfred Tozzer persuaded him to move rather more quickly northward. Willey's initial work in Belize was followed by several other important multiseason projects, in Altar de Sacrificios and Seibal, Guatemala, and then in Copán, Honduras, all of which used multiple approaches and data sets to examine the leading questions of the day and all of which were grounded, as Ashmore notes, in the study of settlements.

Willey's long-term interest in method and theory in archaeology, and in the history of the field, dated from 1937, the year he completed his master's thesis under Byron Cummings at the University of Arizona (see fig. I.2). This fascination with the thought processes of archaeologists and with how they put their thoughts into action in their field research shines through clearly in Willey's memoir, *Portraits in American Archaeology*. Willey's first book to examine these issues was the highly influential *Method and Theory in American Archaeology*, which he wrote with his friend and colleague Philip Phillips. Richard Leventhal and Deborah Cornavaca demonstrate the importance of this often cited volume by carefully considering the context in which it was prepared and published. In his writings and teaching, Willey always emphasized the cumulative aspects of archaeology, rightly noting that all excellent archaeological publications are built upon the solid foundation created by earlier works in the field. While he praised what had been done well in previous archaeological endeavors, he did not shy away from critically evaluating what could have been done better. He and Robert Braidwood put together an important volume called *Archaeological Researches in Retrospect*, in which the contributors were encouraged to examine the positive contributions of their research projects while suggesting ways that similar projects could be improved upon in the future. *A History of American Archaeology*, which Willey and Jeremy Sabloff subsequently produced and so compellingly revised over the years, continues to be a benchmark in the field.

The next great innovation that Willey proposed for the study of the ancient Americas was the archaeological consideration of art as a means of assessing the causative role of ideology in culture change. His presidential

Figure I.2. Gordon Willey, second from the left, and other University of Arizona archaeology students with their mentor, Byron Cummings, circa 1934. Courtesy of the Peabody Museum.

address to the American Anthropological Association (AAA), published in 1961, examined the emergence of what he referred to as the "great art styles" in both Mesoamerica and the Andes, and it considered the role played by these styles' underlying ideology in the rise of civilization in both culture areas. Willey was fascinated with the big picture throughout his life, and he always encouraged his students to pursue a far-reaching approach. Anyone who visited his office was treated to the portraits, on the wall behind him, of distinguished Americanists, of whom he dryly said, "You've gotta be dead to be on that wall." But what Gordon looked at, all the way across the room on the opposite wall, were two very large maps: North and Central America on the left and South America on the right. Despite proudly introducing himself to new acquaintances as "a Maya archaeologist," he retained his grand vision throughout his career.

Willey's presidential address "The Early Great Styles and the Rise of the Pre-Columbian Civilizations" (published in 1962 in *American Anthropologist*) very likely came as a surprise to many of his colleagues in the field of American archaeology. The subject was not one that Willey had previously addressed in any detail, as he had focused on ceramics, space-time systematics on the local and regional scales, the study of settlement patterns, and—most recently—the forms of social structure among the ancient Maya. Yet Willey was always quick to spot new goals on the horizon, and clearly his vision had been broadened by his research of the "high cultures" of both Peru and Mesoamerica. While his search for causality in the ideological realm was an innovative and farsighted attempt at plotting a new course, the rest of the profession clearly wasn't ready for it yet. Unlike the change in tack that Willey successfully led in understanding settlement patterns, this idea was not quickly embraced by his colleagues. Willey himself was not again to tackle the subject of ideology's role in culture change until he published "Mesoamerican Civilization and the Idea of Transcendence" (1976) in the British journal *Antiquity*. Ideology's role in culture change was a direction whose time had not yet come, in American archaeology as practiced in 1961.

At the time of Willey's AAA presidential address, no one else in the profession had the experience and the knowledge needed to tackle such a complex comparative problem. Fortunately, one of the very few people of whom the same can be said today has provided the reader of this volume with a formidable new look at this subject. Joyce Marcus's article provides us with a stunning "update" of both the causative role of ideology and the level of complex society in which Willey's great art styles emerged. She takes advantage of the immense amount of careful research in American archaeology on the subject of art and ideology that has ensued since Willey's address—slowly at first and then rising to a crescendo in the past two decades. She includes comparative work on the chiefdoms of Panama, yet another area where Willey made important contributions.

Gordon Willey's abilities and prowess as a synthesizer of archaeological research were the stuff of legend. The two-volume *An Introduction to American Archaeology* displayed Gordon's mastery at assimilating and synthesizing vast amounts of data and his gift for weaving together the best information and ideas of other scholars as well as his own. With marvelous prose, he seamlessly incorporated what most thought to be diametrically opposed perspectives into a single, coherent treatment that proponents of both sides could accept. Jeffrey Quilter provides us with a perceptive consideration of *An Introduction to American Archaeology*, emphasizing Willey's signal contributions in defining and shaping the archaeology of the Intermediate Area that so captivated his attention and interest as he transitioned from the Andean area northward to Mesoamerica.

Following the Belize Valley work, Willey conducted multiyear investigations at the ruins of Altar de Sacrificios and Seibal (or Ceibal), Guatemala. The Seibal project provided critical new data on both the alpha and the omega of complex society in the southern Maya Lowlands and is the subject of a thoughtful review here by two participants in that work, Gair Tourtellot and Norman Hammond. Willey's field projects were singularly successful in having his students and colleagues tackle a wide array of problems by using multiple, crosscutting data sets and in getting the material into the hands of others in the profession. Tourtellot and Hammond share their views on what made Willey's approach to fieldwork and teaching—at the Seibal project in particular—such a resounding success.

The compelling new data on the collapse of the Classic Maya tradition at Seibal led Willey to help organize the first of many conferences at the School of American Research (SAR), in Santa Fe. The landmark volumes on Maya archaeology that resulted from that series of SAR advanced seminars were to become benchmarks in the history of Maya studies. They began with the seminal volume on the collapse, which was followed by works on the origins of Maya civilization, settlement patterns, and late Lowland Maya civilization, all of which benefited from Willey's ability to bring the best minds in the field together to address the pressing issues of the day. Prudence Rice provides the reader with a powerful review of more recent perspectives on the omnipresent subject of the Classic Maya "collapse." In doing so, she critically evaluates the role played by ancient Maya warfare, a topic that was not highlighted in the working model developed by Willey and Demitri Shimkin in their summary chapter of the SAR advanced seminar. Drawing from a broad spectrum of data sets on and approaches to the role of conflict, Rice shows how prescient Willey and Shimkin proved to be—in the few lines that they devoted to the subject—in her superb synthesis of recent research on both warfare and the Terminal Classic throughout the Maya Lowlands.

Another subject that continues to perplex and fascinate Mesoamericanists is the relationship between the great central highland Mexican metropolis of Teotihuacan and the kingdoms of the Classic Maya Lowlands. Brought to the fore by the Carnegie Institution of Washington's excavations at Kaminaljuyú, Guatemala, the topic of Teotihuacan-Maya relationships kept coming up, as investigations of the Early Classic components of many Lowland Maya sites unearthed clear evidence for "interaction at a distance." Willey's interest in the big picture inevitably led him to focus on this subject, and his article on the collapse of Teotihuacan and the Maya "hiatus" provided an extremely innovative and thought-provoking hypothesis. As David Freidel, Hector Escobedo, and Stanley Guenter's contribution to this volume makes clear, the epigraphic revolution in Maya studies has lent historical data in support of intensive interactions between individual Maya kingdoms and the great urban center of Teotihuacan. The authors' work at Waka' highlights the fascinating ways in which more detailed archaeological, epigraphic, and technological studies have enabled scholars to fine-tune their understanding of the individual site histories and the nature of the highland-lowland exchanges through time and space. It also addresses the broader, more controversial subjects of the degree to which Maya rulers, both individually and collectively, controlled economic resources and of the degree to which Teotihuacan—and other, later Mesoamerican states to the west of the Maya area—played a role in Maya economies.

Freidel and his coauthors, as well as other contributors to this volume, reflect on where Willey placed himself with regard to the many changes that took place in Americanist archaeology over the six decades in which GRW played a leading role. A champion of settlement patterns and the study of how people interacted with their environment, Willey was nonetheless both a humanist and a historian at heart. In his summary of the volume *The Origins of Maya Civilization* (edited by R. E. W. Adams and published by the School of American Research in 1977), Willey waxed philosophical on the model the book's contributors had created.

This model, as cast here, is obviously a very "historical" one. With this historicity stripped away, it places demographic pressure—in its systemic complex with ecology and subsistence productivity—in the position of prime mover or prime cause of the rise of Lowland Maya civilization. This is satisfactory up to a point. Numbers of people and their physical well-being are basic to the maintenance of any society, particularly a large and complex one. But these are self-evident truths—essentially biological conditions. Without these forces and factors, to be sure, nothing would have happened. And yet the forms that they assumed are not, to my mind, really comprehensible from so distant, so superhuman a perspective. Beyond population pressure, a drive for survival through competition represents a second level of causality. Complex social, political, and economic organizations are adaptive mechanisms for survival, but they take many forms. It is at this point that ideas and ideologies enter the picture. When we begin to consider these, and to attempt to achieve understanding on a more human scale, we come to "historical explanation"—something that is decried by some as no explanation at all. Maybe so, but in the study of human events I cannot rid myself of the feeling that this is where the real interest lies. (Willey 1977)

Willey's interest in studying the role of ideology in culture change came to the forefront persuasively once more in what he repeatedly confided to me was his favorite article, "Mesoamerican Civilization and the Idea of Transcendence," published in *Antiquity* in 1976. It is, in this writer's view, sad that Gordon said that the epigraphic revolution in studies of the Classic Maya came so late in his life, when he was retired from teaching and fieldwork. "That's for younger people like you to tackle," he would say, cheerfully stating at one gathering that he "envied" those of us who had access to the historical and religious data recorded in the hieroglyphic texts and pictorial imagery. The *Antiquity* article gives us a brief glimpse at just how skillful Willey was in considering both ideology and (what we would now refer to as) human agency, in the study of ancient Mesoamerican cultures, and history. In the penultimate chapter of this volume, Patricia McAnany critically revisits this influential article in light of more recent research on the subject of the feathered serpent and ideology in ancient Mesoamerica. Her insightful contribution is followed by the modestly titled but magnificently complete conclusion, by Jerry Sabloff, who, following Milanich's assessment of Gordon Willey, "gets it right."

Willey produced dozens of PhD's during his thirty-six years of teaching in the Department of Anthropology at Harvard, two full generations of some of the finest archaeologists in this country. When, at his retirement dinner, so many people commented on his outstanding record of mentoring students in what was an increasingly competitive arena, Willey said that the secret to his success was quite simple: "You just get the best people to the starting line, get them set, and let 'em go." Willey wrote that he learned the value of good teaching from Byron Cummings. He admired the way "the Dean" imparted a sense of right and wrong to his students, in addition to so much of the knowledge and the wisdom accrued from a lifetime of study and field research. He also greatly admired Duncan Strong as a teacher, learning much from him about how to address larger patterns of culture change in the Americas. He was also moved by Strong's devotion to having his graduate students meet and interact with the leading figures of their profession. Late in life, Willey used to joke about his own role in providing "moral guidance," saying that his own longevity could be directly attributed to "all that good, clean living."

On a personal level, Gordon Willey was engaging, modest, and generous, with a marvelous sense of humor, particularly when he made light of himself. His humanism and his humor shine through in his *Portraits in American Archaeology: Remembrances of Some Distinguished Americanists*, in which he took pains to share his observations on the personalities, current events, and ideas that forged the interests and the approaches of each of the colleagues who had a strong impact on his life and his thinking. He never made disparaging or critical remarks in his published work, even about those few who were outspoken in disagreeing with him. In this and countless other ways, he distinguished himself in our field as both a gentleman and an optimist.

Willey's understated but formidable skills as both a mentor and a colleague were recognized when he was elected president of the American Anthropological Association and, later, of the Society for American Archaeology. He was awarded the A. V. Kidder Medal, the Viking Medal, the Huxley Medal, the Order of the Quetzal from the government of Guatemala, and honorary doctorates from the University of Arizona, the University of New Mexico, and Cambridge University, which he and his wife, Katharine, often visited. And how he loved being fitted for all those marvelous suits! Had there been an award for best-dressed archaeologist, Willey would easily have won it (see fig. I.3). Willey was also an esteemed member of the American Academy of Arts and Sciences, the National Academy of Sciences, and the American Philosophical Society. But despite all these accolades and accomplishments, Gordon Willey remained a modest man at heart, who loved hearing or telling a good story, archaeological or otherwise.

Willey enjoyed his retirement years (1987–2002) in Cambridge, answering correspondence and visiting colleagues in the Peabody Museum, having lunch with friends at the Long Table in the Harvard Faculty Club, and writing the occasional scholarly article or review. By this point, however, he was devoting most of his writing time to crafting archaeological mystery novels. Willey's skills as a writer and his human qualities shine in each of these works, the first of which (*Selena*) was published and continues to be

Figure I.3. Studio portrait of
Gordon Willey taken in 1972 by
Bachrach Studio.

widely read. He was proud that he had completed and published all the
final field reports for which he was responsible and for which he had
received funding. He will live on happily in the memories of all who knew
him, through all of the many wonderful tales and turns of phrase, the cour-
teous cupping of his hand on your elbow to guide you through a door, the
hilarious mangling of pronunciations that made us all laugh at our folly and
the trials of the human condition, the timely words of advice, and, always,
the appreciation of the character and the accomplishments of others.
Beyond our own times, lives, and memories, Gordon's scholarly work—
the numerous monographs, the innovative thinking, the transcendent syntheses, the showing of the path—will likely be cited in the great texts of his
field for decades to come. As Bob Sharer thoughtfully wrote to me after
Willey's passing, "It is too often said, but in Gordon's case, quite true, that
we will never see his like again."

With that I will pass the baton to the next writer, in our long-distance relay in this volume, knowing that the fastest American archaeologist to ever run a race was none other than Gordon Randolph Willey. In recalling the time that he ran in a heat with the great Jesse Owens, Gordon loved to recall, "You know, I had him for the first three steps. After that I watched his backside." In looking "back" on Willey's great run, I think I can speak for all who knew him when I say that we will always be grateful for the ways in which he enriched our lives and the profession at large.

References

Steward, Julian H., ed. 1963. *Handbook of South American Indians*. New York: Cooper Square Publishers.

Willey, Gordon R. 1962. "The Early Great Styles and the Rise of Pre-Columbian Civilizations." *American Anthropologist* 64:1–14.

———. 1966–71. *An Introduction to American Archaeology*. 2 vols. Englewood Cliffs, N.J.: Prentice Hall.

———. 1974. *Archaeological Researches in Retrospect*. Cambridge, Mass.: Winthrop Publishers.

———. 1976. "Mesoamerican Civilization and the Idea of Transcendence." *Antiquity* 50 (199/200):205–15.

———. 1977. "The Rise of Maya Civilization: A Summary View." In *The Origins of Maya Civilization*, ed. Richard E. W. Adams, 383–423. Albuquerque: University of New Mexico Press.

———. 1988. *Portraits in American Archaeology: Remembrances of Some Distinguished Americanists*. Albuquerque: University of New Mexico Press.

Willey, Gordon R., and Philip Phillips. 1958. *Method and Theory in American Archaeology*. Chicago: University of Chicago Press.

Chapter One

Gordon R. Willey and the Archaeology of the Florida Gulf Coast

Jerald T. Milanich

ordon Willey's volume *Archeology of the Florida Gulf Coast* (1949a) appeared in late December 1949 in the Smithsonian Institution's Miscellaneous Collection series. Six hundred pages in length with sixty additional full-page plates, the book initially was not widely endorsed by all Willey's colleagues. One "distinguished senior colleague" told Willey the "book has set Florida archaeology back fifty years" (Willey 1998, xxvi). Other archaeologists were said to refer to the book as "The Young Pothunter's Friend and Guide" (Willey 1999, 201). But Willey would have the last laugh; more than fifty years after it was first published, *Archeology of the Florida Gulf Coast* is still in print, and many generations of professional and avocational archaeologists have referred to the book as "the bible."[1]

Why has Gordon Willey's Florida Gulf Coast work achieved almost biblical importance? In this chapter I will try to answer that question. I will start by relating how Willey became involved in southeastern United States archaeology and then will focus on his Florida investigations. Lastly, I will explain why his Gulf Coast research has remained a mainstay for investigators for more than a half-century. In the process I will draw on Willey's writings, as well as a very informative website about his Gulf

Coast work that Katherine Burton Jones created on the Harvard Peabody Museum's website (cited here as Jones). I also want to acknowledge my use of Edwin Lyon's well-researched book (1996) on the history of federal relief archaeology programs in the Southeast.

Willey, a native Iowan, received his bachelor of arts degree in anthropology from the University of Arizona in 1935, when he was twenty-two; the next year he was awarded his master of arts in anthropology from the same institution. At Arizona he became well versed in dendrochronology, southwestern archaeology, and other disciplines. At that time most southwestern United States archaeologists did not adhere to the W. C. McKern cultural classification system, which was born in the Midwest and later raised in the Southeast. Instead, as Willey noted (1999, 203), the emphasis at Arizona was on chronology and stratigraphic excavations. Willey would bring that emphasis to the Southeast, essentially eschewing the McKern system. To quote Willey (1999, 203), "As a case in point, where did the Gulf Florida Weeden Island culture fit into the Midwestern Taxonomic System? . . . Did Weeden Island belong in the Woodland pattern?" Even modern authors are uncertain whether the Weeden Island culture should be placed with Woodland cultures or with Mississippian cultures (see, e.g., Fagan 1991, 385–89).

With degree in hand, Willey went east, where he was a field assistant to Arthur R. Kelley at the Ocmulgee site in Macon, Georgia, about seventy-five miles southeast of Atlanta. During that initial field season in Macon, in the summer of 1936, Willey was one of six outstanding graduate students from U.S. universities selected to participate in the project (see fig. 1.1).

The Macon project was funded and sponsored by the Works Progress Administration (WPA) and the Civilian Conservation Corps (CCC). At the project Willey first was employed as a "laboratory of anthropology field fellow"; he later held the title of senior field foreman and received a salary from the CCC. A laboratory was established in Macon to process the artifacts and data being excavated at Ocmulgee and other federal relief archaeological projects in Georgia and Florida, and Willey was involved with it as well. The National Park Service also was a participant in the Ocmulgee project, and the site was later designated a national monument. The Park Service still administers it.

During the three years he worked in Georgia, 1936–38, Willey directed excavations both at Ocmulgee, including in the village area around Mound

Figure 1.1. Gordon Willey and graduate student colleagues at the Ocmulgee site in Macon, Georgia, in 1936. *Left to right*: Lawrence Angel, Joseph Birdsell, Charles Wagley, Gordon Willey, Walter Taylor, H. Y. Feng. Courtesy of the National Park Service, Southeast Archeological Center, Tallahassee.

C, usually called the Funeral Mound, and at several outlying sites around Macon, in central Georgia (Lyon 1996, 181–83). He clearly knew what he was doing in the field. When Charles H. Fairbanks wrote his 1954 dissertation on the Funeral Mound, at the University of Michigan, he noted he used Willey's field notes extensively, stating they were "an outstanding exception" to the other notes and data with which he had to work and which lacked "stratigraphic detail" (Fairbanks 1954, 30).

During his time in Georgia, Willey met and became a colleague of several young archaeologists who later helped to shape the discipline in the Southeast and beyond. In addition to the men pictured in figure 1.1, they included James A. Ford and Charles Fairbanks. While at Macon, Willey also met Matthew Stirling of the Smithsonian Institution, who had been working in peninsular Florida, and Philip Phillips. In September 1938 Willey married Katharine Whaley, a Macon resident.[2]

Newly married, Willey set out for New Orleans, where he was appointed laboratory supervisor for the WPA Louisiana excavations being directed by James Ford (Lyon 1996, 38–39, 82–83). At the lab on Chartres Street in the French Quarter, Willey encountered other soon-to-be big names in archaeology—people like Robert S. Neitzel, Edward Doran, Arden King, and William Mulloy. In 1937–38 Ford had been a graduate student at the University of Michigan under James B. Griffin's tutelage (Willey 1969, 63), bringing Willey into indirect contact with Griffin, the future doyen of eastern United States archaeology, and a host of new ideas.

Those must have been heady times. In his book *Portraits in American Archaeology*, Willey notes he and Ford planned to "solve all kinds of problems," including "Hopewell origins, the rise of Middle Mississippian, the role of the Caddoan cultures" (1988, 57). Several years later Ford and Willey would publish in *American Anthropologist* their seminal article "An Interpretation of the Prehistory of the Eastern United States" (1943).

In September 1939, after a year in Louisiana, Willey left the project to enroll in graduate school at Columbia University, where he worked with William Duncan Strong. (Back in New Orleans, his laboratory position was taken over first by Preston Holder and then by George Quimby.) Jim Ford joined Willey at Columbia in 1940, leaving for the U.S. Army in 1942 (Willey 1969, 64).

At Columbia University Willey continued to pursue his interest in southeastern archaeology, following up on a spring 1938 visit he had made to Panama City, on the coast of the Florida Panhandle, where he surveyed shell middens at St. Andrew Bay, on the southwest side of town (Willey 1949a, xix). On that 1938 trip, he observed that complicated stamped pottery (Swift Creek ceramics) from the Florida coastal sites looked like the complicated stamped pottery being found in central Georgia. He also noted that this Florida stamped pottery often was found in association with incised and punctated pottery (Weeden Island ceramics), which in turn resembled Lower Mississippi Valley pottery he had seen on an earlier visit to the archaeology laboratory at Louisiana State University, in Baton Rouge. He later wrote, "Here, on the Florida Gulf, were the means of relating the Louisiana and central Georgia culture sequences, in 1938 the only ones known for the lower Southeast" (Willey 1949a, xix).

Funded in part by Columbia University and the National Park Service and supported by Duncan Strong (as well as by Matthew Stirling and Art

Figure 1.2. The wood-paneled station wagon that Willey and Woodbury used in the field in northwest Florida in 1940. Their field hats adorn the hood ornament. Courtesy of Alexandra Guralnick, the estate of Gordon R. Willey, and the Harvard Peabody Museum.

Kelley), graduate student Willey set out in the summer of 1940 to carry out stratigraphic excavations at selected sites on the Florida Panhandle Gulf Coast. He wanted to learn more about that coast so that he could pursue his plan to use northwest Florida ceramic assemblages to help correlate the Georgia and Louisiana assemblages. In this field endeavor, he was accompanied by another Columbia graduate student, Richard B. Woodbury.

During the three months they spent on the coast driving around in their field vehicle (a freshly shellacked, wood-paneled station wagon; see fig. 1.2), Willey and Woodbury conducted stratigraphic excavations at six sites and visited and recorded eighty-seven others. Willey was well acquainted with Clarence B. Moore's turn-of-the-century mound excavations on that coast (see Brose and White 1999) and even encountered residents who still remembered Moore, his stern-wheeler steamboat named the *Gopher*, and its captain, J. S. Rayborn (Willey 1999, 202).

The trials and tribulations, as well as the occasional joys, of working in rural wetland areas on the Florida Panhandle coast in 1940 are well chronicled in field diaries Willey and Woodbury kept, excerpts of which can be read online on the Peabody Museum's website (Jones).

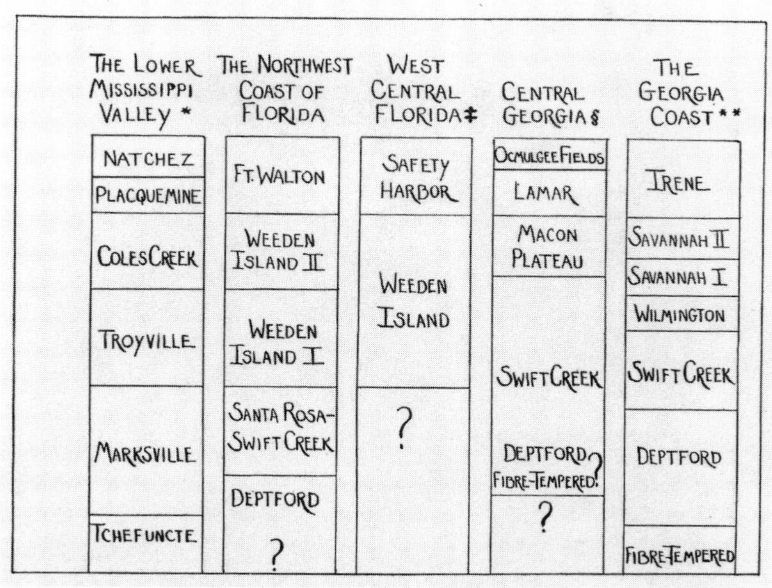

The Lower Mississippi Valley *	The Northwest Coast of Florida	West Central Florida‡	Central Georgia§	The Georgia Coast **
Natchez	Ft. Walton	Safety Harbor	Ocmulgee Fields	Irene
Placquemine			Lamar	
Coles Creek	Weeden Island II	Weeden Island	Macon Plateau	Savannah II
				Savannah I
Troyville	Weeden Island I			Wilmington
			Swift Creek	Swift Creek
Marksville	Santa Rosa–Swift Creek	?	Deptford? Fibre-Tempered?	Deptford
	Deptford			
Tchefuncte	?		?	Fibre-Tempered

Figure 1.3. Comparative chronological chart from Willey and Woodbury's 1942 article, showing correlations among the Lower Mississippi Valley, the Gulf Coast of Florida, and central and coastal Georgia. The hand-drawn chart is just as it appeared in *American Antiquity*. Reproduced by permission of the Society for American Archaeology from Willey and Woodbury 1942.

Returning to Columbia, Willey and Woodbury wrote an article on their work, which they submitted to *American Antiquity* in December 1940, only three months after they exited the field. Entitled "A Chronological Outline for the Northwest Florida Coast," the article appeared in January 1942.

The article provided ceramic-based definitions for a series of temporally ordered archaeological assemblages. The emphasis was on defining periods, not cultures, though descriptions of settlement and subsistence traits also were included. Perhaps most importantly at the time, the northwest Florida coast sequence was tied to the sequences from the Lower Mississippi Valley and central and coastal Georgia (and the central Gulf Coast of Florida; see fig. 1.3). For the first time, archaeologists had a chronological model that encompassed the last two thousand years of Pre-Columbian history over a large portion of the Southeast.

The 1942 publication was one of more than a dozen monographs and articles on southeastern archaeology Willey authored or coauthored. Between 1937 and 1939, he had published three articles on central Georgia archaeology (including an attempt to apply dendrochronology; Willey 1937, 1938, 1939), and in 1940 his classic monograph on the Crooks site in Louisiana, written with Jim Ford, had appeared (the Crooks site is about 180 miles northwest of New Orleans; see Ford and Willey 1940).

In 1941 Willey received a fellowship that allowed him to continue to work on Florida archaeology during the 1941–42 academic year, including writing up the unpublished work carried out previously by Matthew Stirling on the peninsular Florida Gulf Coast in the mid-1930s. The fellowship eventually allowed the integration of those data with Willey's own Panhandle data, resulting in an overview of Florida Gulf Coast archaeology. Another opportunity presented itself first, however, and he put off the Florida work for a year. That opportunity was a chance to work in the Chancay Valley in Peru, a project that provided the data for Willey's dissertation, which was submitted and accepted in 1942.

During the 1942–43 academic year, Willey used the delayed Columbia fellowship to once again take up Florida Gulf Coast archaeology. But the task was set aside again in 1943, when he was hired at the Smithsonian Institution's Bureau of American Ethnology (BAE) to work with Julian Steward on the preparation of the *Handbook of South American Indians*. During the several years he worked on articles that would appear in those volumes, he continued to follow Florida archaeology, though I believe the two Florida-related articles he published in *American Antiquity* in 1944 and 1945 were essentially written before he joined the BAE (Willey 1945; Willey and Phillips 1944). He also returned to Peru, working on the Virú Valley project, where he was joined by old friend James Ford in 1946 (Willey 1969, 64).

In 1947 Willey returned to the task of writing up Matthew Stirling's old excavations and producing a synthesis of Florida Gulf Coast archaeology. While involved in that endeavor, he published several additional articles about the area (Willey 1948a, 1948b, 1948c). As he notes in the introduction to the 1949 Gulf Coast volume (Willey 1949a, xx–xxiii), new information had become available since 1943. In addition, from 1947 until the book went to press in June 1949, Willey had had an opportunity to interact with archaeologists newly working in Florida—people like Ripley P. Bullen, John M. Goggin, John W. Griffin, Irving Rouse, and Hale G. Smith. The final product, I believe, was much more complex than Willey had imagined when he began the book in 1941.

The month after *Archeology of the Florida Gulf Coast* was sent to the printer, Willey returned to the Florida Gulf Coast, spending one day at the Crystal River site, in Citrus County, accompanied by Antonio J. Waring, Jr. (Crystal River is about fifty-five miles southwest of Gainesville, Florida). Willey made a surface collection, which he soon reported in an article that provided a description of the site's mounds and earthworks (1949b).

Remarkably, that very same year (1949), Willey published another monograph on Florida. *Excavations in Southeast Florida* (Willey 1949c) was published with Irving Rouse's blessing in the Yale University Publications in Anthropology series. Willey wrote it while he was with the BAE, where he had access to collections and reports from Matthew Stirling and others. A synthesis like its sister volume on the Gulf Coast, the monograph remains a classic of southeastern archaeology.

In 1950 Willey left the Smithsonian Institution for the Peabody Museum, essentially leaving Florida archaeology, at least in terms of fieldwork. He would continue to read the Florida and Southeast literature for many years.

That was more than five decades ago. Today, Willey's six-hundred-page synthesis is not only still in print and widely cited but also essential for any archaeologist working anywhere along the 645 miles of waterfront property where Willey began work in 1940.

But why is Willey's Gulf Coast work, which he called "historical reconstructive," so influential? Why has it stood the test of time?

I do not think those are difficult questions to answer. Willey had data, he organized and interpreted those data correctly, and he got the results right. In *Archeology of the Florida Gulf Coast*, he detailed the results of his and Woodbury's 1940 excavations of the six Panhandle coastal sites, as well as excavations carried out from 1923 to 1936 by other archaeologists at eleven other sites, all on the peninsular coast. In addition to Matthew Stirling's projects, the eleven projects included investigations that had been supported by various combinations of state and federal programs, including federal relief archaeology programs. Willey also examined and used C. B. Moore's publications and collections—no small database—and he drew on a host of other sources.

Besides evaluating the 17 excavated sites, Willey analyzed and described the collections from 142 additional coastal sites, including many reported by Clarence B. Moore,[3] and he mentions nearly 90 other sites. In the process he looked at a very large quantity of potsherds, intact vessels, and arrowheads. He organized the artifacts into assemblages and the assemblages into culture periods whose names—Weeden Island, Swift Creek, Safety Harbor, Fort Walton—are now venerable. More than 200 of his sites were assigned to one or more of the culture periods. It is an impressive database by any standard.

For each culture period, Willey discussed site types, settlement patterns, sociopolitical organization, ceramics and other artifacts, and burial ceremonialism, and he related the evidence for extra-aerial contacts. If the goal of archaeology is to recognize and record patterns of artifact distributions that reflect patterns of human behavior, Gordon Willey accomplished his task.

Because Willey was first and because he was correct, all post-1949 syntheses of any aspect of Florida archaeology must be measured against and tied to Willey's Gulf Coast cultural chronology and the related information. His was an extraordinary achievement.

Should any of the rest of us expect our books still to be in print in fifty years? Probably not. Gordon Willey was the right person at the right time in the right place, and, again, he got it right. Though we might fine-tune things, the fundamental taxonomies that Willey gleaned from the collections he studied remain basic to interpreting other collections and sites, and they are fundamental to our attempts to model past human behavior.

After 1949 Willey moved on to pursue other archaeological interests. Because he left behind his book *Archeology of the Florida Gulf Coast* as a basic guide, generations of archaeologists in Florida have been able to build on his work in their investigations of a host of research questions.

Acknowledgments

Richard Woodbury was kind enough to read and comment on a draft of this chapter. In a letter to me dated July 2, 2003, he wrote, "My part in the 1940 work in Florida was more learning than contributing. I'd had two summers' archeological experience in Arizona where I learned very little about survey methods or stratigraphy. But I learned a lot from Gordon, and also had the good fortune to become a lifelong friend. His lifetime archeological achievements are wonderfully impressive, a scholar and synthesizer but also a fine dirt archeologist."

Alexandra Guralnick (Gordon Willey's daughter), Katherine Jones, and Scott Mitchell all helped me to acquire the illustrations used in this chapter.

Notes

1. A check of the Vatican Library's online catalog (Biblioteca Apostolica Vaticana) revealed a copy of Willey's book in that repository. A cursory check failed to discover any other Florida archaeology books in the library's holdings.

2. Katharine Whaley was not the only Macon woman to marry one of the out-of-town archaeologists working on the Ocmulgee project. Evelyn Adams Timmerman and Charles H. Fairbanks were married in 1941.

3. Willey acknowledged his use of Clarence B. Moore's publications, stating, "Moore, when you come right down to it, should have been a coauthor of my book, despite the fact that I never gave him credit on the title page" (Willey 1999, 201).

References

Brose, David S., and Nancy M. White, eds. 1999. *The Northwest Florida Expeditions of Clarence B. Moore.* Tuscaloosa: University of Alabama Press.

Fagan, Brian M. 1991. *Ancient North America—The Archaeology of a Continent.* London: Thames & Hudson.

Fairbanks, Charles H. 1954. "The Excavation of Mound C, Ocmulgee National Monument, Macon, Georgia." PhD diss., Department of Anthropology, University of Michigan.

Ford, James A., and Gordon R. Willey. 1940. *Crooks Site: A Marksville Period Burial Mound in La Salle Parish, Louisiana.* New Orleans: Department of Conservation, Louisiana Geological Survey.

———. 1943. "An Interpretation of the Prehistory of the Eastern United States." *American Anthropologist* 43:325–63.

Jones, Katherine Burton. "Pioneers of Southeastern Archaeology: Gordon R. Willey." Harvard Peabody Museum. http://www.peabody.harvard.edu/Willey.

Lyon, Edwin A. 1996. *A New Deal for Southeastern Archaeology.* Tuscaloosa: University of Alabama Press.

Willey, Gordon R. 1937. "Notes on Central Georgia Dendrochronology." *Tree Ring Bulletin* 4:6–8.

———. 1938. "Time Studies: Pottery and Trees in Georgia." *Proceedings of the Society for Georgia Archaeology* 1:15–22.

———. 1939. "Ceramic Stratigraphy in a Georgia Village Site." *American Antiquity* 5:140–47.

———. 1945. "The Weeden Island Culture: A Preliminary Definition." *American Antiquity* 10:225–54.

————. 1948a. "A Prototype for the Southern Cult." *American Antiquity* 13:328–30.

————. 1948b. "Culture Sequence in the Manatee Region of West Florida." *American Antiquity* 13:209–18.

————. 1948c. "The Cultural Context of the Crystal River Negative-Painted Style." *American Antiquity* 13:325–28.

————. 1949a. *Archeology of the Florida Gulf Coast*. Smithsonian Miscellaneous Collections 113. Washington, D.C.: Smithsonian Institution Press.

————. 1949b. "Crystal River, Florida: A 1949 Visit." *Florida Anthropologist* 2:41–46.

————. 1949c. *Excavations in Southeast Florida*. Yale University Publications in Anthropology 42. New Haven, Conn.: Yale University Press.

————. 1969. "James Alfred Ford, 1911–1968." *American Antiquity* 34:62–71.

————. 1988. *Portraits in American Archaeology: Remembrances of Some Distinguished Americanists*. Albuquerque: University of New Mexico Press.

————. 1998. "Preface to the 1998 Edition." In *Archeology of the Florida Gulf Coast*, xxv–xxvi. Gainesville: University Press of Florida. (Orig. pub. 1949.)

————. 1999. "1999 FAS Banquet Address—Inconsequent Thoughts and Other Reflections on Florida Archaeology." *Florida Anthropologist* 52:201–204.

Willey, Gordon R., and Philip Phillips. 1944. "Negative-Painted Pottery from Crystal River, Florida." *American Antiquity* 10:173–85.

Willey, Gordon R., and Richard B. Woodbury. 1942. "A Chronological Outline for the Northwest Florida Coast." *American Antiquity* 7:232–54.

Chapter Two

Peru
Willey's Formative Years

Michael E. Moseley

Gordon Willey's many contributions to Andean studies had a fortu-
itous beginning, for as a young man, Willey had no intention of
engaging in Latin American research. After receiving his master's
from the University of Arizona in 1936, he worked in Louisiana, Georgia,
and Florida. In the Southeast Willey met James Ford, an enduring friend,
and they precociously tried their hand at regional synthesis (Ford and Willey 1941). That they would later end up working jointly in Peru was a
product of curious circumstances. The year Gordon left Arizona, Peru's
energetic archaeologist Julio C. Tello convened a meeting with Wendell
Bennett, Alfred Kroeber, Samuel Lothrop, and other scholars at New
York's American Museum of Natural History. Their goal was to further
Latin American field studies by creating the Institute of Andean Research
(IAR), which initially subsidized some of Tello's important explorations.
Meanwhile, completing graduate classwork at Columbia University during
the 1940–41 academic year, Willey planned to return to Florida for his
dissertation research. Yet securing institutional support that would pay for
field investigations, analysis, and dissertation publication as a monograph
(doctoral degrees were granted only when candidates deposited published

copies of their PhD dissertation with the university library) was not on the immediate horizon.

Coincidentally, the IAR received federal subsidies to expand its activities and add new members, including Junius Bird, Alfred Kidder II, and William Duncan Strong, who was a former graduate student of Kroeber's and Willey's major professor at Columbia. With IAR support to investigate archaeological sites on the central Peruvian coast, Strong invited Gordon to be his assistant. Although Willey was still devoted to the Southeast, participating in Andean fieldwork held exciting intellectual opportunities, would support his dissertation publication, and would allow his wife, Katharine, to accompany him on what would be the first of his two episodes of Andean fieldwork. The Peruvian experience exposed Willey to ideas and concepts that provided the foundations for a marvelous career that ultimately embraced all of New World archaeology.

This essay reviews Willey's enduring contributions to Andean studies. It is divided into two sections, which reflects the different concerns of his two field episodes.

Culture Contact

Strong's goal was to investigate sites that would yield stratified cultural successions. He sought to systematize data recovery by excavating in measured horizontal levels, or so-called artificial stratigraphic units, a procedure that Willey subsequently adopted. At the invitation of Julio C. Tello, Strong initiated his IAR project at Pachacamac, a very large religious center with multiple platform mounds. The site had attractive potentials because a fourfold sequence of Inca and pre-Inca burials had previously been recovered by Max Uhle (1903), the father of Peruvian archaeology. In the summer of 1941, John M. Corbett, a University of Southern California archaeology student, joined Strong's team, and excavations were opened on the flank of the dominant mound at the site (Strong and Corbett 1943).

After Strong returned to Columbia, Gordon and John excavated at a series of sites north of Lima, staying into 1942. Willey wrote about two of the settlements with Early Intermediate period remains in his dissertation, *Excavations in the Chancay Valley* (1943). The young archaeologists were also keen to investigate earlier occupations; their interest was piqued by Tello's stunning discoveries (1929) at Chavín de Huántar and by Uhle's identification (1906) of ancient coastal shell middens. Excavations by the Columbia team at Ancón Bay and at sites around Puerto Supe, to the north, produced early ceramics and established the broad coastal distribution of Chavín-like materials (Willey and Corbett 1954).

Willey personally discussed his finds with Tello. He later recounted that his Peruvian associate viewed Andean civilizations as arising out of a far-flung archaic cultural matrix expressed at Chavín, Paracas, and elsewhere. Furthermore, he saw the evolution of indigenous societies as a highly intertwined process, with basal roots and trunks that branched out but that later often merged again (Burger, forthcoming). Although Tello's vision was rather similar to Kroeber's "tree of culture" that grew back into itself, the Peruvian's view was anathema to his North American colleagues. They subscribed to the interpretative framework, formulated by Max Uhle, that envisioned expansive cultural horizons alternating with long episodes of variable local development. The history of this organizing framework is important because the framework was expanded and refined by Willey and continues to influence archaeological thinking.

Before coming to the Andes, Uhle worked with German museum collections from Inca Cuzco and with records of megalithic artwork at the ancient Bolivian center of Tiwanaku, which was known to predate the Inca (Rowe 1954). Thus, he was familiar with both styles when he began Peruvian coastal explorations around the turn of the century. Focusing on burial recovery and working first at Pachacamac (Uhle 1903) and then at a number of far-flung sites, Uhle found Inca remains preceded by those of different local cultures, which were, in turn, preceded by remains he attributed to Tiwanaku. Impressed by the broad spatial distribution of the latter, he drew upon Cuzco as an ethnohistoric analogy and proposed that Inca and Tiwanaku expansions reflected sweeping archaeological horizons. Each had originated at its respective capital and then spread rapidly over vast areas occupied by numerous locally evolved societies. During the process of analyzing and publishing Uhle's collections deposited at Berkeley, A. L. Kroeber and his students, including Strong, codified this interpretative framework. In the field, American archaeologists found Inca and Tiwanaku materials to be useful tools for sorting out local and regional cultural successions. Lacking radiocarbon dates, they presumed both horizon styles to be relatively similar in terms of short duration and geographic spread by force of arms.

A century after Uhle formulated his horizon model, one must wonder if U.S. investigators of the 1930s and '40s would have accepted it had they known three things that are now apparent. First, although the standardized arts and architecture of the short-lived and highly expansive Inca imperium provided a very attractive archetype for the horizon concept, the Inca phenomenon was an evolutionary end point built upon millennia of prior political development. Furthermore, as the largest empire ever to arise in the Americas, the Inca empire ended prematurely and abruptly due to Spanish conquest. Consequently, the archetype is rather unique and largely without precedent in the annals of New World archaeology. The presumption that earlier horizons and styles would be similar in nature is, therefore, highly questionable. Second, Uhle and his disciples misidentified the origin center of the supposed coastal Tiwanaku horizon. It was not the ancient Bolivian metropolis, as was thought for some fifty years. Rather, it was the nexus of Huari in the central Peruvian Andes. Both centers exerted roughly contemporaneous stylistic and cultural influences over different regions of the Cordillera. Coregency during the so-called Middle Horizon is certainly not comparable with the Inca hegemony of the Late Horizon. Third, and finally, increasing numbers of radiocarbon dates indicate that the development and spread of both Huari and Tiwanaku arts and architecture spanned more than four centuries. Neither was a short-lived phenomenon like the Inca model that Uhle invoked, and neither conforms to the horizon concept that Kroeber implanted in North American archaeology.

Nonetheless, given the times, Willey adopted Uhle's scheme when he analyzed collections from the 1942 excavations. Materials from Ancón and Supe convinced him that Chavín had exerted broad geographical influence. Consequently, he became a pioneering advocate of the proposition that Chavín constituted a distinct horizon style predating those recognized by Uhle. His colleagues accepted the argument, and the interpretative framework expanded from two to three horizons. Willey then spent more than a decade trying to refine the horizon concept and later championed its use elsewhere in the Americas (Willey and Phillips 1958).

Tello's vision of intertwining and merging evolutionary pathways captured long-term Andean cultural continuities that his North American colleagues quite literally straightened out with the concept of archaeological "traditions." Willey compared the notions of horizons and traditions in an *American Antiquity* article (1945) to highlight their contrasting spatial and temporal dimensions. He then addressed the knotty problem of how to delineate horizon styles (Willey 1948). Recognizing that fashion, similar to beauty, tends to lie in the eye of the beholder, Willey cogently proposed (1951) that the Chavín horizon style should be strictly defined by the art and the iconography carved in stone at the origin center of Chavín de Huántar. This remains a highly viable definition, but it won few adherents. Investigators, instead, pursued more idiosyncratic characterizations, to the point that the term "Chavinoid" arose as a catchall for a morass of supposedly early material, including material that is now classified as Initial period. Uhle's Tiwanaku horizon also suffered similar definitional problems.

Whereas Inca authority spread by force of arms, Chavín influence was thought to have diffused by ideological means. Recognizing that the horizon concept subsumed great variation, Gordon convened and chaired a 1955 Harvard seminar entitled "An Archaeological Classification of Culture Contact Situations" (Willey et al. 1956). The intent of the six-member panel of distinguished archaeologists, which included John Rowe and Donald Lathrap, was to formulate a classification that would systematize comparisons of contact cases and facilitate anthropological generalizations about cultural interactions.

Evidence of contact was defined archaeologically by the incursion of elements of one culture into the area of another. An important distinction was made between two categories of intrusive phenomena: site units and trait units. The former entailed intrusive physical occupations by foreign groups, while the latter included incursions of alien ideas, objects, styles, technologies, or complex associations. A fourfold classification for each unit type was based on the outcome of the contact. For site unit intrusions (type A), outcomes included no change in either culture (A1), acculturation with dominance of either the resident (A2) or the intruding (A3) society, and fusion followed by revival of the resident culture (A4). For trait unit intrusions (type B), there was adoption with no change (B1), cultural fusion without (B2) or with (B3) corresponding trait replacement in the recipient culture, and fusion and the emergence of entirely new traits (B4). Archaeological examples for each situation fleshed out the classification.

The seminar's conclusions underscored a number of significant points of continued relevance. First, because archaeological sequences based on seriated percentages of sherd types presume cultural continuity, the sequences will often show continuity where it may not exist, thereby obscuring contact. Although the symposium participants did not state this, the same can hold true for assemblages excavated by artificial levels. Thus, when Willey was conducting Peruvian fieldwork, data recovery methods were not very sensitive to the contact situations implied by the horizon style concept.

Second, the symposium participants opined that, while useful, "the horizon style concept seems a very gross one" (Willey et al. 1956, 25). It was noted that even in horizons with widespread site unit intrusions, such as the Inca, all manifestations of the style and its associated phenomena would not have spread uniformly or with equal speed. John Rowe likely contributed to this tepid assessment. For Andean studies it presaged the replacement of Uhle's framework by one based on fixed units of time defined in the Ica valley. Thus, for example, the last prehistoric temporal entity, the Late Horizon, began in A.D. 1476, when the Inca conquered Ica, and it ended in 1534, when the Spanish assumed control of the valley. Designating the alternate temporal divisions "periods" and "horizons" left the latter at least partially cognitively congruent with the Chavín, Tiwanaku (Huari), and Inca horizon styles of Willey's day. Consequently, archaeologists now use fixed episodes of time and considerations of style to understand the past.

Third, and finally, the seminar participants came to the following conclusion: "It has become fashionable in recent years in some circles to deprecate mere chronology, but until the chronology of an archaeological situation is known in great detail it can offer little to the study of historical processes or cultural dynamics" (Willey et al. 1956, 25). This marvelously prophetic statement applies to still-popular chronology bashing. More importantly, it also foretold revolutionary changes now gripping Peruvian archaeology. Beginning in the 1990s, ever-increasing numbers of radiocarbon dates have demonstrated that certain supposedly sequential archaeological phases, such as Moche I–IV, were, in fact, partially or wholly contemporaneous assemblages! Because Moche has long been considered one of the most secure Peruvian archaeological sequences, its collapse has far-reaching implications for the discipline: distinctions in style and material culture formerly thought to mark temporal differences can instead mark social distinctions and differentiations between contemporary populations.

For example, in the Río Moquegua sierra, three supposedly sequential Tiwanaku phases now are known to have overlapping dates between

A.D. 900 and 1000, and all were discovered to be contemporary with an imperial Huari colony. Thus, this small highland valley conforms to John Murra's ethnohistorical characterization (1972) of Andean multiethnic ecological zones occupied by two or more distinct social groups from outside the areas. The prehistoric Moquegua case is replete with type A1 site unit intrusions distinguished by marked retention of separate group identities. Even though most communities were within eyeshot of one or more of their foreign neighbors' sites, intergroup influences were seemingly minimal and largely limited to Willey's type B1 and B2 trait unit intrusions (Owen and Goldstein 2001).

I predict that it is unlikely that either the Moche or the Moquegua situation is unique. Ethnohistoric sources document widespread ethnic diversity in the Cordillera. Completely ignoring social conditions at the time of contact, Andean archaeology was founded on the presumption that distinctions in styles and material culture were products solely of temporal differences. Consequently, many archaeological sequences rest in part or entirely on seriated assemblages rather than on ones shown to be superimposed stratigraphically. This situation places the discipline in the very precarious position of having concocted a prehistory unrelated to the realities of ethnohistoric diversity. Turning a blind eye to these realities, archaeologists confident in the temporal efficacy of seriated sequence have proposed that Peruvian C-14 dates reflect two separate radiocarbon scales, a short younger one and an older long one. Certainly, radiocarbon assays are not without problems. Equally problematic, however, is the presupposition that differences in fashion and style could not have arisen between contemporary social groups.

As independent chronological controls continue to improve our temporal resolution, the archaeological record will be enlivened with more cases of simultaneous social variation. This will affect many practices, ranging from the way we model indigenous states to the way we interpret communal landscapes. Cultural contact situations will continue to be a common denominator, thereby giving contemporary pertinence to Willey's 1955 seminar proceedings. Still highly relevant, the seminar's classification structure was designed to systematize comparisons of contact cases, thereby facilitating anthropological generalization. Site and trait unit intrusions provide investigators with a common language for theory building. Revealingly, recent studies of prehistoric multiethnic situations, which ignore the 1955 proceedings, continue to generate informative and interesting reports, yet they tend to be treated as unique and not comparable.

Settlement Patterns

After his first episode of Peruvian fieldwork, Gordon completed his doctorate and went to work for the Smithsonian Institution. One of his supervisors was Julian Steward, who was keenly interested in reviving and refining inquiry into cultural evolution. Bringing an evolutionary framework to his editorship of the *Handbook of South American Indians*, he assigned Willey the task of producing archaeological syntheses (1946a, 1946b) for areas such as the pampas. The assignment sparked an enduring interest in formulating regional overviews of cultural development (see, e.g., Willey and Howard 1948) and provided the foundations for subsequent grand syntheses of the entire continent and hemisphere (Willey 1966, 1971).

Steward also assisted Willey and Wendell Bennett with planning for a multidisciplinary investigation of a Peruvian desert drainage, the Virú Valley. Among those joining the project were Smithsonian geographer Webster McBride, ethnologist Alan Holmburg, and a cadre of distinguished archaeologists, including Junius Bird, Donald Collier, Duncan Strong, and two of Strong's graduate students, Clifford Evans and James Ford. The majority of archaeologists focused on excavating sites of different periods. Steward had encouraged Willey to examine the spatial distributions of sites over time. Therefore, Gordon joined his old friend Jim Ford in an archaeological survey of the valley (Ford and Willey 1949). To date sites on the basis of surface shards, Ford employed methods of pottery typing and frequency seriation that he had formulated earlier in the Southeast. Although these procedures were later critiqued in Willey's 1955 seminar, decorated ceramics from looted cemeteries served to identify horizon styles. Furthermore, the Virú project recognized both pre-Chavín sites with early pottery and coastal preceramic sites. This was by far the best long-term archaeological sequence in Peru at the time.

Willey's survey responsibilities were new and broad, but not entirely without precedent. Mapping, classifying, and recording spatial distributions of North American mounds and earthworks had antecedents in studies by Caleb Atwood, as well as by Ephraim Squier and George Davis. The Virú survey operated with far better chronological controls, but the vast majority of sites were not monumental complexes, burial grounds, or special facilities that captured attention. They were, instead, simple settings where common people lived and worked. Lacking elite art and architecture, these unimposing yet abundant remains lay beyond the traditional purview of archaeological inquiry.

Willey's seminal contribution was to bring the demographic majority into archaeological focus. His success was enhanced by newly available aerial photographs of the desert coastal region, taken during World War II because of U.S. fears of a South American invasion. Archaeological applications of the new resource were pioneered by Willey and by Paul Kosok, but to different ends. Kosok thought irrigation fostered social stratification and despotic rule (1965). Therefore, in a precocious but rambling study, he seized upon aerial imagery to investigate ancient canal systems in many northern desert valleys.

Willey used images in a more systematic fashion, focusing on sites and only occasionally on agricultural works. He and Ford relied on air photos to locate their survey targets. Enlarged images were then employed to map architectural remains. Finally, the Virú photos contributed to the plotting of valleywide settlement distributions by time period and site type. Even in the driest of deserts, not all sites can be seen in air photos. Nonetheless, the Virú survey captured a revolutionary cornucopia of settlements that defied expectations. The imagery provided a holistic database for investigating the past and monitoring change. This made Willey's survey report, *Prehistoric Settlement Patterns in the Viru Valley, Peru* (1953), a milestone in New World archaeology.

Explaining why settlement patterns change is always challenging. Willey attributed the shift from preceramic coastal localities to interior ones with early pottery to economic change and the advent of intensive farming (1953). He cogently postulated that irrigation began well inland, where steep river gradients facilitated the construction of relatively short canal systems. Farming then advanced downstream, where successively shallower gradients required building progressively larger irrigation systems (Ford and Willey 1949). This remains a highly viable model pertinent to many desert drainages. Willey proposed that armed conflict and conquest were responsible for a number of later settlement pattern changes. Because ceramic depictions of warriors and combat were found, this theory was tenable when applied to the Moche presence in Virú. There was scant evidence of warfare or subjugation during the Tiwanaku horizon style occupation, but it was presumed to be Inca-like. In the next valley north, the succeeding Chimu populations were stylistically affiliated with Chan Chan, the capital of Chimor, which the Spanish sources portrayed as a conquest state.

Although largely unappreciated, one of the great transformations that Willey documented was a marked population decline during the late prehistoric Chimu occupation. The conspicuous drop in numbers of Virú habitation sites and cemeteries transpired long after the establishment of irrigation agriculture and during the political reign of Chimor, the second largest Andean imperium documented by ethnohistorical sources. This type of transformation was of a different order from a change in style or fashion and was new to the discipline. Casting about for an explanation, Gordon suggested that people from Virú might have resettled around Chan Chan, the capitol of Chimor. This conjecture was reasonable, given the Inca practice of resettling certain subjects. Yet it tended to explain away the population decline, which received little subsequent attention.

Half a century later, I approached Willey with an alternative explanation. Survey in the vicinity of Chan Chan had not revealed a population influx from Virú. However, studies of the irrigation systems surrounding the city indicated that they had atrophied markedly in later Chimu times and that more than 25 percent of the land that was formerly farmed was lost (Ortloff and Kolata 1993). Given these conditions, I suggested that demographic decline in Virú might be better understood as a corollary of the prolonged drought that had enveloped the central Cordillera by A.D. 1200 and then endured for at least two centuries (Moseley 2001). Gordon readily accepted this proposition, pointing out that when his Virú survey was undertaken, no one knew that the Andes had experienced Holocene environmental change. Indeed, proxy records of past climatic conditions in the Cordillera were few until the 1980s. Expectably, this recent information has engendered increasing debate about what role, if any, environmental change played in Peruvian prehistory. Andean archaeology has simply entered a stage of inquiry that southwestern studies passed through some seven decades ago, when tree ring studies first identified ancient catastrophic drought in the region (Douglass 1929).

Willey clearly recognized that demographic decline in Virú and prolonged Andean droughts were, at best, temporal corollaries involving two very different phenomena—one human, the other climatic. Consequently, he challenged me to develop bridging arguments and explore testable propositions that could elicit relationships between the two phenomena. As the potential source of stress, water must be the starting point for this task.

Although not numerous, Andean glacier and lake core proxies document decreased precipitation from about A.D. 1100 to 1500, with a nadir in the 1300s, when rainfall was 10 to 15 percent below long-term norms. If these conditions apply to Río Virú headwaters, then hydrological ramifications must be considered. This is because drought stress is greater on runoff farming and irrigation than on highland rainfall farming. Typically, desert drainages, such as the coastal Virú, receive sufficient precipitation to generate runoff in only 20 percent or less of their basin that lies above three thousand meters. In the lower 80 percent or more of the basin, streamflow is rapidly lost to seepage and evaporation in a relatively linear manner. Along the arid Pacific watershed, headwater soils have a moisture absorbency value of 200 millimeters (mm) or more. Similar to sponges, soils take up a set amount of rainfall before reaching saturation. Only after their saturation point is reached is additional precipitation shed as surface runoff. Because headwater soil absorption values remain constant from year to year, they exacerbate runoff loss when rainfall drops below normal. Thus, for example, if there is normally 300 mm of annual rainfall in a highland basin area and soils take up 200 mm of moisture, then 100 mm runs off. Consequently, when rainfall drops by 10 percent, to 270 mm, and 200 mm is absorbed prior to saturation, only 70 mm becomes runoff. With a 15 percent decline in rainfall, runoff drops by 45 percent, to 55 mm. Similar calculations would have to be made for successively higher elevations in Virú's upper basin to obtain an accurate assessment of drought impact on river discharge at the valley mouth. Nonetheless, it is safe to say that runoff reaching the coast declined by well over 25 percent in late prehistoric dry times. This would be a substantial source of stress, particularly if coastal agriculture had previously expanded to the maximum capacity sustainable with normal long-term runoff.

Taking into account preliminary hydrological constraints, it is essential to consider how decreased river flow might have reverberated through the valley's irrigation systems, flood supplies, and storage facilities and eventually affected local nutrition and demographics. Although this task requires information not generated by the Virú Valley project, it entails testable expectations. To judge from irrigation studies around Chan Chan, the Virú

Chimu relied on open-channel earthbank canals. These conduits typically lose more than half the moisture they take in to seepage and evaporation during the course of water transport. Therefore, distal ends of channels should have been dropped from use first in order to reduce transport losses, and irrigation systems should have gradually contracted upchannel and back toward the river as drought progressed. Traditionally, upstream irrigation systems have had better water supplies and preferential rights over downstream ones, which suffer more during dry years due to greater streamflow losses from filtration and evaporation. Therefore, valley mouth canal systems should have been abandoned first, followed by progressively upstream systems. Unfortunately, the Virú project did not map or date abandoned canal systems in sufficient detail to assess these hydrological propositions.

Loss of irrigated land should prompt development of alternative farming methods, but the desert offers few alternatives other than exploiting groundwater. Willey documented widespread construction and use of sunken gardens in high–water table areas near the coast (1953). Excavating planting surfaces a story or more down to naturally moist sediment is laborious, costly, and only tenable in near-shore localities, where groundwater is relatively shallow. Yet even where the practice was hydrologically tenable, substantial quantities of backdirt from one garden inhibited excavating an immediately adjacent farming pit. Indeed, in many situations mounds of earth spoil exceeded sunken planting surfaces. Thus, although sunken gardens were constructed in many valley mouth settings during later Chimu times, they could not compensate for the pervasive loss of irrigated land.

During the course of prolonged water scarcity, a shift to less-thirsty crops is predictable, as are the consumption of wild foods and the intensification of coastal fishing and maritime exploitation. And because some years produced better yields than others, inhabitants likely expanded food storage facilities during the long-term decline in runoff. Ultimately, if drought contributed to population loss, then this was through dietary duress. Studies of Chimu mortuary populations elsewhere record a high incidence of anemia and poor nutrition. However, the health of Virú's late prehistoric people has not been investigated, nor have their storage facilities, food remains, and canal systems.

In overview, connective pathways running from decreased rainfall levels through nutritional stress to decreased population levels in Virú are complex and poorly explored. Without ever veering toward environmental determinism, Willey accepted the drought scenario for Virú, but not because it was a pat solution. Rather, he recognized that potential influences of climate on society could be evaluated on the basis of testable hypotheses. This, in turn, opens the door to rigorous study of dynamic interactions between nature and culture in the Andes and elsewhere.

Epilogue

Willey's 1953 settlement pattern study became the default synthesis of the larger Virú undertaking because the project's senior participants could not agree on who would author a final overview. Unfortunately, this precocious project turned out to be something of a flash in the pan. The participating archaeologists did not continue active Peruvian field studies, and the dominant focus of U.S.-instigated research shifted to chronological refinement based on seriating of mortuary tomb lots. Nonetheless, Gordon's efforts to understand horizon styles and classify cultural contact situations remain enduring, viable contributions to the field. After his departure, settlement pattern studies languished in the Andes but eventually took hold and were refined. More robust when later resumed in Peru, these studies are now major components of prehistoric inquiry in the Andes, as well as lightening rods for debate about natural versus cultural influences in the shaping of the archaeological record. Thus, Willey cast a long shadow over research in the Cordillera, and his legacy remains unmatched.

References

Burger, Richard, ed. Forthcoming. *The Writings of Julio C. Tello*. Iowa City: University of Iowa Press.

Douglass, Andrew E. 1929. "The Secrets of the Southwest Solved by Talkative Tree Rings." *National Geographic*, December, 737–70.

Ford, James A., and Gordon R. Willey. 1941. "An Interpretation of the Prehistory of the Eastern United States." *American Anthropologist* 43 (3):325–63.

———. 1949. *Surface Survey of the Viru Valley, Peru*. Anthropological Papers, vol. 43, pt. 1. New York: American Museum of Natural History.

Kosok, Paul. 1965. *Life, Land and Water in Peru*. New York: Long Island University Press.

Moseley, Michael, and Gordon R. Willey. 1973. "Aspero, Peru: A Re-examination of the Site and Its Implications." *American Antiquity* 38 (4):452–68.

Murra, John V. 1972. "El 'control vertical' de un máximo de pisos ecológicos en la economía de las sociedades andinas." In *Visita de la provincia de León de Huánuco en 1562 por Inigo Ortiz de Zuniga, Documentos para la historia y etnologia de Huanuco y la selva central*, ed. John V. Murra, 2:427–76. Huánuco, Peru: Universidad Nacional Hermilio Valdizán.

Ortloff, Charles R., and Alan L. Kolata. 1993. "Climate and Collapse: Agro-ecological Perspectives on the Decline of the Tiwanaku State." *Journal of Archaeological Sciences* 20:195–221.

Owen, Bruce, and Paul Goldstein. 2001. "Tiwanaku en Moquegua: Interacciones regionales y colapso." *Boletin de Arqueologia PUCP* (Lima) 5:169–87.

Rowe, John H. 1954. *Max Uhle, 1856–1944: A Memoir of the Father of Peruvian Archaeology*. University of California Publications in American Archaeology and Ethnology, vol. 46, no. 1. Berkeley and Los Angeles: University of California Press.

Strong, William Duncan, and John M. Corbett. 1943. "A Ceramic Sequence at Pachacamac." In *Archaeological Studies in Peru, 1941–1942*, ed. William D. Strong, Gordon R. Willey, and John M. Corbett, 1:27–122. New York: Columbia University Press.

Tello, Julio C. 1929. *Antiguo Perú: Primera época*. Lima: Comisión Organizadora del Segundo Congreso Sudamericano de Turismo.

Uhle, Max. 1903. *Pachacamac; Report of the William Pepper, M.D., LL.D., Peruvian Expedition of 1896*. Trans. Charlotte Grosse. Philadelphia: University of Pennsylvania, Department of Archaeology.

———. 1906. "Los Kjoekkenmoedings del Peru." *Revista Historica* (Lima) 1:3–23.

Willey, Gordon R. 1943. *Excavations in the Chancay Valley: Archaeological Studies in Peru 1941–1942*. Columbia Studies in Archaeology and Ethnology, vol. 1, no. 3. New York: Columbia University Press.

———. 1945. "Horizon Styles and Pottery Traditions in Peruvian Archaeology." *American Antiquity* 11:49–56.

———. 1946a. "The Archaeology of the Greater Pampa." In *Handbook of South American Indians*, ed. Julian H. Steward, 1:25–46. Bureau of American Ethnology Bulletin 143. Washington, D.C.: Smithsonian Institution Press.

———. 1946b. "The Culture of La Candelaria." In *Handbook of South American Indians*, ed. Julian H. Steward, 2:661–75. Bureau of American Ethnology Bulletin 143. Washington, D.C.: Smithsonian Institution Press.

———. 1948. "Functional Analysis of 'Horizon Styles' in Peruvian Archaeology." In *A Reappraisal of Peruvian Archaeology*, ed. Wendell C. Bennett, 8–15. Memoirs of the Society for American Archaeology, no. 4. Menasha, Wis.: Society for American Archaeology.

———. 1951. "The Chavin Problem: A Review and Critique." *Southwestern Journal of Anthropology* 7 (2):103–44.

———. 1953. *Prehistoric Settlement Patterns in the Viru Valley, Peru*. Bureau of American Ethnology Bulletin 155. Washington, D.C.: Smithsonian Institution Press.

———. 1966. *An Introduction to American Archaeology*. Vol. 1, *North and Middle America*. Englewood Cliffs, N.J.: Prentice Hall.

————. 1971. *An Introduction to American Archaeology*. Vol. 2, *South America*. Englewood Cliffs, N.J.: Prentice Hall.

————. 1988. *Portraits in American Archaeology: Remembrances of Some Distinguished Americanists*. Albuquerque: University of New Mexico Press.

Willey, Gordon R., and John N. Corbett. 1954. "Early Ancon and Early Supe Culture: Chavin Horizon Sites of the Central Peruvian Coast." In *Columbia Studies in Archaeology and Ethnology*, ed. Gordon Willey and John Corbett, 3:84–130. New York: Columbia University Press.

Willey, Gordon R., and George D. Howard. 1948. *Lowland Argentine Archaeology*. Yale University Publications in Archaeology, no. 39. New Haven, Conn.: Yale University Press.

Willey, Gordon R., and Philip Phillips. 1958. *Method and Theory in American Archaeology*. Chicago: University of Chicago Press.

Willey, Gordon R., John H. Rowe, Charles C. DiPeso, William A. Ritchie, Irving Rouse, and Donald W. Lathrap. 1956. "An Archaeological Classification of Culture Contact Situations." In *Seminars in Archaeology: 1955*, ed. Robert Wauchope, 1–30. Memoirs of the Society for American Archaeology, no. 11. Salt Lake City: Society for American Archaeology.

Chapter Three

Legacies of Gordon Willey's Belize Valley Research

Wendy Ashmore

The following words are Gordon Willey's, from one of the last conference presentations he prepared, in this case for a multidisciplinary conference on architecture and settlement, held at the University of Pennsylvania in October 2000:

> The manner in which people have arranged themselves over and built upon the surfaces of the earth must inevitably tell us something about the societies and cultures of which they were a part. This, in brief, is the logic behind settlement pattern studies in archaeology. The idea is neither esoteric nor profound but basic and obvious, as is the corollary proposition that settlement arrangements and constructions, in their turn, help form and shape society and culture. In a word, settlement pattern study is a necessary, indeed, an inevitable part of archaeology. (Willey 2005, 27)

In this passage he conveys succinctly the essence of settlement pattern studies—the kind of archaeological inquiry for which his work is widely credited as seminal (see, e.g., Billman 1999; Parsons 1972; Preucel 1998; Sabloff and Ashmore 2001). The usual reference to Willey's settlement pattern work, of course, is to his research in the Virú Valley of Peru. But it is his project in the Belize Valley that I examine here (fig. 3.1 shows Willey in

Figure 3.1. Gordon Willey in excavation at Barton Ramie. Reproduced by permission from Willey et al. 1965, fig. 115. Copyright 1965 by the President and Fellows of Harvard College.

the field there), arguing both that it reflects an expansion of the new approach begun in Peru and, more broadly, that it embodies other critical aspects of his intellectual legacy. Prominent among these are his consummate abilities to synthesize quickly the state of knowledge in a field, to identify crucial problem areas, to act swiftly and constructively to advance both inquiry and understanding, and to stimulate others to think in new ways.

When Gordon Willey joined the Harvard faculty in 1950, his work in the Virú Valley was headed for publication, and he had moved from the Andes to fieldwork in Panama. Accepting the new position as the Bowditch Professor of Mexican and Central American Archaeology and Ethnology, however, he took Alfred Tozzer's advice to shift his research to the Maya area (Willey 1988, 288–89; 2004, 15). In consequence, not only was he plunged immediately into yet another geographic and cultural setting, but also he was thereby provided an opportunity to (among other things) test his settlement pattern approach in a very different context. Within a short time, Willey had assessed the state of understanding of ancient Maya settlement patterns, writing in a 1956 article that it was more "a matter for speculation and debate rather than for statement of fact" (1956a, 113). He highlighted the need for inquiry on several key issues: "the size and composition of the Maya living community, . . . the relationship between the living community and the ceremonial center [and] the changes, if any, . . . in population size and grouping [during] Maya prehistory" (Willey 1956a, 107). In the same article, however, he also moved to stimulate and guide new thinking, proposing three alternative idealized settlement "types," each of which related "ceremonial center to house mounds or locations" (Willey 1956a, 110–11). He also cited his own beginning work in the Belize Valley as "a nibble at one edge of the whole vast problem of prehistoric Maya settlement and its interpretation" (Willey et al. 1965, 6).

This beginning work opened a major new research campaign to examine Maya settlement traces along the lines of his analysis of the field. Together with a diverse set of colleagues—among whom he identified William Bullard as the "mainstay" (Willey 1988, 331)—Willey conducted four seasons of fieldwork in what was then British Honduras, centering surveys and excavations in a cleared stretch of the Barton Ramie plantation, along the northern alluvial terraces of the Belize River (see figs. 3.2 and 3.3). The results of those endeavors served as foundations for multiple lines of research (Willey et al. 1965), and they are still widely cited as such. My goal here is to consider why this is so and, more precisely, what the legacies of the Belize Valley efforts are, with respect to settlement pattern studies, Maya archaeology, and archaeology more generally.

Settlement Patterns

Willey's own recounting of the Virú settlement study portrays it almost as an afterthought within the larger research program (1974, 154; 2005, 27–28). In the "division of problems" addressed by the Virú project, settlement patterns was listed last, at number eight (Ford and Willey 1949, 18; cf. Willey 1946). Willey explicitly identified it as an experiment in a new method, proposed to him in somewhat vague terms by Julian Steward (Willey 1953, 1; 1999a, 10; Willey and Ford 1949, 6). The experiment was, of course, hugely successful. So why does the project at Barton Ramie and environs matter?

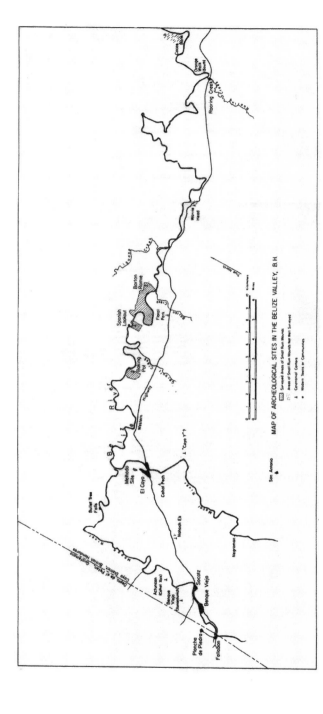

Figure 3.2. Belize Valley reconnaissance map. Reproduced by permission from Willey et al. 1965, fig. 2. Copyright 1965 by the President and Fellows of Harvard College.

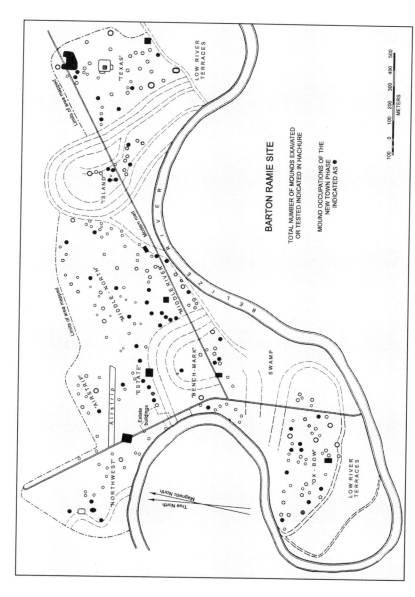

Figure 3.3. Map of Barton Ramie site, showing all mound ruins and highlighting those associated with New Town–phase ceramics. Reproduced by permission from Willey et al. 1965, fig. 172. Copyright 1965 by the President and Fellows of Harvard College.

To be sure, in some historical accounts, Virú's long shadow permits little more than a small glimpse of Barton Ramie. But beyond the later project's significant shifts in setting, culture, and logistics—all of which dealt with new potentials and constraints—at least two features marked the Belize Valley research as different from Virú.

The first was that settlement pattern study got at least equal billing, if it did not take center stage, and other methods were fit within a research program oriented around the promising new method (Willey 2004, 16). Antecedents there certainly were, in the Maya area and beyond; nevertheless, Willey and his colleagues' investigations in the Belize Valley gave both intellectual focus and institutional imprimatur to the study of settlement patterns, on what seemed a new scale.

The second feature is the scope of the Central American research, which Evon Vogt and Richard Leventhal describe succinctly (1983, xviii–xix). The following oft-cited Willey quotation from the Virú monograph addresses the relevance of settlement pattern studies:

> The term "settlement patterns" is defined here as the way in which man disposed himself over the landscape on which he lived. It refers to dwellings, to their arrangement, and to the nature and disposition of other buildings pertaining to community life. These settlements reflect the natural environment, the level of technology on which the builders operated, and various institutions of social interaction and control which the culture maintained. Because settlement patterns are, to a large extent, directly shaped by widely held cultural needs, they offer a strategic starting point for the fundamental interpretation of archaeological cultures.
>
> . . . I have confidence that the settlement-pattern approach to a functional understanding of prehistoric cultures is a sound conception. (Willey 1953, 1–2; cf. Willey 1946, 226–27)

Vogt and Leventhal quote this passage and compare its description with Willey's more expansive statement of purpose for the Belize Valley project. For this research Willey presented goals similar to the ones he described for Virú, but then asserted:

> On higher levels of inference, these problems lead on to larger questions of land utilization, agricultural potential, population densities, urbanism, the districting or zoning of ancient settlement, and the interdependence or independence of communities or community assemblages. And, perhaps, ultimately, the data bearing on these problems and solutions of them will help resolve the mystery of the apparent abandonment of the

southern Maya lowlands at the close of the Classic Period and the "fall" of Maya civilization. (Willey et al. 1965, 15)

To be sure, Willey does treat broadly parallel "higher levels of inference" in closing chapters of the Virú monograph (see also Billman 1999, 1; Preucel 1998, 702–703). Although Willey had apparently intended to include a lengthier treatment of those higher levels, reviewers' critiques led him to shorten drastically that section of the manuscript (Preucel, pers. comm., 2003; Willey 2004, 16–17). For the Belize Valley research, however, those levels were prominent from the project's inception. In that respect, even while the Virú settlement study richly deserves every bit of the widespread acclaim it receives for breaking new ground, the broad purview Willey offered in the Belize Valley statement moved toward presaging more closely the range of interpretive ends to which settlement patterns have come to be applied.

Although several of those interpretive ends are discussed explicitly later in this chapter, what is important to understand at this point is that the Belize Valley project tested the new method, in a new cultural and environmental setting, even as it boldly expanded the range of inquiry. Doubtless, it was the combination of Willey's vision for this project and his demonstrated successes at Virú that earned the Belize Valley research the "first National Science Foundation grant for archaeology" (Preucel 1998, 703), heralding the Carnegie Institution's replacement by NSF "as the major source of funding for U.S. archaeologists working in Mesoamerica" (Nichols 1996, 66–67). The settlement pattern "experiment" was maturing nicely in Willey's capable hands.

Maya Archaeology

Within Maya archaeology, the Belize Valley project has certainly been a shaping force in many areas. The project influenced not only settlement pattern studies but also pottery analysis, and perhaps most significantly it fostered advances in models for demography and for social, political, and economic organization. I mention here only a few salient illustrations.

Willey readily acknowledged that his was not the first instance of what we would now label as Maya settlement pattern studies (see, e.g., Ashmore and Willey 1981; Haviland 1966). In the Belize Valley monograph, he cited instances as early as the 1890s, observing as well that house mound "surveys and explorations and the questions of settlement [had been] a theme of the Carnegie Institution's Maya archaeological program from the 1930s forward" (Willey et al. 1965, 10). Willey's new approach met with some initial resistance, however, because it lacked a known sizeable center as its focus (Willey 1988, 329–30; 2004, 22). Despite receiving advice to change his plan, Willey persevered. By 1966, within a year of the monograph's publication, William Haviland aptly lauded the Belize Valley work as "a milestone, for it was the first full-scale research project concerned specifically with the living patterns of the Classic Maya as opposed to investigation of large and presumably functionally specialized buildings" (1966, 28). Shortly after the end of the next decade, Norman Hammond credited Willey's Belize Valley research as "inaugurating the regional approach that . . . characterized Maya archaeology in the 1970s" (1983, 25)—and, I would add, does so to a significant extent today.

Partly a catalyst, partly a model, the Belize Valley project clearly marked a major threshold, spurring concerted research along multiple avenues. Perhaps the broadest and most dramatic impact in the Maya area was that within a short time after the 1965 publication of the monograph, settlement studies had become essential to research designs in the Maya Lowlands. The vibrancy, diversity, and profusion of such inquiry across the Maya Lowlands led to a stocktaking in 1977 at the School of American Research (Ashmore 1981). Not only has settlement pattern research explored many new areas across the region, but also it has resulted in multiple projects that, in the same stretch of the Belize Valley where Willey and his team worked, continue fruitfully to extend and test findings made by the 1950s research (see, e.g., Chase 2004). The insights from and interpretive resilience of Willey's projects are manifest in a recent volume about the area, *The Ancient Maya of the Belize Valley: Half a Century of Archaeological Research* (Garber 2004). Not surprisingly, the volume is dedicated to Willey.

The wide-ranging research at and around Barton Ramie also produced or inspired models for ancient Lowland Maya social, political, demographic, and economic organization. With regard to social order, many have extolled Willey's settlement pattern studies as democratizing the range of society we study and seek to understand (see, e.g., Rathje 1983). Willey, however, preferred to see the shift "not so much as . . . moving from the 'palace' into the 'hut,' but as a widening of the field of vision to encompass both" (1983, 446; see also Trigger 1989, 310). Willey's approach was "critical to Maya archaeology because of its focus on *all* dwellings, both elite and non-elite, its concern with relating structures to the physical environment, and its attempt to infer function" (Sabloff 1990, 70, emphasis in original; see also Nichols 1996, 66). Importantly, the Belize Valley project immediately led Willey to recognize explicitly a wider diversity among commoner folk (see, e.g., Willey 1956b), a topic still being explored actively (see, e.g., Ashmore, Yaeger, and Robin 2004; Johnston 2002). Moreover, Willey and his colleagues challenged then-current models that sharply separated residents of rural villages from people of privilege in the ceremonial centers (see, e.g., Willey 1956b).

The Barton Ramie project yielded flexibly enduring (if not unchallenged) regional as well as local models of political and social structure, models that seriously engaged, refined, and challenged received wisdom. In 1958 Willey's Belize Valley colleague William Bullard extended the settlement pattern focus westward from the Belize Valley, traversing more than 250 kilometers across northeast Petén. Based on that experience, he systematized the frequent previous observations of house mounds, recognizing formally the "domestic house ruin" as one of the principal Maya settlement forms and positing formally their concomitant household level of social organization (Bullard 1960). Willey lauded his colleague's subsequent paper on Lowland Maya social organization (Bullard 1964) as "a small landmark in Maya settlement archaeology" (Willey 1988, 335), explicitly acknowledging Bullard's two Belize Valley– and Petén-inspired papers as the basis for their joint writings on Lowland Maya settlement patterns (Willey 1988, 336; Willey et al. 1965, 571n8). In these collective foundational works, Willey and Bullard were among the first to write of hierarchies in Maya settlement clustering and to suggest they were indices of successively more inclusive scales of social aggregation and integration (Willey and Bullard 1965; Willey et al. 1965, 571–81; see also Parsons 1972; Trigger 1968).

Directly or indirectly, the Belize Valley project also challenged conventional thinking about Maya land use and demography. Although evidence led Willey generally to support the prevailing view that milpa, or swidden, farming prevailed in Lowland Maya agricultural practice, he also noted evidence of terrace intensification and suggested that hill slopes bordering the Belize Valley alluvium, not the alluvium itself, constituted the fields supporting the dense bottomland occupation (Willey et al. 1965, 573–75).

These insights and the systematic manner of their presentation inspired subsequent research that confirmed preferential use of well-drained uplands *and* a diversity of practices for Lowland Maya cultivation at large (see, e.g., Fedick and Ford 1990; Harrison and Turner 1978; Willey 2004, 23).

Engaging debates about land-use strategies, swidden carrying capacity, and demographic reconstructions, Willey acknowledged what seemed to be high densities in the Belize Valley and environs while still maintaining that these fit within potentials of milpa-based subsistence (Willey et al. 1965, 577). At the same time, he contended that "[surely] the enormous ceremonial center of Tikal drew upon the efforts of many more people" than working estimates at the time proposed (Willey et al. 1965, 578). Findings from the Belize Valley project further spurred systematic settlement studies then beginning at such major centers as Tikal and Dzibilchaltun, where populations were revealed as extensive and dense (see, e.g., Haviland 1970; Kurjack 1974; Puleston 1973). As a catalyst and a model, then, the Belize Valley and northeast Petén research ultimately contributed to fundamentally rethinking the range of strategies and locales ancient Maya farmers had chosen, as well as the numbers and densities their populations reached (see, e.g., Rice and Culbert 1990; Fedick 1996; Turner 1978, 17).

Furthermore, Willey and his colleagues' Belize Valley studies reoriented thinking about political organization, from "treating the [elite] site and its monuments in isolation" to adopting a regional vantage point on settlement, society, and political organization (Hammond 1991, 13). The revolution in text decipherment has turned attention back, at least in part, to apical nodes of political articulation (see, e.g., Culbert 1991; Marcus 1976, 1992; Martin and Grube 2000). Nevertheless, while the understanding of Maya politics and social structure has advanced tremendously by still-expanding glyphic literacy, settlement-based models ultimately descended from the sorts proposed by Willey and Bullard remain vital, complementary sources of political inference (see, e.g., Ashmore and Sabloff 2002; de Montmollin 1989, 1995; Folan, Marcus, and Miller 1995; Hammond 1991; Marcus 1976).

Willey's Belize Valley project broke new ground—by innovating with new methods—in at least one additional domain. Whereas archaeology routinely depends heavily on ceramic analyses for constructing relative chronologies, as well as functional and other inferences, the Belize Valley project was once again noteworthy for reliance on (and nurturance of) a promising experiment. In this instance the experiment was the type-variety-mode method of pottery analysis, introduced to the Belize Valley from the southwestern United States. Radically different from previous analytic practices in the region, it has become the backbone of Lowland Maya ceramic study (Gifford 1976; Rice and Sharer 1987; Smith, Willey, and Gifford 1960). Initiation of the approach is appropriately credited principally to James Gifford, as are wide-ranging and thought-provoking analyses. But throughout, Willey's consistent sponsorship, support, and active collaboration are also quite evident.

General Archaeology

With regard to broader legacies, in an earlier review, Jeremy Sabloff and I characterized settlement pattern studies as perhaps "the single most critical theoretical or methodological innovation in archaeology since World War II" (Sabloff and Ashmore 2001, 14). Settlement study has been central to scientific, functional, and evolutionary archaeological inquiry (Sabloff and Ashmore 2001, 16), and it has been a cornerstone of the New Archaeology of the 1960s and after (see, e.g., Ashmore and Willey 1981; Preucel 1998, 708; Sabloff 1983; Sabloff and Ashmore 2001). The significance of the Belize Valley report in expanding the early purview of such study has been noted already. Directly or indirectly, that project has helped generate many further advances in archaeology at large, as asserted earlier in the chapter.

One of these is the burgeoning study of ancient households and communities (see, e.g., Canuto and Yaeger 2000; Flannery 1976; Robin 2003; Santley and Hirth 1993; Wilk and Ashmore 1988; Wilk and Rathje 1982). Willey's input in this domain was immediate in the Belize Valley, at the household-scale Melhado site as well as the larger site of Barton Ramie, as his findings were reported before or at the same time as the release of the monograph (Willey and Bullard 1956, 1965; Willey, Bullard, and Glass 1955).

Since the 1960s, social, economic, and ecological determinants of household settlement patterns have received concerted and diverse attention (see, e.g., Aldenderfer 1993; Blanton 1994; Flannery 1976; Hodder 1990; Trigger 1968; Ucko, Tringham, and Dimbleby 1972). And two decades after the Belize Valley work, Willey and Leventhal drew on their just-completed settlement pattern study at Maya Copán to define a series of local site types (1979) that, in turn, served unambiguously as a foundation and a stimulus for extensive subsequent household and community studies across the Copán

Figure 3.4. Gordon Willey, Richard Leventhal, and Wendy Ashmore at Copán in 1976, by Structure 10L-22. Photo by and courtesy of John Glavis.

polity (see, e.g., Fash 1983; Sanders 1986; Webster, Freter, and Gonlin 2000). (Fig. 3.4 shows Willey at Copán.) Issues of household and community formation and integration continue to inspire varied programs of new research. Indeed, a host of examples of household and community archaeology, in and well beyond the Maya area, testify eloquently to the profound and multifaceted impact that Willey's studies continue to have on archaeological understanding (see, e.g., Chase and Garber 2004, 9; MacEachern, Archer, and Garvin 1989; Rogers and Smith 1995; Sheets 2002). Willey's work was certainly not the only stimulus for these expanding lines of inquiry. But because of the pathbreaking methodological and interpretive developments in his Belize Valley project and its immediate offshoots, his initial Maya project remains, for many, a fundamental catalyst.

Landscape archaeology is another arena of study inspired by Willey's work. While landscapes have long been a fundamental focus of archaeological inquiry, reviews of current work in this area frequently acknowledge Willey's seminal contributions to the study of the settled landscape (see, e.g., Anschuetz, Wilshusen, and Scheick 2001; Ashmore 2004; Fisher and Thurston 1999; Knapp and Ashmore 1999). Particularly among archaeologists trained in America, landscape archaeology is often either allied with settlement pattern studies or seen as a juncture between the latter and historical ecology (see, e.g., Dunning et al. 1999; Erickson 2000; Kirch 2000; Rossignol and Wandsnider 1992). Although Virú is cited more often than Barton Ramie as a model inspiring landscape study, Willey's move to the Maya Lowlands and his aforementioned extension and test there of the settlement pattern "experiment" underscored the relation of landscape variation to human occupation, settlement, and land use. More inclusively, A. Bernard Knapp asserts that Willey not only "set this entire [settlement study] process in motion," but also by 1991 had "adopted a more humanistic approach . . . to assess 'the landscape of Precolumbian cultural history'" (1997, 13). Paraphrasing comments Sabloff and I made elsewhere (2001, 24), I maintain that settlement pattern research provides a common ground for the productive intersection of multiple perspectives, from culture history to processual and postprocessual views. Like Willey and his writings, settlement pattern studies nurture the intersection of social scientific and humanistic concerns. Indeed, it is such an atmosphere of critical encouragement that typifies Willey's legacy.

Conclusion

The Belize Valley report was unarguably innovative in many ways and constitutes a prominent component of Gordon Willey's legacy to archaeology. The work stands, of course, as an integral part of Willey's wider corpus of achievements, not as a work in isolation. In this chapter I have outlined specific aspects of its particular role, including immediate and particular contributions as well as longer-term and broader implications for settlement patterns, Maya studies, and archaeology more generally. In concluding the discussion, I add two further points.

The first is that Willey repeatedly urged that settlement patterns be studied jointly with artifacts and contexts. In so doing, he acknowledged explicitly "the wisdom or even the inevitability of [Taylor's] 'conjunctive' approach" (Willey et al. 1965, 6; see also Willey 1968; Trigger 1968). Although sometimes taken to task for the culture-historical perspective he steadfastly embraced, Willey was, as suggested earlier, simultaneously adventurously thoughtful—considering new theories and methodologies, probing them critically, if sometimes skeptically, and promoting and adopting those that convinced him of their efficacy. Recent examples are his enthusiastic endorsement (Willey 1999b) of the dual processual theory proposed by Richard Blanton and his colleagues (Blanton et al. 1996) and, more personally, his encouragement (Willey 2005; pers. comm. 2000, 2001) of my studies in landscape archaeology and other humanistic spatial archaeologies (Ashmore 1991, 2002). His frank advocacy of Walter Taylor's initially widely dismissed conjunctive approach is one indication that the same kind of critical openness was already well evident in the Belize Valley report, which had been completed by July 1962 (Willey et al. 1965, ix), while Lewis Binford's revolutionary call for a New Archaeology (1962) was yet in press.

The second and closing point is to emphasize the model for scholarship, which I cited at the outset, in Willey's consummate abilities to synthesize quickly the state of knowledge in a field, to identify crucial problem areas, to act swiftly and constructively to advance both inquiry and understanding, and to stimulate others to think in new ways. The Belize Valley project and report exemplified magnificently his breadth of vision, creativity of thought, encouragement to others, and simultaneous generosity of spirit. He set an admirable standard for his own subsequent research and writing, as well as for the work of his students and colleagues. As noted earlier, Willey wrote of the Belize Valley research—with his characteristic self-deprecating style—as an attempt "to nibble at one edge of the whole vast problem of prehistoric Maya settlement and its interpretations" (Willey et al. 1965, 6, 581). In the same vein, for the 2000 conference from which this chapter's opening quotation came, he wrote: "I can only close by repeating that settlement pattern study is, inevitably and inescapably, a major dimension of archaeology, and I am pleased to have had a small role in its more conscious recognition and development" (Willey 2005, 33).

Like many others, I am immensely indebted to Gordon Willey, and I miss his easy humor, generous counsel, and towering intellect. "Small role" and "nibbles," indeed, Gordon.

Acknowledgments

I thank Jerry Sabloff and Bill Fash for inviting my participation in this volume honoring Gordon Willey and his work, and I thank them as well as Tom Patterson, Bob Preucel, Chelsea Blackmore, and two anonymous reviewers for kindly and critically reading early drafts of this chapter.

References

Aldenderfer, Mark, ed. 1993. *Domestic Architecture, Ethnicity, and Complementarity in the South-Central Andes*. Iowa City: University of Iowa Press.

Anschuetz, Kurt F., Richard H. Wilshusen, and Cherie L. Scheick. 2001. "An Archaeology of Landscapes: Perspectives and Directions." *Journal of Archaeological Research* 9:157–211.

Ashmore, Wendy, ed. 1981. *Lowland Maya Settlement Patterns*. Albuquerque: University of New Mexico Press.

———. 1991. "Site-Planning Principles and Concepts of Directionality among the Ancient Maya." *Latin American Antiquity* 2:199–226.

———. 2002. "'Decisions and Dispositions': Socializing Spatial Archaeology." *American Anthropologist* 104:1172–83.

———. 2004. "Social Archaeologies of Landscape." In *Blackwell Companion to Social Archaeology*, ed. Lynn Meskell and Robert W. Preucel, 255–71. Oxford: Blackwell.

Ashmore, Wendy, and Jeremy A. Sabloff. 2002. "Spatial Order in Maya Civic Plans." *Latin American Antiquity* 13:201–15.

Ashmore, Wendy, and Gordon R. Willey. 1981. "A Historical Introduction to the Study of Lowland Maya Settlement Patterns." In *Lowland Maya Settlement Patterns*, ed. Wendy Ashmore, 3–18. Albuquerque: University of New Mexico Press.

Ashmore, Wendy, Jason Yaeger, and Cynthia Robin. 2004. "Commoner Sense: Late and Terminal Classic Social Strategies in the Xunantunich Area." In *The Terminal Classic in the Maya Lowlands: Collapse, Transition, and Transformation*, ed. Arthur A. Demarest, Prudence M. Rice, and Don S. Rice, 302–23. Boulder: University Press of Colorado.

Billman, Brian R. 1999. "Settlement Patterns in the Americas: Past, Present, and Future." In *Settlement Pattern Studies in the Americas: Fifty Years since Virú*, ed. Brian R. Billman and Gary M. Feinman, 1–5. Washington, D.C.: Smithsonian Institution Press.

Binford, Lewis R. 1962. "Archaeology as Anthropology." *American Antiquity* 28:217–25.

Blanton, Richard E. 1994. *Houses and Households: A Comparative Study*. New York: Plenum Press.

Blanton, Richard E., Gary M. Feinman, Stephen A. Kowalewski, and Peter N. Peregrine. 1996. "A Dual-Processual Theory for the Evolution of Mesoamerican Civilization." *Current Anthropology* 37:1–14.

Bullard, William R., Jr. 1960. "Maya Settlement Pattern in Northeast Petén, Guatemala." *American Antiquity* 25:355–72.

———. 1964. "Settlement Pattern and Social Structure in the Southern Maya Lowlands during the Classic Period." In *XXXV Congreso Internacional de Americanistas*, 1:279–87. Mexico City: Editorial Libros de México.

Canuto, Marcello A., and Jason Yaeger, eds. 2000. *The Archaeology of Communities: A New World Perspective*. London: Routledge.

Chase, Arlen F., and James F. Garber. 2004. "The Archaeology of the Belize Valley in Historical Perspective." In *The Ancient Maya of the Belize Valley: Half a Century of Archaeological Research*, ed. James F. Garber, 1–14. Gainesville: University Press of Florida.

Chase, Diane Z. 2004. "Diverse Voices: Toward an Understanding of Belize Valley Archaeology." In *The Ancient Maya of the Belize Valley: Half a Century of Archaeological Research*, ed. James F. Garber, 335–48. Gainesville: University Press of Florida.

Culbert, T. Patrick, ed. 1991. *Classic Maya Political History: Hieroglyphic and Archaeological Evidence*. Cambridge: Cambridge University Press.

de Montmollin, Olivier. 1989. *The Archaeology of Political Structure: Settlement Analysis in a Classic Maya Polity*. Cambridge: Cambridge University Press.

———. 1995. *Settlement and Politics in Three Classic Maya Polities*. Monographs in World Archaeology, no. 24. Madison, Wis.: Prehistory Press.

Dunning, Nicholas P., Vernon Scarborough, Fred Valdez, Jr., Sheryl Luzzadder-Beach, Timothy Beach, and John G. Jones. 1999. "Temple Mountains, Sacred Lakes, and Fertile Fields: Ancient Maya Landscapes in Northwestern Belize." *Antiquity* 73:650–60.

Erickson, Clark L. 2000. "The Lake Titicaca Basin: A Precolumbian Built Landscape." In *Imperfect Balance: Landscape Transformations in the Precolumbian Americas*, ed. David Lentz, 311–56. New York: Columbia University Press.

Fash, William L. 1983. "Deducing Social Organization from Classic Maya Settlement Patterns: A Case Study from the Copan Valley." In *Civilization in the Ancient Americas: Essays in Honor of Gordon R. Willey*, ed. Richard M. Leventhal and Alan L. Kolata, 261–88. Albuquerque: University of New Mexico Press / Cambridge, Mass.: Peabody Museum of Archaeology and Ethnology, Harvard University.

Fedick, Scott L., ed. 1996. *The Managed Mosaic: Ancient Maya Agriculture and Resource Use*. Salt Lake City: University of Utah Press.

Fedick, Scott L., and Anabel Ford. 1990. "The Prehistoric Agricultural Landscape of the Central Maya Lowlands: An Examination of Local Variability in a Regional Context." *World Archaeology* 22:18–33.

Fisher, Christopher T., and Tina L. Thurston, eds. 1999. "Special Section: Dynamic Landscapes and Socio-political Process: The Topography of Anthropogenic Environments in Global Perspective." *Antiquity* 73:630–88.

Flannery, Kent V., ed. 1976. *The Early Mesoamerican Village*. New York: Academic Press.

Folan, William J., Joyce Marcus, and W. Frank Miller. 1995. "Verification of a Maya Settlement Model through Remote Sensing." *Cambridge Archaeological Journal* 5:277–301.

Ford, James A., and Gordon R. Willey. 1949. "Virú Valley: Background and Problems." In *Surface Survey of the Virú Valley, Peru*, 11–28. Anthropological Papers, vol. 43, pt. 1. New York: American Museum of Natural History.

Garber, James, ed. 2004. *The Ancient Maya of the Belize Valley: Half a Century of Archaeological Research*. Gainesville: University Press of Florida.

Gifford, James C. 1976. *Prehistoric Pottery Analysis and the Ceramics of Barton Ramie in the Belize Valley*. Memoirs of the Peabody Museum of Archaeology and Ethnology, vol. 18. Cambridge, Mass.: Harvard University.

Hammond, Norman. 1983. "Lords of the Jungle: A Prosopography of Maya Archaeology." In *Civilization in the Ancient Americas: Essays in Honor of Gordon R. Willey*, ed. Richard M. Leventhal and Alan L. Kolata, 3–32. Albuquerque: University of New Mexico Press / Cambridge, Mass.: Peabody Museum of Archaeology and Ethnology, Harvard University.

———. 1991. Introduction to *Classic Maya Political History: Hieroglyphic and Archaeological Evidence*, ed. T. Patrick Culbert, 1–18. Cambridge: Cambridge University Press.

Harrison, Peter D., and B. L. Turner II, eds. 1978. *Pre-Hispanic Maya Agriculture*. Albuquerque: University of New Mexico Press.

Haviland, William A. 1966. "Maya Settlement Patterns: A Critical Review." In *Archaeological Studies in Mesoamerica*, 23–47. Middle American Research Institute, Publication 26. New Orleans: Tulane University.

———. 1970. "Tikal, Guatemala and Mesoamerican Urbanism." *World Archaeology* 2:186–98.

Hodder, Ian. 1990. *The Domestication of Europe: Structure and Contingency in Neolithic Societies*. Oxford: Blackwell.

Johnston, Kevin L. 2002. "Protrusion, Bioturbation, and Settlement Detection during Surface Survey: The Lowland Maya Case." *Journal of Archaeological Method and Theory* 9:1–67.

Kirch, Patrick V. 2000. *On the Road of the Winds: An Archaeological History of the Pacific Islands before European Contact*. Berkeley and Los Angeles: University of California Press.

Knapp, A. Bernard. 1997. *The Archaeology of Late Bronze Age Cypriot Society: The Study of Settlement, Survey and Landscape*. Occasional Paper 4. Glasgow: University of Glasgow, Department of Archaeology.

Knapp, A. Bernard, and Wendy Ashmore. 1999. "Archaeological Landscapes: Constructed, Conceptualized, Ideational." In *Archaeologies of Landscape: Contemporary Perspectives*, ed. Wendy Ashmore and A. Bernard Knapp, 1–30. Oxford: Blackwell.

Kurjack, Edward B. 1974. *Prehistoric Lowland Maya Community and Social Organization*. Middle American Research Institute, Publication 38. New Orleans: Tulane University.

MacEachern, Scott, David J. W. Archer, and Richard D. Garvin, eds. 1989. *Households and Communities*. Proceedings of the 21st Annual Chacmool Conference. Calgary, AB: Archaeological Association of the University of Calgary.

Marcus, Joyce. 1976. *Emblem and State in the Maya Lowlands: An Epigraphic Approach to Territorial Organization*. Washington, D.C.: Dumbarton Oaks.

———. 1992. "Dynamic Cycles in Mesoamerican States." *National Geographic Research* 8 (4):392–411.

Martin, Simon, and Nikolai Grube. 2000. *Chronicle of the Maya Kings and Queens: Deciphering the Dynasties of the Ancient Maya*. London: Thames & Hudson.

Nichols, Deborah L. 1996. "An Overview of Regional Settlement Pattern Survey in Mesoamerica: 1960–1995." In *Arqueología Mesoamericana: Homenaje a William T. Sanders*, ed. Alba Guadalupe Mastache, Jeffrey R. Parsons, Robert S. Santley, and Mari Carmen Serra Puche, 59–95. Mexico City: Instituto Nacional de Antropología e Historia / Arqueología Mexicana.

Parsons, Jeffrey R. 1972. "Archaeological Settlement Patterns." *Annual Review of Anthropology* 1:127–50.

Preucel, Robert W. 1998. "Gordon Randolph Willey." In *Encyclopedia of Archaeology: The Great Archaeologists*, ed. Tim Murray, 2:701–12. Santa Barbara, Calif.: ABC-CLIO.

Puleston, Dennis E. 1973. *Ancient Maya Settlement Patterns and Environment at Tikal, Guatemala: Implications for Subsistence Models.* Ann Arbor, Mich.: University Microfilms.

Rathje, William L. 1983. "To the Salt of the Earth: Some Comments on Household Archaeology among the Maya." In *Prehistoric Settlement Patterns: Essays in Honor of Gordon R. Willey*, ed. Evon Z. Vogt and Richard M. Leventhal, 23–34. Albuquerque: University of New Mexico Press / Cambridge, Mass.: Peabody Museum of Archaeology and Ethnology, Harvard University.

Rice, Don S., and T. Patrick Culbert. 1990. "Historical Contexts for Population Reconstruction in the Maya Lowlands." In *Precolumbian Population History in the Maya Lowlands*, ed. T. Patrick Culbert and Don S. Rice, 1–36. Albuquerque: University of New Mexico Press.

Rice, Prudence M., and Robert J. Sharer. 1987. Introduction to *Maya Ceramics: Papers from the 1985 Maya Ceramics Conference*, ed. Prudence M. Rice and Robert J. Sharer, 1–11. BAR International Series 345. Oxford: British Archaeological Reports.

Robin, Cynthia. 2003. "New Directions in Classic Maya Household Archaeology." *Journal of Archaeological Research* 11:307–56.

Rogers, J. Daniel, and Bruce D. Smith, eds. 1995. *Mississippian Communities and Households.* Tuscaloosa: University of Alabama Press.

Rossignol, Jacqueline, and LuAnn Wandsnider, eds. 1992. *Space, Time, and Archaeological Landscapes.* New York: Plenum Press.

Sabloff, Jeremy A. 1983. "Classic Maya Settlement Pattern Studies: Past Problems, Future Prospects." In *Prehistoric Settlement Patterns: Essays in Honor of Gordon R. Willey*, ed. Evon Z. Vogt and Richard M. Leventhal, 413–22. Albuquerque: University of New Mexico Press / Cambridge, Mass.: Peabody Museum of Archaeology and Ethnology, Harvard University.

———. 1990. *The New Archaeology and the Ancient Maya.* Scientific American Library, no. 30. New York: W. H. Freeman.

Sabloff, Jeremy A., and Wendy Ashmore. 2001. "An Aspect of Archaeology's Recent Past and Its Relevance in the New Millennium." In *Archaeology at the Millennium: A Sourcebook*, ed. Gary M. Feinman and T. Douglas Price, 11–32. New York: Kluwer Academic / Plenum Press.

Sanders, William T. 1986. Introduction to *Excavaciones en el area urbana de Copán, tomo 1*, ed. William T. Sanders, 9–25. Tegucigalpa, Honduras: Secretaría de Cultura y Turismo, Instituto Hondureño de Antropología e Historia.

Santley, Robert S., and Kenneth G. Hirth, eds. 1993. *Prehispanic Domestic Units in Western Mesoamerica: Studies of the Household, Compound, and Residence.* Boca Raton, Fla.: CBC Press.

Sheets, Payson, ed. 2002. *Before the Volcano Erupted: The Ancient Cerén Village in Central America.* Austin: University of Texas Press.

Smith, Robert E., Gordon R. Willey, and James C. Gifford. 1960. "The Type-Variety Concept as a Basis for the Analysis of Maya Pottery." *American Antiquity* 25:330–40.

Trigger, Bruce G. 1968. "The Determinants of Settlement Patterns." In *Settlement Archaeology*, ed. K. C. Chang, 53–78. Palo Alto, Calif.: National Press Books.

————. 1989. *A History of Archaeological Thought*. Cambridge: Cambridge University Press.

Turner, B. L. II. 1978. "The Development and Demise of the Swidden Thesis in Maya Agriculture." In *Pre-Hispanic Maya Agriculture*, ed. Peter D. Harrison and B. L. Turner II, 13–22. Albuquerque: University of New Mexico Press.

Ucko, Peter J., Ruth Tringham, and G. W. Dimbleby, eds. 1972. *Man, Settlement and Urbanism*. London: Duckworth.

Vogt, Evon, and Richard M. Leventhal. 1983. Introduction to *Prehistoric Settlement Patterns: Essays in Honor of Gordon R. Willey*, ed. Evon Z. Vogt and Richard M. Leventhal, xiii–xxiv. Albuquerque: University of New Mexico Press / Cambridge, Mass.: Peabody Museum of Archaeology and Ethnology, Harvard University.

Webster, David, AnnCorinne Freter, and Nancy Gonlin. 2000. *Copán: The Rise and Fall of an Ancient Maya Kingdom*. Fort Worth, Tex.: Harcourt College Publishers.

Wilk, Richard R., and Wendy Ashmore, eds. 1988. *Household and Community in the Mesoamerican Past*. Albuquerque: University of New Mexico Press.

Wilk, Richard R., and William L. Rathje, eds. 1982. "Archaeology of the Household: Building a Prehistory of Domestic Life." Special issue, *American Behavioral Scientist* 25, no. 6.

Willey, Gordon R. 1946. "The Virú Valley Program in Northern Perú." *Acta Americana* 4:224–38.

————. 1953. *Prehistoric Settlement Patterns in the Virú Valley, Perú*. Bureau of American Ethnology Bulletin 155. Washington, D.C.: Smithsonian Institution.

————. 1956a. "Problems Concerning Prehistoric Settlement Patterns in the Maya Lowlands." In *Prehistoric Settlement Patterns in the New World*, ed. Gordon R. Willey, 107–14. Viking Fund Publications in Anthropology, no. 23. New York: Wenner-Gren Foundation for Anthropological Research.

————. 1956b. "The Structure of Ancient Maya Society: Evidence from the Southern Lowlands." *American Anthropologist* 58:777–82.

————. 1968. "Settlement Archaeology: An Appraisal." In *Settlement Archaeology*, ed. K. C. Chang, 208–26. Palo Alto, Calif.: National Press Books.

————. 1974. "The Virú Valley Settlement Pattern Study." In *Archaeological Researches in Retrospect*, ed. Gordon R. Willey, 149–79. Cambridge, Mass.: Winthrop.

————. 1983. "Settlement Patterns and Archaeology: Some Comments." In *Prehistoric Settlement Patterns: Essays in Honor of Gordon R. Willey*, ed. Evon Z. Vogt and Richard M. Leventhal, 445–62. Albuquerque: University of New Mexico Press / Cambridge, Mass.: Peabody Museum of Archaeology and Ethnology, Harvard University.

————. 1988. *Portraits in American Archaeology: Remembrances of Some Distinguished Americanists*. Albuquerque: University of New Mexico Press.

————. 1999a. "The Virú Valley Project and Settlement Archaeology: Some Reminiscences and Contemporary Comments." In *Settlement Pattern Studies in the Americas: Fifty Years since Virú*, ed. Brian R. Billman and Gary M. Feinman, 9–11. Washington, D.C.: Smithsonian Institution Press.

————. 1999b. "Styles and State Formation." *Latin American Antiquity* 10:86–90.

————. 2004. "Retrospective." In *The Ancient Maya of the Belize Valley: Half a Century of Archaeological Research*, ed. James F. Garber, 15–24. Gainesville: University Press of Florida.

————. 2005. "Settlement Patterns in Americanist Archaeology." In *Structure and Meaning in Human Settlement*, ed. Tony Atkin and Joseph Rykwert, 27–34. Philadelphia: University of Pennsylvania Museum Press.

Willey, Gordon R., and William R. Bullard. 1956. "The Melhado Site: A House Mound Group in British Honduras." *American Antiquity* 22:29–44.

————. 1965. "Prehistoric Settlement Patterns in the Maya Lowlands." In *Handbook of Middle American Indians*, ed. Robert Wauchope and Gordon R. Willey, 2:360–77. Austin: University of Texas Press.

Willey, Gordon R., William R. Bullard, and John B. Glass. 1955. "The Maya Community of Prehistoric Times." *Archaeology* 8 (1):18–25.

Willey, Gordon R., William R. Bullard, John B. Glass, and James C. Gifford. 1965. *Prehistoric Maya Settlements in the Belize Valley*. Papers of the Peabody Museum of Archaeology and Ethnology, vol. 54. Cambridge, Mass.: Harvard University.

Willey, Gordon R., and James A. Ford. 1949. Preface to *Surface Survey of the Virú Valley, Peru*, 5–7. Anthropological Papers, vol. 43, pt. 1. New York: American Museum of Natural History.

Willey, Gordon R., and Richard M. Leventhal. 1979. "Prehistoric Settlement at Copan." In *Maya Archaeology and Ethnohistory*, ed. Norman Hammond and Gordon R. Willey, 75–102. Austin: University of Texas Press.

Chapter Four

Willey and Phillips
The Social Context and Maturation
of American Archaeology

Richard M. Leventhal and
Deborah Erdman Cornavaca

In 1958 Gordon R. Willey and Philip Phillips's book *Method and Theory in American Archaeology* (Willey and Phillips 1958) was published based upon their 1953 (Phillips and Willey 1953) and 1955 (Willey and Phillips 1955) articles in *American Anthropologist*. This is an important book in the history of American archaeology. Richard Leventhal first read this book in the mid-1970s and at the time wondered why the book was considered so critical in archaeology. It was not a deeply theoretical book, nor was it just culture-historical, nor did it have new insights into and approaches to the methods and the theories of New World prehistory. But that view was from twenty years after the book was published. *Method and Theory in American Archaeology* requires a second look based upon its 1958 context, wherein it sets forth the framework for the discipline during a period where the goals of American archaeology were under question.

Method and Theory in American Archaeology is divided into three parts: an introduction, which focuses upon the nature of archaeology within the discipline of anthropology; part 1, which presents a series of terms and concepts that Willey and Phillips argue underlie the discipline of archaeology; and part 2, which presents a broad cultural evolutionary model with examples of such cultural development from the Americas.

In this chapter we examine Willey and Phillips's book from three perspectives, or contexts. First, we focus upon the American intellectual milieu, specifically the nature of cultural evolutionary models in academia during the Red Scare—that period between 1917 and the mid-1950s. Second, we examine the book as a response to a direct challenge towards American archaeology by Clyde Kluckhohn (1940) and Walter Taylor (1948). Third, and finally, we argue that the book was one of the first clear-cut attempts to create and identify clearly a real archaeology discipline, in Thomas Kuhn's terms (1962).

Cultural Evolutionary Models and the Red Scare

From 1917 to the 1950s, the United States was in the grip of an antisocial-ism and anticommunism movement. The socialist takeover of Russia in 1917 initiated the first period of the Red Scare (1917–20). This period was particularly focused upon the fear of communism and socialism and the influence of these two movements upon American society. This fear lessened slightly after 1920 but continued through World War II and the Korean War, and a second major period of the Red Scare lasted from the late 1940s to the mid-1950s. Anticommunism grew in ferocity over the years and culminated in the 1950s with Joseph McCarthy's very public attack on individuals throughout the United States through the Committee on Un-American Activities (Schrecker 1986; Hodgson 1976; Belfrage 1989). The Red Scare became the underlying framework for American politics not only during the two periods of heightened public display but all throughout the period from 1917 to the late 1950s. Most relevant here, this strong movement against the influence of socialism and a socialist government structure included a political isolationist stance and an antievolutionary perspective.

This antisocialist, anticommunist movement within the United States had a huge impact upon academia, with faculty being targeted and fired for their political preferences and as a result of overly simplistic interpretations of intellectual work that found connections to Marxism almost everywhere. The impact upon anthropology is visible in a variety of shifts in the focus of anthropological research. Prompted by Franz Boas's theory of historical particularism, anthropology moved away from cultural evolutionary models towards a focus upon new research and fieldwork (Harris 1968).

Researchers during this period focused less upon theories of culture and change and more upon gathering new data from the field. Boas, certainly, was not opposed to either biological evolutionary or cultural evolutionary models. Although Boas intellectually supported evolutionary models, he argued for the need to develop broader historic and cultural models about past and present societies.

We believe that this apparent reluctance to work with evolutionary models was partly due to the chilly climate (between 1917 and the 1950s) for such research, which was seen as Marxist in origin. But by the end of the 1940s and beginning of the 1950s, this reluctance began to diminish with McCarthy's final, very public assault upon socialists and communists within the U.S. government. Although the attacks were virulent and very public, McCarthy's attempt to further his own career through these assaults was the final gasp of this Red Scare (Belfrage 1989). In American archaeology one of the first articles to return to a strong cultural evolutionary perspective on the prehistory of a region was authored by James Ford and Gordon Willey. It was published in 1941, prior to the final period of the Red Scare, in *American Anthropologist* and was titled "An Interpretation of the Prehistory of the Eastern United States" (Ford and Willey 1941). Several other articles followed this one, and the cultural evolutionary perspective was again becoming accepted within American archaeology and anthropology.

We are not proposing that Gordon Willey and James Ford were politically motivated or were consciously trying to make a statement to break the lock against cultural evolutionary models. In Leventhal's discussions with Gordon Willey about the changes in anthropology and the development of new cultural evolutionary models in the 1940s and 1950s, Willey saw them purely as intellectual developments, explaining, "It was the right time for new models. We had gathered enough data to begin creating these new evolutionary pictures." Willey and Ford and then Willey and Phillips did not present an overt evolutionary model in their respective articles and book but rather presented their culture-historical structure for the development and change of human cultures in the New World. We believe that this caution in proposing evolutionary models was the result of the cultural and political environment of the 1940s and 1950s. Other scholars do not see a strong evolutionary framework within these works by Willey and his colleagues (O'Brien, Lyman, and Schiffer, 2005; Willey and Sabloff, 1993).

In many respects the early article by Ford and Willey was one of many early attempts to begin the creation of new, broad cultural evolutionary models for the New World. A variety of additional models appeared over the next decade, including the Willey and Phillips articles in *American Anthropologist* (Phillips and Willey 1953; Willey and Phillips 1955; see also Steward 1947; Armillas 1948).

In fact, the 1958 book that is examined here was a clear attempt to create a broad evolutionary framework as part of the discipline building of the 1950s (discussed in more detail later in the chapter). A book such as this one, with its discipline-wide impact, would have been unthinkable in the sociopolitical context of the country even a decade earlier.

A Response to Challenges

Another context in which to view *Method and Theory in American Archaeology* involves the variety of challenges to Americanist archaeology, circulating in the United States in the 1940s, from both within and beyond the bounds of the archaeological discipline. The initial challenge came from two scholars at Harvard, one of the centers of anthropology and Americanist archaeology. The two individuals who threw down the glove were a Harvard professor, Clyde Kluckhohn, and one of his students, Walter Taylor.

Clyde Kluckhohn received his bachelor's from the University of Wisconsin in 1928, a master's from Oxford in 1932, and then a PhD from Harvard in 1936. He began as an instructor at Harvard in 1935 and then became an assistant professor of anthropology in 1937. Walter Taylor, one of Kluckhohn's students at Harvard, received his PhD in 1943 with a dissertation entitled "A Study of Archaeology: A Dialectic, Practical and Critical Discussion with Special Reference to American Archaeology and the Conjunctive Approach." This dissertation was first published as part of the American Anthropological Association memoir series in 1948 and then republished by Southern Illinois University Press in 1967.

Kluckhohn initiated the challenge to Americanist archaeology in 1940 with the publication of a book article entitled "The Conceptual Structure in Middle American Studies" (1940). This essay was highlighted in the book's table of contents as "a criticism of the intellectual basis on which Middle American archaeologists conduct their research" (Hay et al. 1940, iv). Interestingly, this essay was published right in the belly of the beast.

Kluckhohn presented his criticism in the Festschrift for Alfred Marston Tozzer entitled *The Maya and Their Neighbors: Essays on Middle American Anthropology and Archaeology*, edited by Clarence L. Hay, Ralph L. Linton, Samuel K. Lothrop, Harry L. Shapiro, and George C. Vaillant. Tozzer, the editors of this volume, and the other contributors were all part of a core group of traditional American archaeologists and anthropologists.

Kluckhohn begins his critique of Mesoamerican studies and American archaeology in general with a disclaimer—that he does not really know Middle American research and is an outsider. That, however, does not stop him from first creating a mission for Middle American studies and archaeologists and then critiquing the performance of researchers in the past.

> First, however, I must be careful to state and discuss briefly two postulates upon which my analysis will rest: 1. archaeologists and ethnologists wish to be "scholarly" at least in the sense of working systematically (with provision verification by other workers) toward the end of enriching our intellectual grasp of human experience; 2. In scholarly procedure there is a rational or conceptual element as well as a factual or evidential element. The first postulate implies that Maya archaeologists, for example, should not be interested merely in any set of facts as such—no facts are, from this point of view, their own justification simply because they satisfy our intellectual curiosity on a given point. Gathering, analyzing, and synthesizing all the data on, let us say, the calendar system of the Aztecs is justified only if all this industry can be viewed as contributing, however indirectly, toward our understanding of human behavior or human history. (Kluckhohn 1940, 41–42)

With this initial statement, Kluckhohn sets his agenda and then proceeds to state, rather clearly, that Maya studies, Middle American studies, and American archaeologists in general were not focused on the key points as set forth in his propositions. It is best to use Kluckhohn's own words to demonstrate his concerns.

> Let us now turn directly to Middle American studies. To begin with, I should like to record an overwhelming impression that many students in this field are but slightly reformed antiquarians. To one who is a layman in these highly specialized realms there seems a great deal of obsessive wallowing in detail of and for itself. No one can feel more urgently than the writer the imperative obligation of anthropologists to set their descriptions in such a rich context of detail that they can properly be used for comparative purposes. Yet proliferation of minutiae is not its own justification . . .
>
> Personally, I suspect that unless archaeologists treat their work quite firmly as part of a general attempt to understand human behavior they will, before many generations,

find themselves classed with Aldous Huxley's figure who devoted his life to writing a history of the three-pronged fork. (Kluckhohn 1940, 42–43)

This Maya essay was one of Kluckhohn's few forays into the field of archaeology, but it was a strong challenge to the field. Kluckhohn also had a huge impact upon Walter Taylor, a student at Harvard, in the creation of his dissertation (1943) and then his book *A Study of Archaeology* (1948). Taylor's book challenged much of the discipline of archaeology along the lines of Kluckhohn's Maya article while setting forth a more detailed set of concerns and challenges; it extended Kluckhohn's thinking.

In this short chapter, we cannot examine adequately all the detailed comments and criticisms found within Taylor's book, but a brief discussion is warranted. *A Study of Archaeology* can be broken into two main parts. Part 1 focuses upon an assessment of the history and background of Americanist archaeology and the study of the past. Taylor starts from the same position as did Kluckhohn.

> For even within academic and scholarly circles, what passes for archaeology has a compass that is truly Jovian, and the resultant confusion of theoretical precepts is largely responsible for the false position which, in many instances, the discipline of archaeology has come to assume. (Taylor 1948, 3)

In part 2 Taylor sets forth his own models for the nature of the archaeological discipline and specifically presents his "conjunctive approach." Taylor contrasts what he perceives to be the dominant model, the "comparative or taxonomic approach," with his conjunctive approach.

> The conjunctive approach, on the other hand, has as its primary goal the elucidation of cultural conjunctives, the associations and relationships, the "affinities," *within* the manifestation under investigation. It aims at drawing the completest possible picture of past human life in terms of its human and geographic environment. It is chiefly interested in the relation of item to item, trait to trait, complex to complex (to use Linton's concepts) *within* the culture-unit represented and only subsequently in the taxonomic relation of these phenomena to similar ones outside of it. (Taylor 1948, 94, emphasis in original)

Within this conjunctive approach, Taylor argues for a combination of archaeology with both ethnohistory and ethnography. These are combined in a format to emphasize the long continuities that connect the present to the past material found on the ground. This was less a new theoretical push than a strong methodological reassessment of how American archaeology could become more forceful with new interpretive rigor.

Taylor's book, which followed the completion of his dissertation in 1943, was published in 1948. It was eventually reviewed in a few journals and mentioned in a few articles of the late 1940s and the 1950s. (Taylor's book was also discussed in the 1960s and 1970s following Lewis Binford's use of Taylor's argument as the backdrop for Binford's "processual archaeology" [Binford 1968].) But generally, there was little response in the archaeological discipline to this challenge.

The two Willey and Phillips articles were published in 1953 and 1955 and were followed three years later by their book. Willey and Phillips do not refer to the Taylor book more than once. But the structure and the format of their book were clearly designed to offer a response to criticisms and challenges leveled at Americanist archaeology by both Taylor and Kluckhohn. Even without mentioning either Taylor or Kluckhohn, Willey and Phillips were, from the center of the discipline, responding to jabs and challenges from what was perceived to be the periphery of archaeology.

Defining the Discipline of American Archaeology

Willey and Philips attempted to define the basic structure, vocabulary, concepts, and framework for the discipline of American archaeology. They did this, following the publication of Taylor's book, but in a very different way from Taylor's.

As mentioned previously, in addition to its introduction, *Method and Theory in American Archaeology* has two major sections. The first focuses upon the identification of a variety of terms and concepts related specifically to the nature of archaeology as a discipline. The second part sets forth a broad cultural evolutionary model that is, in concept, viable for an entire range of societies and cultures across the globe. How did this book move the archaeological discipline forward, especially in light of the comments, criticisms, and strong language of the earlier writings of Clyde Kluckhohn and Walter Taylor?

The short answer is that Willey and Phillips were beginning the process of defining the discipline. They seemed to be reacting both to the criticisms leveled at American archaeology and to a trend in the broad American culture towards evolutionary models.

Considering the work of Thomas Kuhn helps illustrate the importance and the position of Willey and Phillips's book. Kuhn's book *The Structure of Scientific Revolutions* (1962) sets forth a model for the nature of theoretical change within scientific disciplines. Kuhn's broad model focuses upon the development of a paradigm within a scientific discipline; Kuhn then examines the nature of this paradigm and how paradigms shift. This model has been applied to many disciplines, including archaeology and anthropology, which has resulted in much controversy over its applicability to these social science disciplines.

The concept of paradigm is a critical one for the use of Kuhn's model, for it is the basis of his entire argument. A paradigm, according to Kuhn, is the overarching theoretical structure that provides the framework within which scientists function. Kuhn discusses paradigm as a shared set of rules, methods, and techniques. This definition is very similar to the way culture has often been defined within anthropology (see, e.g., Kuper 1999).

Following criticism of his book and confusion about this concept of paradigm, Kuhn attempted to split his definition into two parts (1974). The term "paradigm" continued to refer to a shared set of questions and values (culture). In addition, Kuhn created a new term, "disciplinary matrix," which referred to three things: (1) symbolic generalizations, (2) models, and (3) exemplars. These are, in fact, the set of rules, methods, and techniques mentioned earlier.

We believe that American archaeology in the 1950s was, in fact, in what Kuhn would call a "pre-paradigmatic state." There was no cohesion or paradigm that brought people and the discipline together. Competing schools of thought set the agenda within the discipline. The Willey and Phillips book, therefore, moved American archaeology towards its initial paradigm as the field was being defined for the first time.

Kuhn's 1974 reformulation of his paradigm theory as a two-part concept relates, we believe, to the two main sections of the Willey and Phillips book. Part 1 of that book, as mentioned earlier, is an attempt to define the methods, procedures, and terms associated with the day-to-day functioning of archaeology. Willey and Phillips define culture history and the nature of archaeological interpretation. They create a working model for how archaeological research can be done. This model includes three operational levels: (1) observation, (2) description, and (3) explanation. These levels are very much the rules, methods, and techniques that relate to the Kuhn model for his disciplinary matrix.

Part 2 of the Willey and Phillips book sets forth the shared set of questions and values for American archaeology of the 1950s. The authors present their very broad cultural evolutionary model, which consists of five major phases: (1) Lithic, (2) Archaic, (3) Formative, (4) Classic, and (5) Postclassic. This specific cultural evolutionary model was not itself the paradigm. What is significant, rather, is that the presentation and the acceptance of cultural evolution as the primary point of assessment and comparison for future studies led to archaeology's moving from a preparadigmatic state to a discipline in its initial throes of creation. The reemergence of this archaeological paradigm in the 1950s has arguably led to a long-lasting paradigm for American archaeology. The concepts of cultural evolution are under question and are constantly being reassessed. However, cultural evolution, as it was defined during the 1950s, has become a bedrock concept and shared belief within anthropology and archaeology across the globe (Trigger 1990).

What Willey and Phillips did within their book was to define the youthful discipline of archaeology. Their definition fulfills all the requirements of Thomas Kuhn's paradigm for a scientific discipline.

We do not think that Willey and Phillips specifically set out to create this paradigm within American archaeology. Rather, they were responding, in their own way, to the issues raised by Clyde Kluckhohn and Walter Taylor, and they were trying to bring consensus to the archaeological table. Many of the ideas and concepts presented in the Willey and Phillips book had been part of the discussion within the discipline during the previous decade or two. But for the first time, Willey and Phillips brought these ideas together in a clean and coherent statement of both the methods and the techniques of archaeology as well as of the primary questions relating to the cultural evolution of human groups throughout the world.

Conclusion

Ultimately, the Gordon R. Willey and Philip Phillips book *Method and Theory in American Archaeology* is a critical work for many reasons. It was written at a time when cultural evolutionary models were just returning to the mainstream of anthropological and archaeological thought. It responded, in an indirect way, to the criticism and challenges thrown at Americanist archaeology by Clyde Kluckhohn and Walter Taylor. Finally, it formed the basis for the creation of a real discipline by defining the concepts and the basic mission for an American archaeology of the future.

American archaeology was thus set up with a paradigm within which archaeologists could work and create interpretive and comparative models for the cultural evolution of human societies.

Interestingly, in the 1960s there was an attempt to argue that New Archaeology, or processual archaeology, brought about a paradigmatic shift within the archaeological discipline. But the creation of the paradigm of the 1950s, as seen within the Willey and Phillips book, carried over into the 1960s and beyond. It was the discipline's initial paradigm, and it is perhaps the only paradigm that has existed for American archaeology.

References

Armillas, Pedro. 1948. "A Sequence of Cultural Development in Meso-America." In *A Reappraisal of Peruvian Archaeology*, ed. W. C. Bennett, 105–12. Society for American Archaeology Memoir 4. Menasha, Wis.: Society for American Archaeology.

Belfrage, Cedric. 1989. *American Inquisition 1945–1960: A Profile of the "McCarthy Era."* New York: Thunder's Mouth Press.

Binford, Lewis R. 1968. "Archaeological Perspectives." In *New Perspectives in Archaeology*, ed. Sally R. Binford and Lewis R. Binford, 5–33. Chicago: Aldine.

Ford, James A., and Gordon R. Willey. 1941. "An Interpretation of the Prehistory of the Eastern United States." *American Anthropologist* 43:325–63.

Harris, Marvin. 1968. *The Rise of Anthropological Theory*. New York: Crowell.

Hay, Clarence L., Ralph L. Linton, Samuel K. Lothrop, Harry L. Shapiro, and George C. Vaillant, eds. 1940. *The Maya and Their Neighbors*. New York: Appleton-Century.

Hodgson, Godfrey. 1976. *America in Our Time*. New York: Vintage Books.

Kluckhohn, Clyde K. M. 1940. "The Conceptual Structure in Middle American Studies." In *The Maya and Their Neighbors*, ed. Clarence L. Hay, Ralph L. Linton, Samuel K. Lothrop, Harry L. Shapiro, and George C. Vaillant, 41–51. New York: Appleton-Century.

Kuhn, Thomas S. 1962. *The Structure of Scientific Revolutions*. Chicago: University of Chicago Press.

———. 1974. "Second Thoughts on Paradigms." In *The Structure of Scientific Theories*, ed. Frederick Suppe, 459–82. Urbana: University of Illinois Press.

Kuper, Adam. 1999. *Culture: The Anthropologists' Account*. Cambridge, Mass.: Harvard University Press.

O'Brien, Michael J., R. Lee Lyman, and Michael B. Schiffer. 2005. *Archaeology as a Process: Processualism and Its Progeny*. Salt Lake City: University of Utah Press.

Phillips, Philip, and Gordon R. Willey. 1953. "Method and Theory in American Archaeology: An Operational Basis for Culture-Historical Integration." *American Anthropologist* 55:615–33.

Schrecker, Ellen W. 1986. *No Ivory Tower: McCarthyism and the Universities*. New York: Oxford University Press.

Steward, Julian H. 1947. "American Culture History in the Light of South America." *Southwestern Journal of Anthropology* 3:85–107.

Taylor, Walter W. 1943. "A Study of Archaeology: A Dialectic, Practical and Critical Discussion with Special Reference to American Archaeology and the Conjunctive Approach." PhD diss., Harvard University.

———. 1948. *A Study of Archaeology*. American Anthropological Association Memoir 69. Menasha, Wis.: American Anthropological Association.

Trigger, Bruce G. 1990. *A History of Archaeological Thought*. Cambridge: Cambridge University Press.

Willey, Gordon R., and Philip Phillips. 1955. "Method and Theory in American Archaeology, 2: Historical-Developmental Interpretation." *American Anthropologist* 57:723–819.

———. 1958. *Method and Theory in American Archaeology*. Chicago: University of Chicago Press.

Willey, Gordon R., and Jeremy A. Sabloff. 1993. *A History of American Archaeology*. 3rd ed. New York: W. H. Freeman.

Chapter Five

Great Art Styles and the Rise of Complex Societies

Joyce Marcus

More than forty years ago, Gordon Willey published a paper (1962) that was as ambitious as it was comparative. Called "The Early Great Styles and the Rise of the Pre-Columbian Civilizations," it is both a product of its time and an enduring challenge for today's generation of archaeologists.

Willey noted that in both Mesoamerica and the Andes, the rise of first-generation states had been preceded by a period in which flamboyant and well-executed art styles had become multiregional in extent. He emphasized that these early art styles—called Olmec in Mesoamerica and Chavín in the Andes—had emerged at about the same time, peaking between 1000 and 600 B.C.[1] (in uncalibrated radiocarbon years).

Appropriately enough, both styles became known to the modern world at about the same time. In 1869 José María Melgar y Serrano published a paper describing the first Olmec colossal head (Monument A of Tres Zapotes) to be discovered (Melgar y Serrano 1869, 293). In 1871 the first Chavín sculpture (the Raimondi Stone) was found by José Polo in the town of Chavín (Tello 1960, 188).

Willey posed three key questions about Olmec and Chavín art: (1) What were the motivations behind the craftsmen's work? (2) What accounts for any similarity between Olmec and Chavín? (3) Might the Olmec style, believed to have emerged slightly earlier, have diffused southward and stimulated the Chavín style? Willey answered the last question in the negative. He argued that "stimulus diffusion" could not explain either style, since the landmass separating Mexico and Peru (the so-called Intermediate Area of Central America) lacked either style. He further noted that although Chavín and Olmec art often featured similar themes, these themes were expressed in different styles.

Willey concluded that the two styles had arisen independently, a position with which most of us agree. In fact, in today's theoretical milieu, we would see the development of the Olmec and Chavín societies as a case of *parallel evolution*, involving two sets of chiefdoms whose styles display similarities to those of rank societies as far away as New Zealand.

It is worth asking why Willey would have linked the "rise of civilization" to "great art styles" in the first place. In this endeavor he was following in the footsteps of two influential scholars of the 1950s, V. Gordon Childe and Alfred L. Kroeber. Childe had included the presence of a great art style as one of his criteria for civilization (1950). Kroeber saw such art styles as civilization's precursors (1951).

Willey's interpretation was that the symbols appearing in Chavín and Olmec art demonstrated the presence of a shared ideology within each region. He suspected that the presence of this shared ideology ultimately led to civilization by enlarging the social field, incorporating more individuals and more social segments into a larger network. By uniting what had formerly been separate segments, shared ideology becomes an ecumenical, or universal, style. Willey therefore concluded that Olmec and Chavín societies featured two multiregional "ecumenical religions" (1962, 7, 10).

Models for Chiefly Interaction

Archaeologists have tried in various ways to model the interregional interaction implied by the spread of early "horizon styles." Willey himself borrowed the concepts of "introgression" and "hybridization" from plant genetics to model Olmec and Chavín societies (1962, 8), but his biological and botanical analogies have not been pursued much in the last forty years.

One approach that *has* been widely used is that of Colin Renfrew and John Cherry, who developed a model of "peer-polity interaction" (1986). The key word in their model is "peer," a term that acknowledges that although interacting societies may be heterogeneous, they are roughly at the same level of sociopolitical development.

This 1986 model describing interaction among many roughly equal polities stands in contrast to older models in which a single precocious society served as the mother culture for its neighbors. The older view is typified by the work of Julio C. Tello (1942, 1943, 1960), who saw the highland site of Chavín de Huántar as the center of a *cultura matriz*. Today—based on the accumulated data of the last half-century—Richard Burger, a leading expert on Chavín, sees the style as the product of many interacting Andean societies of different sizes and origins, no one of which possessed all the elements of the style (1988, 1995).

Similar to Tello's view of Chavín as a cultura matriz was Miguel Covarrubias's view of the Olmec (1942, 1944, 1946), whom he regarded as a *cultura madre*. Today—based on the accumulated data of the last half-century—most Mesoamericanists prefer to see the numerous chiefdoms of 1200–800 B.C. as *culturas hermanas* (Hammond 1988), noting that none of them possessed all the elements of a widespread Olmec style (Demarest 1989; Flannery and Marcus 1994, chap. 20; Grove 1989, 1993, 1997; Marcus 1989).

Three years after Renfrew and Cherry's peer-polity model was proposed, Arthur Demarest developed a model of interregional interaction specifically tailored to Formative Mesoamerica (1989). In a more recent essay (Flannery and Marcus 2000), Kent Flannery and I borrowed a model from geneticist Sewall Wright (1939, 46), who had shown that one of the most favorable scenarios for rapid evolutionary change is one in which a species is divided into multiple local units, each adapted to its region but still in periodic contact with other units. The near-autonomy of each unit enables it to adapt to its local setting. The periodic contact between units increases the likelihood that should a favorable innovation occur in one unit, it will ultimately be transmitted to the entire population.

Just as the units in Wright's model all belong to the same species, interacting chiefdoms in an area like Mexico or Peru often shared a common cultural background. Groups sharing the ideology of a common ancestor are quicker to accept iconographic referents to that ideology than to some other. David Grove has suggested that the iconography on Mesoamerican pottery of 1200–800 B.C. referred to shared concepts of great antiquity (1989, 1997). Similarly, Andeanists would say that the roots of Chavín can be seen in the art of societies that preceded it, such as the art at Moxeke and Cerro Sechín in the Casma Valley and Punkurí in the Nepeña Valley (Burger 1995; Larco Hoyle 1941; Tello 1943, 136–40).

Robert Carneiro, in describing the competing chiefdoms of Colombia's Cauca Valley (1991), makes it clear that there were considerable differences in size, settlement patterns, and other sociocultural variables among them; nevertheless, all of them drew on each other until broad regional similarities emerged. In similar ways the various chiefdoms of the Andes and Mesoamerica were not uniform in size, local adaptation, preferences in crafts, repertoire of motifs, or artistic media. Their widespread styles were the product of an interaction that could be voluntaristic and peaceful when the societies cooperated in long-distance trade in exotic items, or competitive and violent when rivalry and raiding dominated.

The often-violent nature of chiefly interaction has been the subject of studies that emphasize not only its antiquity but also its effect on sociopolitical evolution (Carneiro 1998, 2002; Johnson and Earle 2000; Keeley 1996; Kelly 2000; Marcus 2000; Redmond 1994, 1998; Spencer 1993). Competition drove chiefdoms to intensify agriculture, concentrate manpower, elevate the level of craft production, raise enduring monuments of their own, and destroy the monuments of others.

Allen Johnson and Timothy Earle have described the role of raiding and warfare as follows:

> In local group villages, warfare pits small groups of warriors against one another in raids; sometimes these groups attack each other within the village, fissioning it. In clan-based local groups, warfare is organized by leaders and at least partly regulated by the intergroup collectivity. In chiefdoms, a chief imposes order within the chiefdom, bringing a highly valued peace to his subjects, but then wages violent and systematic warfare against neighboring chiefdoms and states. In short, warfare is no one phenomenon but the varying expression of aggression in varying institutional settings.
>
> We explain the nature of warfare, then, when we explain the level of sociopolitical integration at which it takes place. War itself explains some integration, but other principles (risk management, capital technology, trade) are required for a full explanation of the evolution of society. (Johnson and Earle 2000, 15–16)

Mesoamerica: How Many Style Horizons?

At the time Willey's 1962 paper was published, most Mesoamericanists regarded Olmec as the first style that was widespread and uniform. Today, we know that there were widespread pre-Olmec ceramic styles (1400–1150 B.C.), that the Early Horizon style that emerged throughout Mesoamerica at about 1150 B.C. displayed heterogeneity in time and space, and that chiefdoms of the Gulf Coast contributed only some of the motifs used during the Early Horizon (figs. 5.1–5.3 show Formative themes and motifs). Other regions, most notably the Basin of Mexico and nearby Morelos, may even have contributed more, including complex ceramic masterpieces (see fig. 5.1j).

Mesoamerica's first widespread style appeared on ceramics between 1400 and 1150 B.C. (Clark 1991; Flannery and Marcus 2000). Over a large area stretching from the Basin of Mexico to the Isthmus of Tehuantepec, villages of this period shared a complex of red-on-buff bowls, bottles, and jars (Flannery and Marcus 2000, fig. 3). To the east, the Veracruz-Tabasco lowlands, the Grijalva Depression, and the Chiapas coast shared a complex of neckless jars, or *tecomates*, with bichrome slips, fluting, and cross-hatching. The occupants of both style areas were aware of each other and exchanged products such as obsidian, shell, stingray spines, mica, and kaolin pottery.

A second set of widespread styles emerged between 1150 and 850 B.C., a period sometimes referred to as the Early Horizon (Flannery and Marcus 1994, chap. 20). Some of the most widespread motifs, often carved or incised on pottery, were stylized or abstract referents to Earth (especially in its angry form, Earthquake) and Sky (especially in its angry form, Lightning) (see figs. 5.1 and 5.2). As widespread as these motifs were, no single site had the complete repertoire: highland Mexican sites like Tlapacoya and San José Mogote had thousands of depictions of Earth/Earthquake incised on white-slipped or negative white vessels, whereas inhabitants at San Lorenzo in the Olmec region made no incised white-slipped or negative white pottery at all during this time. San Lorenzo did export gray pottery with carved designs, but the motifs seem to have been restricted to a sunburst and a narrow range of Lightning motifs (Flannery and Marcus 2000, 27). San Lorenzo's single greatest exportware, Xochiltepec White, reached many highland villages, but this *undecorated*, white monochrome pottery bore no iconography.

Despite efforts to credit the Gulf Coast Olmec with all of this iconography, we can see the full repertoire of Early Horizon motifs only when we look at the products of *both* highland and lowland Mexican sites. Significantly, sites located to the west of the old 1400 B.C. style boundary still

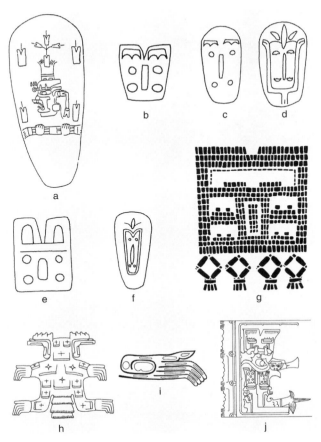

Figure 5.1. Mexican motifs representing Earth and the four world directions: *a*, celt from Río Pesquero, Veracruz, showing four openings in the earth, surrounding a face whose headdress includes four world directions (Benson and de la Fuente 1996, 269); *b*, four world directions below a cleft (Drucker 1952, fig. 47b); *c*, celt from Offering 2, La Venta (Drucker, Heizer, and Squier 1959, fig. 35c); *d*, celt from cache in Mound A-2, La Venta (Drucker 1952, fig. 47b); *e*, four world directions below a cleft (Kelley 1966, fig. 2a); *f*, celt from cache in Mound A-2, La Venta (Drucker 1952, fig. 47c); *g*, pavement beneath East Platform of Ceremonial Court, A-1, from La Venta (Drucker 1952, plate 10); *h*, crocodile skin worn as a cape by the Atlihuayán figure (Covarrubias 1957, fig. 21); *i*, foot of crocodile on Tlatilco vessel (Covarrubias 1957, fig. 10); *j*, elaborate design on Tlapacoya vessel (Niederberger 1987, 552).

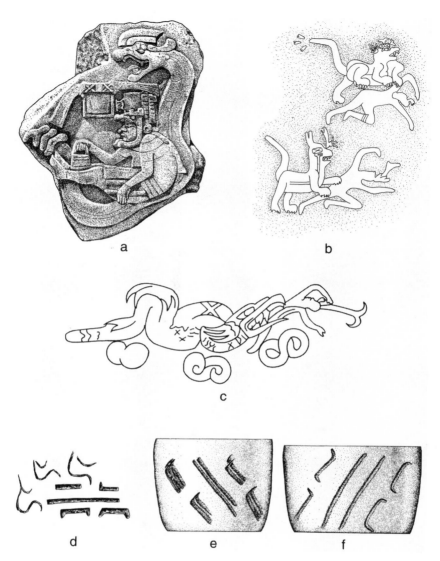

Figure 5.2. Artists of Formative Mexico depicted humans' relationships with fierce animals and supernatural forces, including Lightning: *a*, a serpent encircles a man (Monument 19, La Venta) (Drucker, Heizer, and Squier 1959, fig. 55); *b*, two jaguars, each trampling a human body (Relief 4, Chalcatzingo) (Grove 1972, fig. 2); *c*, reptilian creature devouring human (Relief 5, Chalcatzingo) (Grove 1968, fig. 6); *d–f*, depictions of Lightning on pottery from the Valley of Oaxaca (Flannery and Marcus 1994, figs. 12.39, 12.49).

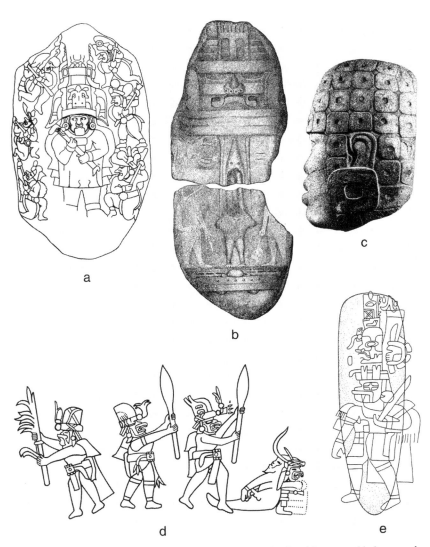

Figure 5.3. Gulf Coast Mexican artists depicted men wearing headdresses and helmets and carrying weapons and trophy heads: *a*, a central figure holds a possible weapon and is surrounded by six smaller figures, also holding apparent weapons (Stela 2, La Venta) (Drucker 1952, fig. 49); *b*, mask panel above three individuals, two in profile facing a central figure; the figure on the right holds a possible trophy head, while the other grasps a dagger (Stela A, Tres Zapotes) (Stirling 1943, fig. 3); *c*, colossal head, 1.8 meters high, showing possible chief wearing a helmet and large ear spools (Head 10, San Lorenzo) (Cyphers 1996, 53); *d*, three men appear to hold weapons, while the fourth seems to be the victim (Relief 2, Chalcatzingo) (Grove 1968, fig. 3); *e*, possible chief or warrior wearing an elaborate headdress and carrying a weapon (Benson and de la Fuente 1996, 273).

79

tended to share more ceramic attributes with each other than they did with sites to the east of the boundary. What villages on both sides of the style boundary did share was an enormously escalated interest in receiving sumptuary goods from other regions, which included obsidian, marine shell, iron ores, jadeite, mica, stingray spines, shark teeth, turtleshell drums, and conch shell trumpets (Flannery and Marcus 1976; Marcus and Flannery 1996). Without question, the reasons for this escalation in inter-regional exchange had to do with the rise of societies with a chiefly elite whose appetite for sumptuary goods was insatiable.

In other words, Mexico's Early Horizon (1150–850 B.C.) was not the first period to witness widespread sharing of styles, nor was it as homogeneous as once thought. During the Early Horizon, each region of Mesoamerica was distinct in its preferred medium of display and its repertoire of motifs. Certain media, like three-dimensional stone sculpture (see figs. 5.3a–c), were virtually restricted to the Gulf Coast, while most large, hollow whiteware "dolls" found in museums come from the central Mexican Highlands (Benson and de la Fuente 1996; Flannery and Marcus 2000, 29; Grove 1987; Marcus 1998; Niederberger 1987; Piña Chan 1955; Vaillant and Vaillant 1934).

After 850 B.C. many of the goods and motifs that had circulated during the Early Horizon disappeared or were replaced. With the collapse of San Lorenzo and the rise of La Venta, highland areas like the Basin of Mexico, Puebla, Morelos, and Oaxaca seem to have become far less interested in sumptuary goods from the Gulf Coast. Giant blades of Basin of Mexico obsidian, chipped to resemble stingray spines, became more frequent in highland Oaxaca temples than spines from actual stingrays (Marcus and Flannery 1996, fig. 132). Instead of depicting fantastic composite animals and abstract symbols of Lightning and Earth, as had the artists of the Early Horizon, the artists of the Middle Formative period seem to have been more interested in depicting elite individuals holding weapons (see fig. 5.3) and galleries of sacrificed prisoners (Marcus 1974, 89–90; Marcus and Flannery 1996, 152). Evolving social hierarchies and genuine military power, which were leading toward the formation of early states in several highland regions, changed both the cultural landscape and the design repertoire. In the last two centuries leading up to the formation of highland Mesoamerica's earliest states, there were many regional styles but no "great" one.

The Andes: How Many Horizon Styles?

Just as Mesoamerica's Early Horizon art, including that of the Olmec, was preceded by other widespread styles, so was the art of Chavín. One of the most dramatic venues for this early art was the exterior walls of public structures. For example, buildings at the site of Punkurí, in the Nepeña Valley on Peru's north coast, featured painted reliefs. One impressive clay sculpture was that of a jaguar placed in the middle of a staircase; its head was painted green, its pupils blue, its gums red, and its interlocking canines white. At the base of the giant feline was an offering that included the skeleton of a decapitated woman, buried with a kilogram of turquoise beads, a stone bowl and pestle, an engraved *Strombus* shell trumpet, and a pair of *Spondylus* shells (Tello 1943, 137).

The Casma Valley is one of the best-known areas featuring an impressive pre-Chavín style. It is most notably displayed at Cerro Sechín, which dates to roughly 1400 B.C.; there, we find a striking set of sculptures on the exterior of a public building fifty-three meters on a side (Samaniego, Vergara, and Bischof 1985; Tello 1943). Set into its walls are more than four hundred carved stones depicting both triumphant warriors holding weapons (fig. 5.4a) and victims who had been mutilated, quartered, or disemboweled (figs. 5.4b–f).

Another large center in the Casma Valley was Moxeke, known since Tello discovered (1956) painted monumental clay sculptures on a thirty-meter-tall, multitiered pyramid with rounded corners. Moxeke is architecturally similar to Cerro Sechín, and there are similarities in art style and motifs that link Cerro Sechín, Punkurí, Moxeke, and other sites during the pre-Chavín era (Burger 1995; Pozorski and Pozorski 1990; Tello 1943, 1956).

Here, as in Mesoamerica, traces of earlier distinctive regional pottery styles survived even during the peak of the region's great art style. As Burger puts it (1995, 60), "Generated by a high degree of community self-sufficiency and reinforced by competition with neighboring groups, there developed a strong sense of local identity which was expressed through these myriad pottery assemblages." The emergence of a widespread Chavín style subdued, but did not eliminate, that heterogeneity. The latter continued to be expressed in at least three ways—in the repertoire of motifs used in each region, in the use of different media, and in the popularity of different themes. Not only was there synchronic variation from

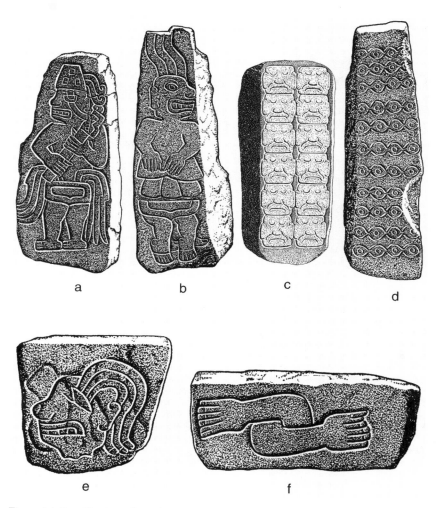

Figure 5.4. Pre-Chavín art from Cerro Sechín, Peru, featured warriors, trophy heads, and the butchered remains of victims: *a*, warrior carrying a club (Tello 1956, fig. 74); *b*, unfortunate fellow cut in half (Tello 1956, fig. 62); *c*, a dozen human heads stacked in two piles (Tello 1956, fig. 56); *d*, eleven strings of human eyeballs, representing forty-four eyes of twenty-two captives (Tello 1956, fig. 75); *e*, victim with blood spurting from eye socket (Tello 1956, fig. 89); *f*, arms of a victim (Tello 1956, fig. 88).

region to region during the Chavín horizon, but there was even variation over time at the type site of Chavín de Huántar. To express what was occurring during this time, Burger aptly entitled a 1988 paper "Unity and Heterogeneity within the Chavin Horizon."

Temporal and regional variability are often de-emphasized once scholars have invested effort into confirming that the label "horizon" fits an era. Once the art of a period has been declared a horizon, subsequent work tends to emphasize everything that is shared, rather than what differentiates each site from others (Demarest and Foias 1993; Rice 1993). Often, the differences are glossed over by subsuming them under a term such as "Chavinoid" or "Olmecoid." The late Pedro Armillas showed me graphically what he thought of the term "Olmecoid." Pointing to the metal tips of his field boots, he said, "This material is described by the manufacturer as 'silveroid.' It contains no silver."

The use of the term "Chavinoid" in the Andean literature is analogous to the use of the term "Olmecoid" in the Mesoamerican literature; both terms indicate that we are glossing over heterogeneity. As Burger puts it (1995, 211), "The sphere of [Chavín] interaction was multifocal and included a host of roughly equivalent regional centers, each continuing to serve as the center of more limited social systems." As was the case in Mesoamerica, the Andes at this time were characterized by a series of chiefdoms engaged in competitive interaction, exchanging products, and driving each other to achieve at a higher level. Chavín de Huántar was no more the sole source of artistic inspiration for this horizon than the Gulf Coast Olmec were for Early Horizon Mexico.

A Glimpse at the Art of Chiefdoms

In the sections that follow, I look not only at the art styles of Early Horizon Mexico and Chavín-era Peru but also at the styles of two other flamboyant chiefdoms, the Coclé of Panama and the Maori of New Zealand. My purpose is to show how differently these art styles would be viewed today as compared to Willey's era. In 1962 such art was assumed to reflect "religious cults" and to characterize societies on the verge of becoming "civilizations." Although we still see a lot of cosmological information in Early Horizon art, we now realize that a great deal of it referred to the military prowess of the individuals who commissioned the art, as well as to their relationships with supernatural ancestors. We also know that many chiefly societies with equally "great" styles, in other parts of the world, did not give rise to "civilizations."

Mexico's Early Horizon Chiefdoms

Mexico had multiple Early Horizon chiefdoms and multiple artistic media. While the Olmec chiefdoms of the Gulf Coast were leaders in three-dimensional sculpture, the greatest masterpieces of ceramic art come from the central Mexican Highlands (Benson and de la Fuente 1996; Cyphers 1996; Flannery and Marcus 2000; Niederberger 1987).

One widespread iconographic theme was the powerful forces of nature. Such depictions could be naturalistic or abstract. Some of the most wide-spread motifs, often carved or incised on pottery, were abstract referents to Earth (especially in its angry form, Earthquake) and Sky (especially in its angry form, Lightning). To show that these forces were supernatural, Early Horizon craftsmen combined parts of different animals to depict them, thereby creating fantastic creatures not seen in nature (Marcus 1989). For example, parts of crocodiles or snakes could be combined with parts of birds, fish, sharks, or felines (see, e.g., figs. 5.1j, 5.2c). In many cases artists used the principle of *pars pro toto* (the part stands for the whole); thus, a jaguar's canine teeth could stand for the jaguar, or a crocodile's foot could stand for the crocodile (see fig. 5.1i).

Earth could be depicted as an anthropomorphic or a zoomorphic being. It sometimes was depicted as having a cleft in its head, and occasionally, vegetation was shown sprouting from that cleft (see figs. 5.1d, 5.1f). Earth could also be depicted as a crocodile (or symbolized by a crocodile's foot), a reference to the widespread Mesoamerican belief that the surface of the earth was the back of a giant crocodile (see figs. 5.1h–i).

Petitioning Earth, or honoring it as a remote ancestor of the chiefly elite, could also be achieved by creating pavements of green celts and adzes, some bearing the symbols of supernatural forces. By so doing, the chiefly line could assert its supernatural ties to Earth, one source of its supernatural power. A Middle Formative example can be seen at La Venta, where enormous pavements of serpentine blocks show Earth with its head cleft at the top and four "world directions" pendant at the bottom (fig. 5.1g). This massive offering was dedicated to Earth, covered with clays of different colors, and then buried in such a way that Earth alone could see it (Drucker, Heizer, and Squier 1959).

A second way that a chiefly individual might link himself to Earth was to wear the skin of a crocodile as a cape, as seen in a ceramic figure from Atli-huayán, in the Valley of Morelos (fig. 5.1h).

Lightning, on the other hand, could be depicted by combining the gums of one creature with the eyebrows of another (Marcus 1989). The lightning bolt could be represented as a zigzag across the surface of a vessel or as a serpent with fiery eyebrows in the darkened sky. Particularly common on central highland pottery, these depictions, whether excised or incised, were often filled with dry red pigment, serving to contrast the fiery serpent motif with a clouded black or gray ceramic background (Marcus 1999, 78). Such vessels could be used to show descent from Lightning by placing them in burials (see figs. 5.2d–f).

Another major Early Horizon theme is the depiction of elite individuals wielding weapons and wearing helmets or headdresses (see figs. 5.3a–e). In addition to claiming descent from supernatural forces, chiefly individuals linked themselves to powerful predators (see figs. 5.2a–c) because one of their crucial roles was war leader (Carneiro 1998, 2002).

While the chiefly elite of Mexico's chiefdoms sought to tie themselves to natural forces and to predatory creatures who symbolized their military prowess, there were regional differences in the media emphasized. Stone sculpture in the Olmec lowlands was often freestanding and in the round, while highland Mexican sculpture was either incorporated into buildings (as in Oaxaca) or carved onto living rock (as in Morelos) (Grove 1968, 1972, 1987; Marcus 1989). The vast majority of Earth motifs in the high-lands occurred on incised white-slipped pottery of a type not found at the Olmec center of San Lorenzo during the Early Horizon (Flannery and Marcus 2000).

To be sure, stone sculptures were often set in public places and could be viewed by many more people than could the smaller objects used, worn, or exchanged by the elite. Different media sent different messages; we simply do not know what all the messages were.

The Chavín Chiefdoms

The Chavín art style is named for the site of Chavín de Huántar, and the term "Chavín" has often been extended to regions where it is not appro-priate, just as the term "Olmec" has often been extended to regions where it is not appropriate. While the region of Chavín de Huántar is probably the epicenter for stone monuments, other regions excelled at gold working, feather working, ceramics, and weaving.

Chavín de Huántar is situated at 3,150 meters in the Mosna Valley (works about sites in this valley include Bennett 1943, 1944; Carrión Cachot 1948; Lothrop 1941, 1951; Roe 1974; Tello 1943, 1960). There, Julio C. Tello recovered more than one hundred stone sculptures (1960). Additional sculptures have been found at secondary centers below Chavín, such as Runtu, Pojoc, Waman Wain, Gotush, and Yura-yako (Espejo Núñez 1955; Tello 1960).

Chavín art was fundamentally representational (Rowe 1962, 1967). It used similes, metaphors, and what Rowe called "kennings" (comparison by substitution) to combine human figures with the attributes of raptorial birds, pumas or jaguars, caymans, snakes, and spiders (see figs. 5.5–5.7). An example of a simile in Chavín art, put into words, would be "his hair is like snakes," as shown on a monument from Chavín de Huántar (Rowe 1967, fig. 21). The corresponding metaphor would be "his snaky hair." On the other hand, comparison by substitution would be "a nest of snakes," without the word "hair" being mentioned. Common Chavín metaphors included combining the talons of an eagle with the body of a man to convey the image of a successful warrior (Tello 1960, fig. 61) and combining the features of a spider, a man, and a bag of trophy heads to convey the same image (see fig. 5.6b). Chavín art often emphasized an animal's most frightening body part, such as the jaw or the foot of a cayman, the canines of a jaguar, or the talons of a hawk (see figs. 5.5a–c, 5.6a, 5.7a–b).

In addition to using images combining human and animal attributes, Chavín artists made the war leader's role particularly clear by depicting individuals holding trophy heads (see fig. 5.6e) or weapons (see fig. 5.6d). A good example of an image of an individual holding weapons comes from the secondary site of Yura-yako, less than ten kilometers from Chavín de Huántar (fig. 5.6d). Both the predatory animals and the human figures holding trophy heads emphasize ferocity and aggressiveness, associating these attributes with successful warriors (see figs. 5.6b, 5.6e). Of course, the association of men with weapons and trophy heads was not a new convention; as we have seen, it occurred at pre-Chavín sites like Cerro Sechín.

As in Mesoamerican art, supernatural forces were featured in Chavín art. Perhaps the closest approximation by Chavín artists to Mesoamerica's focus on Earth and Sky can be seen on monuments like the Tello Obelisk,

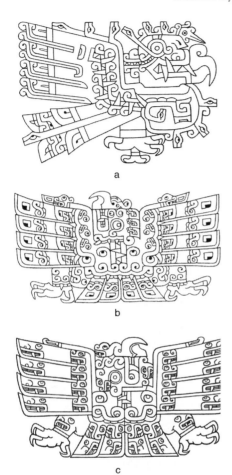

a

b

c

Figure 5.5. Images of raptorial birds (eagles, hawks) are important in Chavín art, often combining bird, snake, and other animal attributes (redrawn from Rowe 1967, figs. 11, 12, 15).

where primordial Earth and Sky are seemingly symbolized by two super-natural caymans, each 2.5 meters long (fig. 5.7b). Donald Lathrap origi-nally suggested (1973) that one of the caymans represented the Lower World and was associated with *Spondylus* shells, while the other repre-sented Sky and was associated with a raptorial bird. This interpretation is not dramatically different from seeing them as Earth and Sky. Signifi-cantly, the cayman depictions are *split representations*—either a single cay-man split into two halves, or two paired caymans. These split caymans

Figure 5.6. Chavín art features fierce animals and warriors: *a*, Sculpture 34, from Chavín de Huántar, a realistic jaguar whose powerful claws and canines are emphasized (Tello 1960, fig. 62); *b*, composite spider/jaguar holding a trophy head in one hand, with ten decapitated heads in net bag; carved on bowl, probably from Limoncarro, Jequetepeque Valley, Peru (Burger 1995, fig. 82); *c*, procession of animals that combine attributes of raptorial birds, serpents, and jaguars; found in southwest corner of New Temple, Chavín de Huántar (Kan 1972, fig. 2); *d*, Sculpture 52 from Yura-yako depicts a man holding weapons (Tello 1960, fig. 80); *e*, Sculpture 53 from Yura-yako shows a man holding a trophy head (Tello 1960, fig. 81).

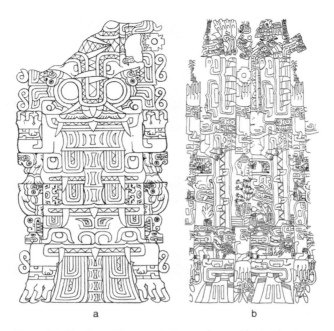

Figure 5.7. Similar to Mesoamerica's use of crocodiles is Chavín
art's use of caymans: *a*, Yauya Stela showing fish associated with
cayman (Tello 1960, fig. 34); *b*, Tello Obelisk, depicting two caymans—one at left associated with land and sea (with serpents and
Spondylus at the top), and one at right associated with the sky (represented by an eagle) (Tello 1960, fig. 31).

depicting the Andean cosmos seem to be a case of parallel evolution, analogous to Mesoamerica's dichotomy of Earth and Sky.

Though jaguars are often cited as the key animal in Chavín art, several
Andean experts have emphasized that the cayman was actually the most
important animal in the corpus of Chavín sculpture (Burger 1988, 120;
Lathrap 1973; Rowe 1962, 18). Impressive depictions of this reptile are
found at widely separated localities—in a tomb at Karwa on the Paracas
Peninsula, more than five hundred kilometers from Chavín de Huántar; on
the Tello Obelisk at the Chavín site itself; and on the Yauya Stela from the
Marañon River region, far to the east (fig. 5.7a).

The trophy head theme is evident on a Chavín vessel made of steatite
(fig. 5.6b) that shows a supernatural spider with trophy heads inside a bag

Figure 5.8. The facade of the Old Temple, Chavín de Huántar, Peru, originally displayed tenoned heads; three are shown at top (Tello 1960, figs. 7, 94, 95, 100).

(Salazar-Burger and Burger 1983). These heads are such blatant referents to the role of the chief as war leader that any attempt to see them as religious iconography seems unconvincing. They lead us to a new interpretation of the tenoned heads of Chavín de Huántar's Old Temple, which have been the subject of considerable speculation.

These tenoned heads, displayed at the impressive height of ten meters, look down on all who approach the wall of the Old Temple (fig. 5.8, bottom). Some of them have contorted faces and nasal extrusions, some look like starved captives, some look like tattooed warriors, and some look like the heads of monsters (fig. 5.8, top). What they remind me of are the frightening wooden figures used in a variety of Polynesian chiefdoms, including in the Maori chiefdom (discussed later), where carvings of fierce-looking tattooed chiefs or grotesque monsters with protruding tongues were placed at the top of the posts forming the defensive palisade surrounding the village. These wooden sculptures were mounted on high, to be seen by those approaching the village and to discourage them from attacking.

Comparisons with Other Chiefdoms

We have now looked at the art styles of Chavín and Early Horizon Mexico, not as the product of religious cults but as a display of chiefly attributes. The authority of the chief was rooted in his descent from powerful supernatural ancestors and tied to great cosmological divisions like Earth and Sky. Moreover, it was necessary for both his subjects and his enemies to know that in his role as war leader, he possessed the attributes of ferocious beasts, devouring his foes (see, e.g., fig. 5.2c) or harvesting their heads (see, e.g., figs. 5.4c, 5.4e).

This view of the early great art styles becomes even more plausible when we expand our sample by looking at the art of two more chiefdoms from very different world regions. These two chiefdoms—the Coclé of Panama and the Maori of New Zealand—have the advantage of ethnohistoric or ethnographic contexts that aid in the interpretation of their art.

THE COCLÉ CHIEFDOMS OF PANAMA

One of the best analyses of a body of chiefly art was that of Olga Linares (1977), who studied the Coclé style, which flourished in Panama from A.D. 400 to 800. Her analysis, informed by ethnohistory, focused on painted elite burial vessels from the provinces of Veraguas, Coclé, Herrera, and Los Santos (see, e.g., fig. 5.9d). These mortuary vessels were placed in such a way that their polychrome motifs could be viewed by mourners who came to feast before each chiefly grave was filled.

Linares argued that Coclé art was "a rich symbolic system using animal metaphors to extol aggression in several spheres of political and social life" (1977, 9). Knowing that sixteenth-century Panamanian chiefdoms featured a high level of warfare with intense competition for positions of leadership, Linares suggested that earlier chiefdoms had also experienced numerous conflicts, using depictions of fierce animals as metaphors for the bravery of warriors. Among those animals were potential predators of humans, such as crocodiles, sharks, and jaguars; dangerous species such as stingrays and scorpions; poisonous snakes and toads; and raptorial or notably aggressive birds, such as hawks, guans, and curassows. Crocodiles were particularly common (Bray 1981; Helms 1977; Lothrop 1937), appearing on gold helmets (figs. 5.9b, 5.10b), in bone and resin (figs. 5.9c, 5.10c), and on pottery (fig. 5.9d).

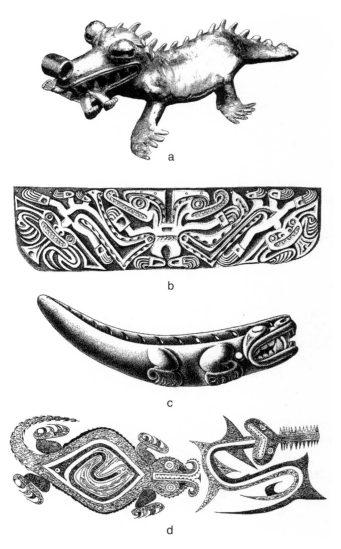

Figure 5.9. The crocodile was a metaphor for aggression and predatory behavior in chiefly art: *a*, gold pendant from Costa Rica, showing a man being eaten by a crocodile (drawn from photo in Bray 1981, plate 97); *b*, double-headed crocodile god depicted on a gold helmet worn by the man in Grave 5, Sitio Conte, Panama (Lothrop 1937, fig. 108); *c*, whale ivory carved into the shape of a crocodile (Lothrop 1937, fig. 158a); *d*, crocodile pursuing a sawfish on polychrome vessel, Panama (Linares 1977, fig. 37).

To reinforce the qualities of powerful animals, Panamanian warriors wore ornaments made from the bones or the teeth of those species, including the teeth of whales and sharks (Lothrop 1937). These body parts were included in graves, either as funeral gifts or as personal jewelry worn by dead warriors. In contrast to the dangerous animals mentioned, docile animals or prey species were essentially ignored in Coclé art. Much the same can be said of Chavín and Early Horizon Mexican art. Panamanian warriors could also be shown with trophy heads (see fig. 5.10a).

Chiefly art from nearby Costa Rica also featured fierce animals, especially crocodiles; in some cases, a crocodile is shown eating a man (see fig. 5.9a), as is the reptile in Relief 5 from the Mexican site of Chalcatzingo (fig. 5.2c). Costa Rican stone sculptures, like Chavín art, show warriors and trophy heads (Aguilar Piedra 1952; Snarskis 1981, figs. 193, 195, 206, 212, 245). Also featured are mace heads, axes, and daggers (Snarskis 1981, figs. 44–51, 140–142). Warriors might also be depicted with captives tied up with rope (Abel-Vidor et al. 1981). Though Panama and Costa Rica are far from Peru, these militaristic themes are remarkably similar.

THE MAORI OF NEW ZEALAND

The Maori are a wonderful comparative case because they provide both living informants and historical records. Thus, we have not only their "great style" but also data on what artists meant to convey. Maori artists told the anthropologists who studied them that their goal was to imbue their work with *wehi* (fear), *wana* (authority), and *ihi* (power) (Mead 1985, 23). (It would have been interesting to hear what an Olmec, Chavín, or Coclé artist would say.)

The best Maori artists and woodcarvers were usually men of high rank, and some are shown carrying clubs or wearing pendants (see fig. 5.11a). One of the important qualities associated with chieftainship was knowledge of carving, a skill used to ornament chiefs' houses, canoes, and war clubs (figs. 5.11c–f). Carving was performed by men in high-ranking families—the people closest to the gods, the bearers of political authority. Carving was considered a sacred activity that related the community as a whole to its gods and ancestors, putting the community in touch with supernatural sources of power.

The Maori had the custom of naming personal houses, meeting houses, and even storehouses. When an orator stood up to speak in front of a meeting house, he addressed the house by its name, which was often taken from a

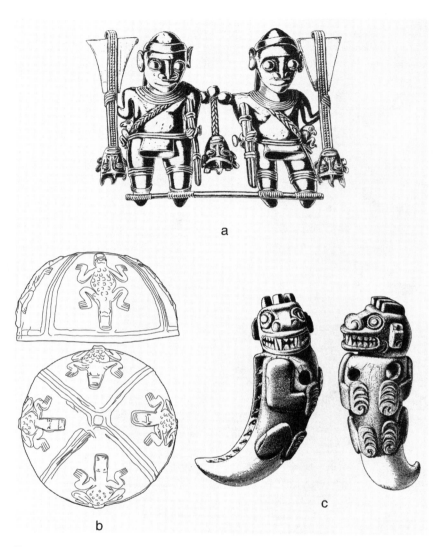

Figure 5.10. Fierce animals and warriors from Panama and Colombia: *a*, gold-copper alloy pendant from Sitio Conte, Panama, depicts two warriors carrying clubs, spears, and the heads of three enemies (Lothrop 1937, fig. 150); *b*, two views of Colombian gold helmet, divided into quadrants, each with a crocodile (drawn from photo in Lothrop 1937, fig. 110); *c*, crocodile pendant carved out of whale ivory (Lothrop 1937, fig. 158c-c').

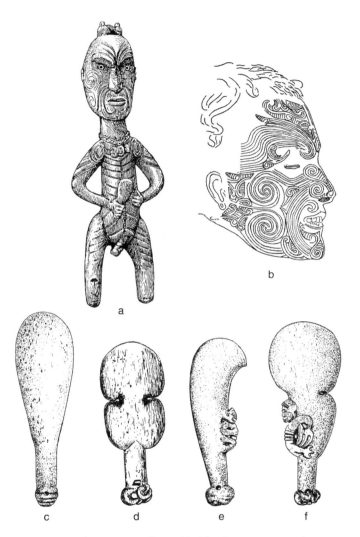

Figure 5.11. Ancestors and warriors are featured in Maori art: *a*, ancestor shown as a tattooed warrior with a club (*patu*) in his right hand and a pendant around his neck. This wooden figure was carved at the top of a palisade post, where it served to protect the village (Simmons 1985, 218); *b*, man tattooed with the same spirals that characterize Maori wood-carving (Buck 1949, fig. 96a); *c–f*, clubs used by chiefs to challenge other chiefs (Buck 1949, figs. 78b, 78e–g).

great ancestor. When the kin group assembled inside the meeting house and lay there enclosed by its carved side posts, the descent group—living and dead—was said to have come together in the belly of its ancestor (Salmond 1985, 120). Carved images were in fact placed inside these buildings to summon the ancestors. The meeting house itself was considered the body of a distant ancestor, with the ridgepole serving as his backbone; the carvings on the house posts depicted more recent ancestors (Simmons 1985, 198).

Like their Mesoamerican counterparts, the Maori elite wore pendants (*hei tiki* or *tiki*) around their necks (figs. 5.12a–f show these and other pendants). Each carved pendant was known by a personal name since it carried the mana of the individual who owned it. When such tiki were brought to the courtyard in front of a meeting house, they were greeted as people, as though the ancestors they represented were physically present (Simmons 1985, 192).

The naming of structures, posts, statues, and pendants accomplished many things. Naming denoted ownership, personalized and animated the objects, and connected living descendants with their ancestors. Ancestors could frighten enemies away from palisaded villages. The carving of a chief might be placed on the top of posts at the main gate leading through the palisade (Simmons 1985, 195–96). These depictions of the chief, in addition to carvings of grotesque monsters, were intended to frighten away potential attackers, much as I suspect the tenon heads of Chavín's Old Temple were. One Maori meeting house, called a Kai Tangata (Eat Man) house, was adorned with grotesque human figures whose faces were tattooed and whose eyes were inlaid with shell. George Angas described these grotesque figures as follows:

> The tongues of all these figures are monstrously large, and protrude out of the mouth, as a mark of defiance toward their enemies who may approach the house. . . . Within the house is a carved image, of most hideous aspect, that supports the ridge-pole of the roof: This is intended to represent the warlike proprietor, and is said by the natives to be entirely the work of Rangihaeata's [the chief's] own hand. (Angas 1847, 1:24. Quoted in Kernot 1985, 147)

Rangihaeata was known as a fighting chief embroiled in the politics of his time.

Because of the wealth of ethnographic and ethnohistoric data available on the Maori, we know that their great art style was not the result of a religious cult. Like the Coclé (and, I suspect, like the Chavín and Early Horizon

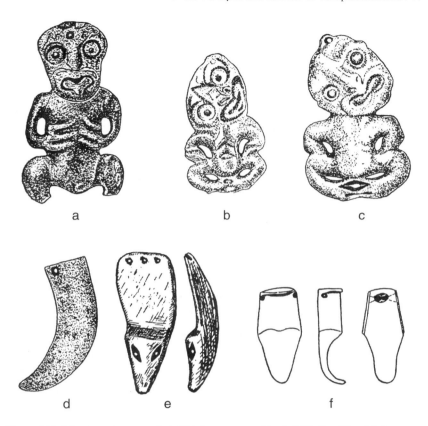

Figure 5.12. Maori pendants: *a–c*, hei tiki jade ornaments (Buck 1949, figs. 84a–c); leftmost pendant features a protruding tongue and wide eyes, a facial expression used by Maori warriors to scare off rivals; *d*, whale tooth drilled for suspending; *e*, *rei puta* (*rei*, whale ivory; *puta*, hole) made into a valuable ornament by cutting away a portion of the tooth to form a flat surface extending to the root; three holes were drilled so a cord could be attached; *f*, pendant carved to imitate a whale tooth. (Figs. 5.12*d–f* redrawn from Buck 1949, figs. 81a–c).

Mexicans), the Maori were sending the message that their chiefs were powerful in war, too fearsome to be attacked, and granted authority by their revered ancestors—hence the desire for the art they commissioned to be imbued with ihi, wehi, and wana. The art style spread not through religious proselytizing, but because of the widespread competition among rival chiefs, all of whom wanted to have authority, wield power, and inspire fear.

The Maori and Coclé have another lesson to teach. Both regions featured powerful competing chiefdoms, out of which first-generation states could have emerged. That no state emerged in either case shows us that having a widespread great art style is no guarantee that further social evolution will take place.

The Early Great Styles and the Nature of Chiefdoms

Forty-five years ago, Willey concluded his paper on early great art styles by predicting that "local prototypes of Chavín and Olmec may eventually be found, although these will only carry the story back a little in time and leave the startling florescences unexplained" (1962, 10). The first part of his prediction has come true since we now know that Chavín and Olmec were preceded by earlier widespread styles. I do not believe that the second part of his prediction—that the florescences will remain unexplained—will survive our accumulating data on how chiefdoms work.

Forty-five years ago, "religious cult" was a popular archaeological phrase, and prehistorians envisioned art styles spreading the way the Mediterranean empires spread their religion and art. But Olmec and Chavín were not empires. They were sets of competing chiefdoms, and one of the things we have learned about chiefdoms from the ethnographic record is that proselytizing was not high on their list of goals. Their chiefly ancestors, and the supernatural beings from whom they derived their power, were not to be shared with strangers and enemies.

What *were* the things that chiefs wanted to accomplish and that might have motivated the art they commissioned? First, they wanted to attract as many followers as possible, surrounding themselves with laborers, artisans, and potential warriors. Second, they wanted their art to express the very things Maori artists claim to have aimed for—that the chief had *authority*, wielded *power*, and could sow *fear*. Fear was engendered by scenes of trophy heads, by grotesque figures atop palisades, by scowling tenon heads, and perhaps even by colossal stone heads of chiefly ancestors who watched over the village. Power was shown by metaphorically associating chiefs with crocodiles, caymans, jaguars, pumas, and other creatures capable of devouring humans (see fig. 5.2c) or by portraying chiefs grasping clubs, axes, or maces.

It was in the depiction of *authority* that chiefly art touched religion—not in the sense of a cult, but in the belief that chiefly authority came from supernatural beings through important ancestors. The depictions began with cosmological references to Earth and Sky, the four world directions with the chief at the center, primordial white-slipped babies, and the great crocodile whose back was the surface of the earth. Intervening between the great beings of the cosmos and humans were venerated ancestors, some of them former chiefs that became heroic figures. Through these heroes, supernatural authority flowed to the living chief—and, of course, to the brothers, half-brothers, and cousins who struggled to compete with him.

Today, we can respond to Willey's 1962 challenge concerning "startling florescences." As we have seen, such florescences are not necessarily predictors that a "civilization" is about to appear; in fact, Martin Doornbos has suggested (1985) that in some cases, a full flowering of ceremonialism may actually mask the fact that a given chiefdom is on the verge of decline. What Chavín and Early Horizon Mexican art probably reflect is a sudden escalation in hereditary rank. To be sure, the pre-Olmec and pre-Chavín styles of Nuclear America are skillful and aesthetically pleasing. It would seem, however, that the "startling florescences" of which Willey spoke reflect a quantum leap in the need to portray the power, authority, and fearsome nature of society's leaders. As such, they present the archaeologist with one more clue to an important plateau in social evolution. It is this clue that may be the most enduring legacy of Willey's 1962 essay.

Acknowledgments

I sincerely thank K. Clahassey and J. Klausmeyer for their excellent drawings, Jerry Sabloff and Bill Fash for asking me to participate in this volume, and Dr. Willey for teaching Anthro 211r.

Note

1. All dates in this chapter are uncalibrated.

References

Abel-Vidor, Suzanne, Ronald L. Bishop, Warwick Bray, Elizabeth Kennedy Easby, Luis Ferrero A., Oscar Fonseca Zamora, Héctor Gamboa Paniagua, et al. 1981. *Between Continents/Between Seas: Precolumbian Art of Costa Rica*. New York: Harry N. Abrams.

Aguilar Piedra, Carlos H. 1952. "El complejo de las cabezas-trofeo en la etnología costarricense." *Revista de la Universidad de Costa Rica* (San José) 7:39–63.

Angas, George F. 1847. *Savage Life and Scenes in Australia and New Zealand*. 2 vols. London: Smith, Elder.

Bennett, Wendell C. 1943. "The Position of Chavín in Andean Sequences." *Proceedings of the American Philosophical Society* 86:323–27.

―――. 1944. *The North Highlands of Peru: Excavations in the Callejón de Huaylas and at Chavín de Huántar*. Anthropological Papers of the American Museum of Natural History, vol. 39, pt. 1. New York: American Museum of Natural History.

Benson, Elizabeth P., and Beatriz de la Fuente, eds. 1996. *Olmec Art of Ancient Mexico*. Washington, D.C.: National Gallery of Art.

Bray, Warwick. 1981. "Gold Work." In *Between Continents/Between Seas: Precolumbian Art of Costa Rica*, 153–66. New York: Harry N. Abrams.

Buck, Sir Peter (Te Rangi Hiroa). 1949. *The Coming of the Maori*. Wellington: Whitcombe & Tombs.

Burger, Richard L. 1988. "Unity and Heterogeneity within the Chavín Horizon." In *Peruvian Prehistory*, ed. Richard W. Keatinge, 99–144. Cambridge: Cambridge University Press.

―――. 1995. *Chavín and the Origins of Andean Civilization*. London: Thames & Hudson.

Carneiro, Robert L. 1991. "The Nature of the Chiefdom as Revealed by Evidence from the Cauca Valley of Colombia." In *Profiles in Cultural Evolution*, ed. A. Terry Rambo and Kathleen Gillogly, 167–90. Anthropological Papers of the University of Michigan Museum of Anthropology 85. Ann Arbor: University of Michigan Museum of Anthropology.

―――. 1998. "What Happened at the Flashpoint? Conjectures on Chiefdom Formation at the Very Moment of Conception." In *Chiefdoms and Chieftaincy in the Americas*, ed. Elsa M. Redmond, 18–42. Gainesville: University Press of Florida.

―――. 2002. "Was the Chiefdom a Congelation of Ideas?" *Social Evolution and History* 1 (1):80–100.

Carrión Cachot, Rebeca. 1948. "La cultura Chavín: Dos nuevas colonias: Kuntur Wasi y Ancón." *Revista del Museo Nacional de Antropología y Arqueología* 2 (1):99–172.

Childe, V. Gordon. 1950. "The Urban Revolution." *Town Planning Review* (University of Liverpool) 21 (1):3–17.

Clark, John. 1991. "The Beginnings of Mesoamerica: *Apologia* for the Soconusco Early Formative." In *The Formation of Complex Society in Southeastern Mesoamerica*, ed. William R. Fowler, 13–26. Boca Raton, Fla.: CRC Press.

Covarrubias, Miguel. 1942. "Origen y desarrollo del estilo artístico 'Olmeca.'" In *Mayas y Olmecas*, 46–49. Mexico City: Sociedad Mexicana de Antropología.

―――. 1944. "La Venta: Colossal Heads and Jaguar Gods." *DYN, The Review of Modern Art* (Coyoacán, Mexico) 6:24–33.

―――. 1946. "El arte 'Olmeca' o de La Venta." *Cuadernos Americanos* 28 (4):153–79.

―――. 1957. *Indian Art of Mexico and Central America*. New York: Alfred A. Knopf.

Cyphers, Ann. 1996. "The Colossal Heads." In "Olmecs," special issue, *Arqueología Mexicana* (INAH, Editorial Raíces), 48–55.

Demarest, Arthur A. 1989. "The Olmec and the Rise of Civilization in Eastern Mesoamerica." In *Regional Perspectives on the Olmec*, ed. Robert J. Sharer and David C. Grove, 303–44. Cambridge: Cambridge University Press.

Demarest, Arthur A., and Antonia E. Foias. 1993. "Mesoamerican Horizons and the Cultural Transformations of Maya Civilization." In *Latin American Horizons*, ed. Don S. Rice, 147–91. Washington, D.C.: Dumbarton Oaks.

Doornbos, Martin R. 1985. "Institutionalization and Institutional Decline." In *Development and Decline: The Evolution of Sociopolitical Organizations*, ed. Henri J. M. Claessen, Peter van de Velde, and M. Estellie Smith, 23–35. South Hadley, Mass.: Bergin and Garvey.

Drucker, Philip. 1952. *La Venta, Tabasco: A Study of Olmec Ceramics and Art*. Bureau of American Ethnology Bulletin 153. Washington, D.C.: Smithsonian Institution.

Drucker, Philip, Robert F. Heizer, and Robert J. Squier. 1959. *Excavations at La Venta, Tabasco, 1955*. Bureau of American Ethnology Bulletin 170. Washington, D.C.: Smithsonian Institution.

Espejo Núñez, Julio. 1955. "Gotush: Nuevos descubrimientos en Chavín." *Baessler-Archiv* (Berlin) 3:123–36.

Flannery, Kent V., and Joyce Marcus. 1976. "Formative Oaxaca and the Zapotec Cosmos." *American Scientist* 64:374–83.

———. 1994. *Early Formative Pottery of the Valley of Oaxaca*. Memoirs of the University of Michigan Museum of Anthropology 27. Ann Arbor: University of Michigan Museum of Anthropology.

———. 2000. "Formative Mexican Chiefdoms and the Myth of the 'Mother Culture.'" *Journal of Anthropological Archaeology* 19:1–37.

Grove, David C. 1968. "Chalcatzingo, Morelos, Mexico: A Reappraisal of the Olmec Rock Carvings." *American Antiquity* 33:486–91.

———. 1972. "Olmec Felines in Highland Central Mexico." In *The Cult of the Feline*, ed. Elizabeth P. Benson, 153–64. Washington, D.C.: Dumbarton Oaks.

———, ed. 1987. *Ancient Chalcatzingo*. Austin: University of Texas Press.

———. 1989. "Olmec: What's in a Name?" In *Regional Perspectives on the Olmec*, ed. Robert J. Sharer and David C. Grove, 8–16. Cambridge: Cambridge University Press.

———. 1993. "'Olmec' Horizons in Formative Period Mesoamerica: Diffusion or Social Evolution?" In *Latin American Horizons*, ed. Don S. Rice, 83–111. Washington, D.C.: Dumbarton Oaks.

———. 1997. "Olmec Archaeology: A Half Century of Research and Its Accomplishments." *Journal of World Prehistory* 11 (1):51–101.

Hammond, Norman. 1988. "Cultura hermana: Reappraising the Olmec." *Quarterly Review of Archaeology* 9 (4):1–4.

Helms, Mary W. 1977. "Iguanas and Crocodilians in Tropical American Mythology and Iconography with Special Reference to Panama." *Journal of Latin American Lore* 3 (1):51–132.

Johnson, Allen W., and Timothy Earle. 2000. *The Evolution of Human Societies: From Foraging Group to Agrarian State*. 2nd ed. Stanford, Calif.: Stanford University Press.

Joralemon, Peter D. 1976. "The Olmec Dragon: A Study in Pre-Columbian Iconography." In *Origins of Religious Art and Iconography in Preclassic Mesoamerica*, ed. Henry B. Nicholson, 27–71. Latin American Studies 31. Los Angeles: UCLA Latin American Center.

Kan, Michael. 1972. "The Feline Motif in Northern Peru." In *The Cult of the Feline*, ed. Elizabeth P. Benson, 69–85. Washington, D.C.: Dumbarton Oaks.

Keeley, Lawrence H. 1996. *War before Civilization*. New York: Oxford University Press.

Kelley, David H. 1966. "A Cylinder Seal from Tlatilco." *American Antiquity* 31:744–46.

Kelly, Raymond C. 2000. *Warless Societies and the Origin of War*. Ann Arbor: University of Michigan Press.

Kernot, Bernard. 1985. "Nga Tohunga Whakairo O Mua: Maori Artists of Time Before." In *Te Maori: Art from New Zealand Collections*, ed. Sidney M. Mead, 138–55. New York: Harry N. Abrams.

Kroeber, Alfred L. 1951. "Great Art Styles of Ancient South America." In *The Civilizations of Ancient America*, ed. Sol Tax. Selected Papers of the 29th International Congress of Americanists, vol. 1. Chicago: University of Chicago Press.

Larco Hoyle, Rafael. 1941. *Los Cupisniques*. Lima: Casa Editorial La Crónica y Variedades.

Lathrap, Donald W. 1973. "Gifts of the Cayman: Some Thoughts on the Subsistence Basis of Chavin." In *Variation in Anthropology: Essays in Honor of John C. McGregor*, ed. Donald W. Lathrap and Jody Douglas, 91–103. Urbana: Illinois Archaeological Survey.

Linares, Olga F. 1977. *Ecology and the Arts in Ancient Panama: On the Development of Social Rank and Symbolism in the Central Provinces*. Studies in Pre-Columbian Art and Archaeology 17. Washington, D.C.: Dumbarton Oaks.

Lothrop, Samuel K. 1937. *Coclé: An Archaeological Study of Central Panama, Part 1*. Memoirs of the Peabody Museum of Archaeology and Ethnology 7. Cambridge, Mass.: Harvard University.

———. 1941. "Gold Ornaments of Chavin Style from Chongoyape, Peru." *American Antiquity* 6 (2):250–61.

———. 1951. "Gold Artifacts of Chavin." *American Antiquity* 16 (3):226–40.

Marcus, Joyce. 1974. "The Iconography of Power among the Classic Maya." World Archaeology 6:83–94.

———. 1989. "Zapotec Chiefdoms and the Nature of Formative Religions." In *Regional Perspectives on the Olmec*, ed. Robert J. Sharer and David C. Grove, 148–97. Cambridge: Cambridge University Press.

———. 1998. *Women's Ritual in Formative Oaxaca: Figurine-making, Divination, Death and the Ancestors*. Memoirs of the University of Michigan Museum of Anthropology 33. Ann Arbor: University of Michigan Museum of Anthropology.

———. 1999. "Men's and Women's Ritual in Formative Oaxaca." In *Social Patterns in Pre-Classic Mesoamerica*, ed. David C. Grove and Rosemary A. Joyce, 67–96. Washington, D.C.: Dumbarton Oaks.

———. 2000. "Cinco mitos sobre la guerra Maya." In *La guerra entre los antiguos Mayas*, ed. Silvia Trejo, 225–43. Mexico City: Instituto Nacional de Antropología e Historia.

Marcus, Joyce, and Kent V. Flannery. 1996. *Zapotec Civilization: How Urban Society Evolved in Mexico's Oaxaca Valley*. London: Thames & Hudson.

Mead, Sidney M. 1985. "Nga Timunga Me Nga Paringa o Te Mana Maori: The Ebb and Flow of Mana Maori and the Changing Context of Maori Art." In *Te Maori: Art from New Zealand Collections*, ed. Sidney M. Mead, 20–36. New York: Harry N. Abrams.

Melgar y Serrano, José María. 1869. "Antigüedades mexicanas, notable escultura antigua." *Boletín de la Sociedad Mexicana de Geografía y Estadística* 2 (1):292–97.

Niederberger, Christine. 1987. *Paléopaysages et archéologie pré-urbaine du Bassin de Mexique*. Etudes Mésoamericaines 11. Mexico City: Centre d'Etudes Mexicaines et Centroamericaines.

Piña Chan, Román. 1955. *Las culturas preclásicas de la Cuenca de México*. Mexico City: Fondo de Cultura Económica.

Pozorski, Thomas, and Shelia Pozorski. 1990. "Reply to 'The Pre-Chavín Stone Sculpture of Casma and Pacopampa.'" *Journal of Field Archaeology* 17:110–11.

Redmond, Elsa M. 1994. *Tribal and Chiefly Warfare in South America*. University of Michigan Museum of Anthropology Memoir 28. Ann Arbor: University of Michigan Museum of Anthropology.

———. 1998. "In War and Peace: Alternative Paths to Centralized Leadership." In *Chiefdoms and Chieftaincy in the Americas*, ed. Elsa M. Redmond, 68–103. Gainesville: University Press of Florida.

Renfrew, Colin, and John F. Cherry, eds. 1986. *Peer Polity Interaction and Socio-Political Change*. Cambridge: Cambridge University Press.

Rice, Don S. 1993. "The Making of Latin American Horizons: An Introduction to the Volume." In *Latin American Horizons*, ed. Don S. Rice, 1–13. Washington, D.C.: Dumbarton Oaks.

Roe, Peter. 1974. *A Further Exploration of the Rowe Chavin Seriation and Its Implications for North Central Coast Chronology*. Studies in Pre-Columbian Art and Archaeology 13. Washington, D.C.: Dumbarton Oaks.

Rowe, John H. 1962. *Chavín Art: An Inquiry into Its Form and Meaning*. New York: The Museum of Primitive Art.

———. 1967. "Form and Meaning in Chavín Art." In *Peruvian Archaeology: Selected Readings*, ed. John H. Rowe and Dorothy Menzel, 72–103. Palo Alto, California: Peek Publications.

Salazar-Burger, Lucy, and Richard Burger. 1983. "La araña en la iconografía del horizonte temprano en la costa norte del Perú." *Beiträge zur Allgemeinen und Vergleichenden Archäologie* (Mainz) 4:213–53.

Salmond, Anne. 1985. "Nga Huarahi O Te Ao Maori: Pathways in the Maori World." In *Te Maori: Art from New Zealand Collections*, ed. Sidney Mead, 109–37. New York: Harry N. Abrams.

Samaniego, Lorenzo, Enrique Vergara, and Henning Bischof. 1985. "New Evidence on Cerro Sechín, Casma Valley, Peru." In *Early Ceremonial Architecture of the Andes*, ed. Christopher Donnan, 165–90. Washington, D.C.: Dumbarton Oaks.

Simmons, David R. 1985. "Te Rarangi Taonga: Catalogue." In *Te Maori: Art from New Zealand Collections*, ed. Sidney Mead, 175–235. New York: Harry N. Abrams.

Snarskis, Michael J. 1981. "Catalogue." In *Between Continents/Between Seas: Precolumbian Art of Costa Rica*, 178–227. New York: Harry N. Abrams.

Spencer, Charles S. 1993. "Human Agency, Biased Transmission, and the Cultural Evolution of Chiefly Authority." *Journal of Anthropological Archaeology* 12:41–74.

Stirling, Matthew W. 1943. *Stone Monuments of Southern Mexico*. Bureau of American Ethnology Bulletin 138. Washington, D.C.: Smithsonian Institution.

Tello, Julio C. 1942. "Origen y desarrollo de las civilizaciones prehistóricas andinas." *Actas y Trabajos Científicos del XXVII Congreso Internacional de Americanistas, 1939* (Lima) 1:589–720.

———. 1943. "Discovery of the Chavín Culture in Peru." *American Antiquity* 9 (1):135–60.

———. 1956. *Arqueología del Valle de Casma. Culturas: Chavín, Santa o Huaylas Yunga u sub-Chimú*. Lima: Publicación Antropológica del Archivo "Julio C. Tello" de la Universidad Nacional Mayor de San Marcos.

————. 1960. *Chavín: Cultura matriz de la civilización andina*. Lima: Publicación Antropológica del Archivo "Julio C. Tello" de la Universidad Nacional Mayor de San Marcos.

Vaillant, Suzannah B., and George C. Vaillant. 1934. *Excavations at Gualupita*. Anthropological Papers of the American Museum of Natural History, vol. 35, pt. 1. New York: American Museum of Natural History.

Willey, Gordon R. 1962. "The Early Great Styles and the Rise of the Pre-Columbian Civilizations." *American Anthropologist* 64:1–14.

Wright, Sewall. 1939. "Statistical Genetics in Relation to Evolution." *Actualités Scientifiques et Industrielles* (Paris) 802:37–60.

Chapter Six

The Intermediate Area and Gordon Willey:
An Assessment

Jeffrey Quilter

Introduction

For any archaeologist active in the last half-century, Gordon R. Willey is remembered as a dominant figure with an impressive breadth of intellect and interests that spanned the New World. For many, he is the grand synthesizer, as is in evidence in his two monumental books on the archaeology of North and Middle America and of South America. Mesoamericanists look to him as the great field archaeologist who brought Maya studies to a new level of comprehension. For Andeanists, he is the pioneer of the Virú Valley who set new standards for settlement pattern studies in the river oases of the Peruvian coast. But for those scholars working in the Intermediate Area, he is "the one that got away."

It is a tribute to the man that at meetings of the Society for American Archaeology and at similar venues, many a bar conversation by a handful of Intermediate Area archaeologists often drifts towards what-if scenarios regarding what might have transpired if Willey had stayed working in Panama instead of accepting the Bowditch Chair, at Harvard, with the proviso that he shift his interests to Maya archaeology. The same lament could be made, however, by Floridian archaeologists or Central Andeanists.

Gordon once said to me, only half in jest, I think, that as a young man his intention was to dig his way, gradually, from Panama up to Mexico City. One might argue that if he had maintained an active research program in southern Central America, published as prolifically and influenced as many students as he did, and occupied the Bowditch Chair, the landscape of contemporary American archaeology would be very different than it is. But such kinds of conjectural histories are generally frowned upon by scholars. To engage in them seems particularly inappropriate for prehistorians, whether of processualist or postprocessualist persuasion. Several long essays might be written that place in sociological or biographical contexts Willey's turning away from Panama and towards the Maya, and the result is the same: the fact is that Willey did not continue active field research in Intermediate Area archaeology. Nevertheless, his ongoing interest in the region, as was in evidence by his participation in conferences on the topic and occasional articles, probably has had a great influence in keeping interest in the region alive among nonnationalist archaeologists of southern Central America and northern South America.

It thus may be of value to present and future scholars to offer a summary and some thoughts on Gordon Willey and the Intermediate Area. Other authors have prepared or are preparing extensive treatments on the historiography of the Intermediate Area or its subregions (Hoopes and Fonseca 2003) and on Willey's involvement with the scholarship of the region (Lange, forthcoming). I see no reason to duplicate their efforts. Therefore, my aim in this essay is to summarize Willey's activities in the field and in print and then follow the summary with a discussion of a meeting held at Dumbarton Oaks in 1997. That was the last occasion on which Willey visited Dumbarton Oaks, which, in itself, is a testament to his continuing interest in issues regarding the Intermediate Area.

"By No Means Drab"

Between 1943 and 1950, Willey was at the Smithsonian Institution, in the Bureau of American Ethnology. In 1948 he served as an assistant to Matthew W. Stirling, who led a Smithsonian–National Geographic expedition to Panama. No articles with substantive results of the research were published: much of Stirling's writings on his "explorations" in Panama and Costa Rica consisted of general summaries (1949a, 1949b), brief reports

(1950, 1953a), or titillating articles in the society's magazine, such as "Hunting Prehistory in Panama Jungles: Tracing Lost Indian Civilizations, an Archeologist and His Wife Narrowly Escape Disaster on the Isthmus' Wild North Coast" (1953b). These outnumber Stirling's more serious treatments of Central American archaeology. Those appeared later and were coauthored with his wife, Marion Stirling (Stirling and Stirling 1964a, 1964b, 1964c).

Willey did conduct fieldwork in Panama in 1948 that yielded substantive results, however, with test excavations in a Pacific coast shell mound, named Monagrillo, on Parita Bay. He returned to the site in 1952, accompanied by graduate students Charles R. McGimsey and James N. East. The large shell mound contained stratified deposits that allowed the investigators to recover and reconstruct a sequence of artifacts, particularly ceramics. Significantly, Willey had accepted the Bowditch Chair by the time of the second field season and was apparently finishing work in Panama before concentrating on the Maya. McGimsey continued to work in Panama for a while longer, notably at his excavations at Cerro Mangote (1956), a preceramic site predating Monagrillo. McGimsey soon shifted his research interests to New Mexico, however, and wrote his 1958 doctoral dissertation on Mariana Mesa. East does not appear to have completed his PhD at Harvard.

The aim of the Monagrillo research was straightforward: to develop artifact sequences in order to build basic temporal-spatial frameworks for the construction of culture history. Willey and McGimsey co-wrote an article (1952) for *Archaeology* magazine that offered a nonspecialist readership a broad picture of their research and its context. Many of the statements in that article expressed ideas and attitudes that Willey appears to have maintained for the rest of his life and that are not as generally summarized in the technical report of the research, although they are implicit in it (Willey and McGimsey 1954). It is therefore worthwhile, I believe, to briefly outline some of the main points made in the *Archaeology* article.

In the opening sentence of the article, the authors state that Panamanian archaeology is significant because of its potential to reveal "interconnections" between the "great native civilizations of Mexico and Central America [and] those of the Andes" (Willey and McGimsey 1952, 173). Interest is specifically focused on discovering traits that will help solve problems of inter-American diffusions. After a little more than a page of this kind of introductory material, the authors provide an overview of regional archaeology.

Panamanian archaeology is by no means drab, but it should be stated at the outset that the aboriginal remains in this country are not of the same order as those of Mexico-Guatemala or Peru. There are no great mounds, and if temples and palaces once existed they were built of perishable materials and have long since disappeared. But this absence of impressive above-ground architecture is deceptive as an indicator of the cultural status and accomplishments of the Indians in the area. (Willey and McGimsey 1952, 174)

They then proceed to state that both archaeology and early Spanish chronicles attest to the presence of petty states ruled by powerful and wealthy monarchs who had enormous quantities of gold and other riches buried with them. After a brief discussion of the few archaeological studies previously carried out in the region, the article shifts to discussing mostly the Monagrillo mound and its excavation. It concludes by noting that the plain and simply incised pottery suggests that the site is quite ancient. The question of a chronometric date was moot in this pre-radiocarbon-dating era. So, too, the authors cautiously state that the pottery style is such that it might indicate a Mexican-Peruvian connection or might be an expression of local invention.

The longer, more technically detailed report on Monagrillo is written in the same tone as the shorter article. The final subsection of the conclusions chapter is entitled "Problems," and its emphasis is on the need for more research and more data.

As we conclude, it is even more obvious that the overwhelmingly important theme for the future of Panamanian archaeology is chronology. . . . Moving out from the Parita Bay region these same chronological problems confront us on every side of Panama. There is still no culture sequence in Chiriquí, Veraguas, or Darien. Going into the larger frame of Central American prehistory, the establishment of broader relationships is not possible without a sounder chronologic basis on the local scene. (Willey and McGimsey 1954, 136–37)

Willey pursued those broader relationships, nonetheless, in an article commemorating the seventy-fifth anniversary of the Anthropological Society of Washington, in 1954: "The Interrelated Rise of the Native Cultures of Middle and South America" (1955). In it, he reviews the appearance of six traits in both Mesoamerica and South America: rocker-stamped pottery decoration, platform mounds, resist-dye pottery painting, mold-made figures, tall tripod vessels, and miscellaneous traits. Citing the work of Junius Bird at Huaca Prieta (see Bird 1985), he notes that Peruvian culture was on a pre-Formative level, while the selected traits mostly occurred first in Mesoamerica, concluding that diffusion of them brought civilization to Peru (Willey 1955, 44).

In his introductory remarks, Willey states that the "peaks of native American civilization were attained in . . . Mexico and Guatemala and in Peru" (Willey 1955, 28). He cites the study of the issues of diffusion as starting with Herbert J. Spinden, who saw an underlying Archaic unity to the New World. He claims that Alfred Kroeber first identified Mexico-Guatemala and Peru as the "climax" cultures of the New World. William Duncan Strong emphasized chronology building, while Julian H. Steward had been able to compare cultures through his interest in "functional development." Interestingly, in a footnote, Willey states that he is following Paul Kirchoff in defining Middle America as "one-third of Mexico, all of Guatemala and British Honduras, parts of Salvador, Honduras, and perhaps Nicaragua and Costa Rica" (Willey 1955, 28n1).

In 1958 Willey attended the Thirty-Third International Congress of Americanists, which was held in San José, Costa Rica. The paper he delivered there was published a year later (Willey 1959). It is important in that it directly addresses a number of issues that continued to be of interest to Willey in later years. By the time of the conference, he was using the term "Intermediate Area," noting at the beginning of the paper that the term is a geographic one, referring to the lands between western Honduras and northern Peru. Immediately following this statement, he uses a negative construction, and a very long sentence, to justify working in the area.

> I do not mean to imply that Lower Central America and the North Andes are significant only as a conduit through which influences or peoples passed between the two areas of the American high civilizations: but by the logic of geography these interlying lands were a vital part of the affairs of all of Nuclear America and it is evident that we will not understand properly what went on in any one part of the heartland of agricultural native America until we can view this part with relation to the whole. (Willey 1959, 184)

This sentence is hard to interpret and might be read in many ways. The phrasing of the beginning of the sentence suggests that such an implication of the Intermediate Area as important only as a conduit could easily be made, undercutting the importance of the region by the way the issue is framed. It is something of a backhanded compliment: "There are other important things to discuss, but I want to discuss the most important thing," he seems to say. This is borne out by the rest of the article, which is mostly concerned with reviewing the evidence for the earliest New World pottery.

Willey's discussion of early pottery is based on an assumption that it and agriculture were part of a larger Formative-period complex that diffused throughout the New World in the first millennium, B.C. He concludes that the trait complex probably originated in Mesoamerica and then spread southward. He is struck by the fact that early pottery should be present in lower Central America but is apparently absent, save for at Monagrillo. He nominates Middle America as the origin point of diffusion because he assumes that the Formative agricultural complex was earliest there.

In closing his article, Willey turns to the "cultural significance of the formative 'Great Styles'" (1959, 189), a topic that he would raise in the future. His use of quotation marks around "Great Styles" suggests a distancing of his own views from the term; it implies that the idea is someone else's, not his own, and is one to which he does not fully subscribe but is using as a heuristic device. Indeed, at the end of his article, he links great art styles—the "horizon" markers of Peru and Mesoamerica—as the expressions of "universal idea systems or moral orders" (Willey 1959, 190). Willey's main point, however, is that no great art style similar to Olmec or Chavín is present in the Intermediate Area.

Willey's comment on art was made at a time when radiocarbon dating was still in its infancy. As a result of this limitation and the paucity of information on many of the archaeological cultures of the region, Willey was unable to assess which art styles may have been candidates for contemporaneity with Olmec or Chavín. Because of this and in spite of it, too, Willey's remarks are based much more on aesthetic judgments than on temporal priority.

> San Agustín may be relatively early. . . . but compared to . . . Olmec . . . or . . . Chavín its area of geographical distribution is tiny, and its intrinsic qualities are inferior. Kroeber (1951, p. 214) has described San Agustín as "crude in conception and execution. Everything wavers in this art . . ." I think that these same statements could be made about Manabí art or the stone sculptures of Nicaragua and Costa Rica. (Willey 1959, 190)

Willey's use of the term "Great Art Styles" appears to have been borrowed directly from Alfred Kroeber, who used the term in the title of the cited 1951 publication. Interestingly, however, Willey uses Kroeber's remarks in a more critical discussion than in the older scholar's text. For Kroeber appreciated Manabí stone carving.

> The chairs, or thrones, without backs, are executed in a single graceful sweep of seat and arms, resting on an Atlantean pedestal of a crouching human figure. (Kroeber 1951, 213)

And while Kroeber critiques San Agustín stone carving, he qualifies his negative remarks by noting a saving grace not cited by Willey.

> Compared with Chavín and Tiahuanaco, San Agustín is crude in conception and execution. Everything wavers in this art. Eyes may be circles, semicircles, crescents, almonds or commas. Mouths may have tusks or be miniature narrow slits. . . . [The sculptures] seem less channeled into a coherent style. Each piece begins all over again to express its own idea in its own way. The size of the statues . . . results in an effect of monumentality, of stolid weight, of labored feeling, of barbaric strangeness verging on the monstrous, of minimal organization and almost no beauty of line or flow of surface; and yet, an effect of indubitable impressiveness. (Kroeber 1951, 214)

Kroeber's quote, in full, has a very different tone from that of Willey's abbreviated citation of it. In fact, Kroeber gives high marks to only two art styles in South America for their "successful naturalism": the Mochica of northern Peru and what he termed Manabí-Esmeraldas, presumably referring to Jama Coaque and similar figurines (Kroeber 1951, 213). Willey cited Kroeber for an authoritative reference but edited him to express his own views. Those views were much more sharply diffusionist and evolutionary than those of the senior scholar. Kroeber, in the same essay, spends little time on issues of origins, although he implies regional traditions and stimulus diffusion as causative agents (Kroeber 1951, 213–15). This stands in contrast to Willey's claims of a single source of diffusion of Formative culture from Middle America. Willey's stance was founded on a belief that cultural traits are interrelated, whereas Kroeber held to the Boasian proposition that various traits, such as mortuary customs, were unconnected (Kroeber 1927). Of these different theoretical positions, Kroeber's represented the "old school," while Willey was expressing the future: he was "preadapted" to New Archaeology. But the old school was much more open to considering the cultures of the Intermediate Area to be as interesting as those of Nuclear America.

Although Willey credits Kroeber as having identified the "climax" cultures of the New World, Wendell Bennett seems to have been much more strongly in favor of viewing American prehistory through such a lens. Bennett was a generation ahead of Willey, and the latter clearly admired him, considering him the "leading North American Andean Archaeologist" conducting field research at the time (Willey 1988, 128), a fully justifiable accolade. It was Bennett who wrote the introduction to *The Civilizations of Ancient America* (Tax 1951), claimed by its editor to be the first book to consider all of the ancient civilizations of Middle and South America "between the covers of one book."

In his introduction Bennett refers to the "Intermediate Subdivision" and includes Ecuador, Colombia, and lower Central America in this area. Referring to Colombia, Bennett states the following: "The Chibcha development has often been classed, with the Inca and Aztec, as a third high civilization of the New World. Evidence for this is based largely on the accounts of the early Spanish conquerors. The archaeological data do not verify this high development, and the recent excavations by Haury have failed to reveal any significant time depth to the known Chibcha materials" (Tax 1951, 5). He continues, "The archaeological situation in lower Central America is like that in Colombia" (Tax 1951, 5). In his assessment, interestingly, Bennett did not take into account factors of preservation or the few archaeological projects that had occurred in the regions in question, even for the time. More interesting, however, is that Bennett's dismissal of Chibcha developments rests on the apparent lack of time depth for archaeology there.

At the very beginning of his introduction, Bennett cites Mesoamerica and the Central Andes as the places of the "highest cultural development" (Tax 1951, 1). This, taken with the statement about lack of time depth for Colombia–southern Central America, clearly created a framework in which archaeology in the region was directed towards viewing the area as one of movement of peoples and ideas between the two primary areas of Nuclear America and emphasizing chronology building for the Intermediate Area.

In the 1950s, then, Willey's chief perspective on the prehistory of the Intermediate Area was based upon his experiences in Panama as well as his thinking on broader issues of cultural evolution and diffusion in the New World, which appears to have been strongly influenced by William Bennett. Bennett himself had worked in the Bay Islands and written key articles on the archaeology of Honduras and of Costa Rica and Nicaragua in volume 4 of *Handbook of South American Indians* (Steward 1948). The senior scholar's interests in the region likely fueled and supported Willey's own interests.

Willey saw the long-term benefit of research in the Intermediate Area as addressing questions of interrelations between the core areas of Nuclear America and was concerned with basic chronology building and time-space synthesis. He was firmly in the "Classificatory-Historical Period," as he and Jeremy Sabloff later termed it (Willey and Sabloff 1993), both in a strict chronological sense—the second phase in *History of American Archaeology* is from 1940 to 1960—and in terms of the kind of research he carried out. In some of his positions, though, he was arguably concerned with classification and description, an even earlier stage in the evolution of the discipline. At the same time, however, his view of the interconnectedness of culture traits, tied to evolutionary theory, was a perspective that presaged New Archaeology.

James A. Ford was certainly another strong influence on Willey's thinking. Ford was a classmate at Columbia University, entering the anthropology program in 1940, a year later than Willey. Willey clearly admired him, stating that he was one of the few archaeologists to whom the term "genius" could be applied (1988, 51). Ford was enthusiastically interested in pursuing issues of wide-ranging patterns and cultural diffusion in the Americas throughout his career, which was capped by his posthumous publication comparing American Formative cultures (1969). Willey's association with Ford was very likely part of the reason for his own interest in Central America as a key to understanding the spread of culture traits.

With respect to Willey's own field research, the Monagrillo ceramic complex is still considered the earliest pottery in central Panama and, possibly, in southern Central America (Cooke 1995, 179). Between 1959 and 1961, Willey conducted his last fieldwork in southern Central America, working with his graduate student Albert Norweb in southern Nicaragua (Norweb 1964). In many ways this was Willey's most ambitious effort because his and Norweb's work was coordinated with that of another graduate student, Michael Coe, who was working with Claude Baudez in northwestern Costa Rica (Coe and Baudez 1961). Together, the two projects spanned a crucial area of the Intermediate Area, establishing basic information still of value today. Norweb did not continue in archaeology, however, and the interests of the others moved to other areas.

"Bewildering Diversity"

By the late 1950s, Willey's time and energy were increasingly being taken up by Maya archaeology. The publication of *Method and Theory in American Archaeology* (Willey and Phillips 1958) demonstrates his continuing interest in larger theoretical issues, however. In 1962, four years after that publication and eight years after the Monagrillo report, his attentions turned to pan-American issues of space-time synthesis when he began to write *An Introduction to American Archaeology*, which was published in two large volumes.

Willey's approach to the role of grand synthesizer in his two big books was straightforwardly empirical. He aimed to provide an equal amount of culture history for all of the major culture regions, utilizing the concept of geographical-cultural regional divisions well established by William Henry Holmes (1914), with variations by subsequent scholars. He notes that factors of preservation give a "technological slant" to writing culture history and tend to lead to an emphasis on "man and his relations to his natural environment" (Willey 1966, 2). Inference is of two kinds, General—of the "common sense" variety—and Specific Historical Analogy (Willey 1966, 3). The latter refers to the Direct Historical Approach.

The idea of cultural tradition was a major organizing principle of Willey's magnum opus. From the discussion of Specific Analogy, he proceeds directly to a section called "Methodology and Organization," in which he argues for the value of culture areas because they are geographically bounded regions that maintained long-term cultural traditions (Willey 1966, 4–7).

Volume 1 is devoted to North and Middle America and Volume 2 covers South America and the Intermediate Area. Mesoamerica is the focus of the first volume, while Peru holds an analogous position in Volume 2. Each was a "major cultural tradition" for its part of the continent.

> The book is organized around this conception of major cultural traditions and the general chronological progression of history. The chapter on "The Early Americans" examines the earliest of the major cultural traditions. . . . Then, chapters are arranged in a certain geographic order so that the Mesoamerican cultural tradition and culture area is dealt with first and then followed by treatments of North American cultural traditions. (Willey 1966, 5)

But by the time Willey wrote the introduction to volume 2, the emphasis was less on the idea of major cultural traditions and more on the availability of literature.

> The course of the presentation swings back and forth, from such abstractions as "major cultural traditions" to the specifics of individual archaeological sites and the man-made objects found within them. . . . As in Volume One, the scheme of organization moves first to the early inhabitants and then takes up, in order, the later cultural traditions. . . . The intention has been to review the archaeology of all parts of South America . . . An area such as the Peruvian, where there is a vast literature—comparable to Mesoamerica in Volume One—receives much more attention than the huge East Brazilian area about which archaeologists yet know very little. (Willey 1971, 2–3)

Two points regarding Willey's general theoretical concerns in relation to the Intermediate Area may be garnered from these two introductory statements in *Introduction to American Archaeology*. First, his understanding of the units by which the past is discussed is geographical in nature, as noted by Frederick Lange (forthcoming). Second, Willey waffles between seeing "core" areas of cultural development, on the one hand, and, on the other, treating such areas mainly as places where the greatest amount of work had been done. He seems to have struggled between seeing the primacy of Mesoamerica and the Central Andes as the result of their being the places of greatest cultural development and admitting that the preponderance of literature on those areas had raised their status, as noted in his remarks about eastern Brazil.

When Willey turns to introducing the Intermediate Area in section 5 of volume 2 of *Introduction to American Archaeology*, he notes that the region's geographical position between Mesoamerica and Peru means that currents of influence could be recognized from both areas and, combined with the great environmental variation in the region, produces "a bewildering subareal and regional diversity in archaeological cultures" (1971, 255). Some fifteen years earlier, in his 1952 publication with McGimsey, Willey had noted the paucity of information on prehistoric Panama. (The second volume of *Introduction to American Archaeology* was written in the academic year of 1968–69, with some additions being made in the following two years.) We must take into account that in the later statement, Willey is referring to the entire Intermediate Area, not simply Panama. Nevertheless, the contrast between the two assessments is stark.

Reviewing Willey's bibliographic notes (1971, 352–59) underlines the fact that, indeed, the years that had elapsed between his Panamanian research and the writing of volume 2 of *Introduction to American Archaeology* had been a time of active research and publication. The scholarship of previous generations is cited frequently: names such as Spinden, Jijón y Caamaño, Linné, and Hartman are common. Nevertheless, the overwhelming majority of citations are to publications that appeared in the 1950s and, especially, the 1960s. For Ecuador, many citations are made to the works of Betty J. Meggers, Clifford Evans, and Emilio Estrada, and various combinations of them. For Colombia, Gerardo Reichel-Dolmatoff is the researcher Willey cites most. Panama citations include work by the Stirlings and by John Ladd, as well as Willey's own investigations. Costa Rica is mostly represented by Samuel Lothrop, Doris Stone, Olga Linares de Sapir, and Wolfgang Haberland. Claude Baudez and Michael Coe are cited for northwestern Costa Rica and for Pacific Nicaragua.

By citing numerous recent publications, Willey indicated that he had kept close watch on research in the area. He may have been particularly attuned to developments in the Intermediate Area not only because of personal interest but also because of the proximity of Samuel Lothrop, at Harvard's Peabody Museum, as well as the sponsorship of that institution in publishing Doris Stone's *Pre-Columbian Man Finds Central America: The Archaeological Bridge* (1972), which was issued only a year after Willey's second volume of *Introduction to American Archaeology* was published.

"Some Developmental Questions and Hypotheses"

The next major event in Willey's engagement with the Intermediate Area was an advanced seminar at the School of American Research, in Santa Fe, New Mexico, held April 8–14, 1980. Willey was on the planning committee with Frederick Lange and Doris Stone. While Willey agreed to chair the discussion sessions, the other two served as co-organizers of the symposium. The resulting book (Lange and Stone 1984) included articles by those who had attended the meeting, plus some additional contributions. Willey contributed part 5, called "Summary Statement," which consists of a single, almost forty-page-long chapter: "A Summary of the Archaeology of Lower Central America" (Willey 1984, 339–78).

Willey's summary chapter is a tour de force in absorbing, organizing, and cogently summarizing a great deal of information during the course of the seminar. The text is worth reading in its revelation of the issues raised and discussed by the participants at the meeting. The first section of his summary, "Archaeological Cultures, Space, and Time," reviews the current state of information for major regions of lower Central America, such as El Salvador, Honduras, and Greater Nicoya. The short second section, "A Chronological-Developmental Scheme for Lower Central America," presents a sequence of periods proposed for use throughout the entire region. A third section is entitled "Interpretations," and it discusses the roles of ecological adaptations and subsistence, sociopolitical inferences, and trade. This section mostly raises issues internal to the scholarship of the region, such as the nature of political organization and questions regarding the origins and circulation of jade and gold.

The final section in Willey's summary is entitled "Some Developmental Questions and Hypotheses." Issues of the constraints and opportunities provided by the environment are raised, as are questions as to why the Mesoamerican presence is not more strongly in evidence than it is. The closing remark turns to the question of whether "we can conceive of lower Central America as a culture-area-with-time-depth" (Willey 1984, 377). The answer is in the negative due to the absence of horizons like those present in Mesoamerica (Olmec, Teotihuacan, Toltec, Aztec) and Peru (Chavín, Huari-Tiahuanaco, Inca).

> To be sure, we do not yet understand the meanings of these horizons nor the processes which they signify; however, they serve to forge what Bennett (1948) once referred to as a "co-traditional" unity for their respective areas. Lower Central America does not present a similar phenomenon or set of phenomena. In this it is like Ecuador and Colombia, and for the time being, at least, the archaeologist is forced to view the whole of Ecuador-Columbia-lower Central America as an Intermediate Area of considerable regional diversity and great cultural complexity. (Willey 1984, 377–78)

"You Should Write This Up"

Willey does not appear to have participated in any extended discussion about the Intermediate Area after the School of American Research seminar and the volume that it produced. His next and final engagement with the issue occurred at a meeting at Dumbarton Oaks (DO). As I was personally involved with this enterprise, from now on I will use the first person perspective as much as possible.

The meeting at DO was entitled "The Gran Chibcha as a Culture Area(?): Horizon Styles, Cultural Traditions, and Temporal Depth at the Center of the Pre-Columbian World." John Hoopes and I organized it, and it was held on November 22 and 23, 1997. The purpose of the meeting was to develop a topic for a symposium at DO. The concept of having a workshop at which there could be extensive discussion seemed appropriate.

The only major meeting at DO that had specifically addressed the Intermediate Area previously had been "Wealth and Hierarchy in the Intermediate Area," which had been organized by Frederick W. Lange and held as a DO symposium in 1987. The resulting book (Lange 1992), published in 1992, was widely recognized as a landmark publication for studies of the region. We believed it was time for another event such as that one at Dumbarton Oaks, but we felt that the net had been cast rather wide in the 1987 symposium, extending from Honduras through the isthmus and well into Colombia and beyond. We felt that research was sufficiently advanced that a tighter geographic focus was possible and appropriate. Consequently, we decided to concentrate on the region comprising Costa Rica, Panama, and Colombia. It was generally agreed that this area was less under the influence of Mesoamerica than were lands to the area's north, with the exception of the northwestern corner of Costa Rica and some spotty intrusions and influences. We also mostly ignored Ecuador, given that, at various times in prehistory, its peoples and cultures participated in the Central Andean cotradition and, elsewhere, in the western Amazonian realm.

The proposition put to the members of the workshop was whether it was appropriate to consider renaming a great portion of the Intermediate Area as the Gran Chibcha or some similar name. John Hoopes and I felt that the question was not one simply of semantics. Instead, it impinged upon real issues of how we conceive of the units by which we frame the archaeological remnants of the fluid realities that comprised the living, breathing peoples and the places of this part of ancient America and how we study all of these. Rather than fully explicate the reasons for holding the conference, however, I will summarize what the participants said.

Six formal papers were presented over a day and a half of meetings in order to allow for opportunities to discuss the ideas presented and to develop thoughts derived from the papers. Fellows-in-residence for the year, DO staff, and guests contributed to the discussion, although the speakers participated the most.

As is common with such meetings, many more questions were raised than were posed at the outset. Nevertheless, the idea of proposing the Gran Chibcha as a culture area met with a range of opinions that ran the gamut from cautious uncertainty to strong feelings against the proposal.

Interestingly, the two scholars who were farthest apart in their approaches to prehistory were the participants most strongly in agreement in regards to *not* employing the term. Dick Drennan argued that worries about terminology distracted from the anthropological mission of archaeology to understand human societies. He noted that the concept of Mesoamerica was in jeopardy due to more focused studies on particular archaeological cultures and their dynamics. He also questioned the purpose of defining a culture area: what kinds of questions would doing so answer?

Mark Miller Graham argued that there was a danger in establishing a Chibchan culture area of creating an essentialist paradigm that would inhibit research rather than help it. Like Drennan, he cited recent research on the Maya as helping to break the barriers of typology. While Drennan suggested detailed archaeological area studies, Miller Graham championed mapping iconographic themes in the Intermediate Area, such as the way in which feline imagery was expressed and, through recourse to ethnography, its possible symbolic meanings.

Others at the meeting expressed different ideas about employing the concept. John Hoopes had begun the meeting by noting that recent research has shown strongly consistent patterning and homogeneity in the linguistics and biological anthropology of Costa Rica and Panama in particular (Barrantes 1993; Barrantes et al. 1990; Constenla Umaña 1991, 1994, 1995), suggesting that the region was a hearth of development and not simply a way station for developments from elsewhere. As the meeting progressed, however, the participants generally agreed that the problem of applying a concept such as the Gran Chibcha was that culture areas are archaeological constructs, not biological or linguistic ones or constructs of the three disciplines, since race, language, and culture are not consistently correlative.

As the meeting concluded, the issue that Gordon Willey originally raised resurfaced: the key to applying the designation of culture area to the Central

Andes and Mesoamerica was the presence of horizon styles. It was agreed, however, that the closest thing to a horizon style that is currently recognizable for the Intermediate Area is the widespread use of gold in jewelry, particularly as expressed in the International Style manifest throughout the region between about A.D. 600 and 900. Rather than continue to push for a larger meeting on nomenclature, John Hoopes and I subsequently decided that exploring the theme of the uses and symbolism of gold would be the best way to advance the study of the Intermediate Area through a conference at DO. Thus, the idea of the symposium "Gold and Power in Ancient Costa Rica, Panama, and Colombia" was born, resulting in a symposium in 1999 and a subsequent publication (Quilter and Hoopes 2003).

Gordon Willey was a guest at the presymposium meeting. It was the last time he visited Dumbarton Oaks, and it was after a long absence, too. He was quiet through most of the meeting but clearly interested in the issues debated. At the end of the meeting and a few times afterwards, he urged, "You should write this up!" as he thought that many worthy points had been raised. I hope that this essay's synopsis of the discussion at the meeting partly satisfies Willey's request.

The day after the meeting ended, when he had returned to the Peabody Museum, Gordon sent his expenses list for reimbursement to me and included a letter, which stated, in part, the following:

> I thought the meetings went very well—in spite of the fact that some of the boys tended to take things too seriously. This whole "Intermediate Area" business is a large question that faces Americanists, and will continue to face them for some time. To my mind the only unfortunate thing is that it has taken them too long to start thinking about it . . . there is a concern here to be addressed from many standpoints. (Willey, pers. comm., 1997)

Conclusion

This chapter has briefly sketched some of Gordon Willey's more important engagements with the archaeology of the Intermediate Area. At the beginning of this essay, I mentioned the bar talk concerning what might have happened if Gordon Willey had continued to work, long term, in Panama. Such conjectural histories are appropriate for bars but not for much else and are of the same order as questions of what might have happened to the Inca or Aztec empire if the Europeans hadn't arrived or had come to the New World later than they did.

Rather than regret the fact that Willey did not continue in southern Central American archaeology, we might take comfort that he worked there at all, for throughout his life he maintained a strong interest in the archaeology of the region and encouraged others to pursue research there. In addition to his own research, he produced a steady stream of graduate students who worked in the region, including Olga Linares, Paul Healy, John Hoopes, and Arthur Demarest. The latter worked on the edge of the Maya zone, in El Salvador, which was considered lower Central America at the time. Furthermore, the Peabody Museum's press published a number of important books on the topic, among which are Doris Stone's two synthetic works, *Pre-Columbian Man Finds Central America: The Archaeological Bridge* (1972) and *Pre-Columbian Man in Costa Rica* (1977), as well as *Adaptive Radiations in Prehistoric Panama* (Linares and Ranere 1980), which still serve as foundation documents for research in the area. With his catholic interests, Willey clearly actively supported and maintained interest in work in the region throughout his career. The fact that he journeyed to Washington, D.C., to attend his last meeting at DO on the issue of the Intermediate Area is a testament to his commitment to the field.

Gordon Willey's successful career in some senses spanned the classificatory-descriptive, classificatory-historical, and modern modes of archaeological discourse (though not, of course, the time periods assigned to these phases, as outlined by Willey and Sabloff). His fieldwork was straightforward chronology building, and that is the reason why it remains relevant to contemporary scholarship. When he interpreted the Intermediate Area in larger theoretical frameworks early in his career, his approach was historical, via his concern with diffusion. Later, his interests were evolutionary, as expressed by his concerns with great art styles and horizon markers.

That Willey could shift from one theoretical framework to the other is a demonstration that the "older" archaeology and New Archaeology were not different paradigms, but rather slightly different modes of analysis. Most proponents of New Archaeology never denied the role of diffusion— they just found the term too generalized and sought more specific, detailed explanations of how ideas spread from one society to another. The Intermediate Area or subregions of it likely will continue to be ranked as "secondary" or "peripheral" so long as the criteria by which such judgments are made are based upon assumptions that state-level societies and their material products (such as elite art) represent an evolutionary advancement over other, so-called less-complex modes of life. And such views are unlikely to change so long as those making the assessment are themselves inhabitants of highly hierarchical states and institutions, such as universities.

Gordon R. Willey contributed to the incremental advances increasing knowledge of the prehistory of the region because of his early experiences in Panama and because he was a man with wide-ranging interests. We should not bemoan what he didn't do but be thankful for all that he did.

Acknowledgments

Many thanks to Jeremy Sabloff and William Fash for inviting me to partici-pate in the Society for American Archaeology panel and for offering me the opportunity to contribute to this volume. I have gained much, through the years, in conversations with Frederick Lange and John Hoopes regarding things Intermediate. The former was kind in letting me read and cite his unpublished manuscript. John Hoopes reminded me of many things that had slipped my memory or that I had overlooked. I also offer special thanks to those who participated in the various workshops and symposia at Dumbar-ton Oaks and elsewhere that, whatever their long-term contributions, raised the profile of Intermediate Area studies at least a little higher than before.

And this one's for Gordon, of course, who, in addition to giving us his fine scholarship and sharing his great sense of humor, was very kind to me in my years at Dumbarton Oaks.

References

Barrantes, Ramiro. 1993. *Evolución en el trópico: Los amerindos de Costa Rica y Panama*. San José: Editorial de la Universidad de Costa Rica.

Barrantes, Ramiro, Peter E. Smouse, Harvey W. Mohrenweiser, Henry Gershowitz, Jorge Azofeifa, T. D. Arias, and James V. Neel. 1990. "Microevolution in Lower Central Amer-ica: Genetic Characterization of the Chibcha-Speaking Groups of Costa Rica and Panama and a Taxonomy Based on Genetics, Linguistics, and Geography." *American Journal of Human Genetics* 46:63–84.

Bird, Junius B. 1985. *The Preceramic Excavations at the Huaca Prieta, Chicama Valley, Peru*. Ed. John Hyslop. Anthropological Papers of the American Museum of Natural History, vol. 62, pt. 1. New York: American Museum of Natural History.

Coe, Michael D., and Claude Baudez. 1961. "The Zoned Bichrome Period in Northwestern Costa Rica." *American Antiquity* 26:505–15.

Constenla Umaña, Adolfo. 1991. *Las lenguas del Aacute*rea Intermédia: Introducción a su estudio areal. San José: Editorial de la Universidad de Costa Rica.

———. 1994. "Las lenguas de la Gran Nicoya." *Vinculos* 18–19:209–27.

———. 1995. "Sobre el estudio diacrónico de las lenguas chichenses y su contribución al conocimiento del pasado de sus hablantes." *Boletín del Museo de Oro* 38–39:13–56.

Cooke, Richard. 1995. "Monagrillo, Panama's First Pottery." In *The Emergence of Pottery: Technology and Innovation in Ancient Societies*, ed. William K. Barnett and John W. Hoopes, 169–98. Washington, D.C.: Smithsonian Institution Press.

Ford, James A. 1969. *A Comparison of Formative Cultures in the Americas: Diffusion or the Psychic Unity of Man?* Washington, D.C.: Smithsonian Institution Press.

Holmes, William Henry. 1914. "Areas of American Culture Characterization Tentatively Outlined as an Aid in the Study of the Antiquities." *American Anthropologist* 16 (3):413–46.

Hoopes, John W., and Oscar Fonseca Z. 2003. "Goldwork and Chibchan Identity: Endogenous Change and Diffuse Unity in the Isthmo-Colombian Area." In *Gold and Power in Ancient Costa Rica, Panama, and Colombia*, ed. Jeffrey Quilter and John W. Hoopes, 49–90. Washington, D.C.: Dumbarton Oaks.

Kroeber, Alfred L. 1927. "Disposal of the Dead." *American Anthropologist* 29:308–15.

———. 1951. "Great Art Styles of Ancient South America." In *The Civilizations of Ancient America*, ed. Sol Tax, 207–15. Selected Papers of the 29th International Congress of Americanists, vol. 1. Chicago: University of Chicago Press.

Lange, Frederick W., ed. 1992. *Wealth and Hierarchy in the Intermediate Area: A Symposium at Dumbarton Oaks, 10 and 11 October, 1987.* Washington, D.C.: Dumbarton Oaks.

———. Forthcoming. "Gordon R. Willey y el Aacuterea Intermédia: Conceptos, contribuciones, y direciones futuros." In Arqueología del *Aacuterea Intermédia*. Vol. 5. Bogota: Instituto Colombiano de Antropología e Historia y Sociedad Colombiana de_Arqueología.

Lange, Frederick W., and Doris Z. Stone, eds. 1984. *The Archaeology of Lower Central America.* School of American Research Advanced Seminar Series. Albuquerque: University of New Mexico Press.

Linares, Olga F., and Anthony J. Ranere. 1980. *Adaptive Radiations in Prehistoric Panama.* Cambridge, Mass.: Peabody Museum of Archaeology and Ethnology, Harvard University.

McGimsey, Charles Robert. 1956. "Cerro Mangote: A Preceramic Site in Panama." *American Antiquity* 22:151–61.

Norweb, Albert. 1964. "Ceramic Stratigraphy in Southwestern Nicaragua." In *Actas y Memorias del XXXV Congreso Internacional de Americanistas (Mexico, 1962)*, 1:551–61. Mexico City.

Quilter, Jeffrey, and John W. Hoopes, eds. 2003. *Gold and Power in Ancient Costa Rica, Panama, and Colombia: A Symposium at Dumbarton Oaks, 9 and 10 October 1999.* Washington, D.C.: Dumbarton Oaks.

Steward, Julian H., ed. 1948. *Handbook of South American Indians.* Vol. 4, *The Circum-Caribbean Tribes.* Washington, D.C.: GPO.

Stirling, Matthew W. 1949a. "Exploring the Past in Panama." *National Geographic*, March, 373–99.

———. 1949b. "The Importance of Sitio Conte." *American Anthropologist* 51:514–17.

———. 1950. "Exploring Ancient Panama by Helicopter." *National Geographic*, February, 227–46.

———. 1953a. "Exploring Panama's Unknown North Coast." *Royal Canadian Institute, Proceedings* (Toronto) 18:29–30.

———. 1953b. "Hunting Prehistory in Panama Jungles: Tracing Lost Indian Civilizations, an Archeologist and His Wife Narrowly Escape Disaster on the Isthmus' Wild North Coast." *National Geographic*, August, 271–90.

Stirling, Matthew W., and Marion Stirling. 1964a. "El Limón, an Early Tomb Site in Coclé Province, Panama." In *Anthropological Papers, Numbers 68–74*, 247–54. Bureau of American Ethnology Bulletin 191. Washington, D.C.: GPO.

———. 1964b. "Archeological Notes on Almirante Bay, Bocas del Toro, Panama." In *Anthropological Papers, Numbers 68–74*, 255–84. Bureau of American Ethnology Bulletin 191. Washington, D.C.: GPO.

———. 1964c. "The Archeology of Taboga, Urabá, and Taboguilla Islands, Panama." In *Anthropological Papers, Numbers 68–74*, 285–348. Bureau of American Ethnology Bulletin 191. Washington, D.C.: GPO.

Stone, Doris. 1972. *Pre-Columbian Man Finds Central America: The Archaeological Bridge*. Cambridge, Mass.: Peabody Museum of Archaeology and Ethnology, Harvard University.

———. 1977. *Pre-Columbian Man in Costa Rica*. Cambridge, Mass.: Peabody Museum of Archaeology and Ethnology, Harvard Universityarvar.

Tax, Sol, ed. 1951. *The Civilizations of Ancient America*. Selected Papers, 29th International Congress of Americanists, vol. 1. Chicago: University of Chicago Press.

Willey, Gordon R. 1955. "The Interrelated Rise of the Native Cultures of Middle and South America." In *New Interpretations of Aboriginal American Culture History*, 28–45. Washington, D.C.: Anthropological Society of Washington.

———. 1959. "The 'Intermediate Area' of Nuclear America: Its Prehistoric Relationships to Middle America and Peru." In *Actas del XXXIII Congreso Internacional de Americanistas, San José, 20–27 Juilo 1958*, 1:184–94. San José: Lehmann.

———. 1966. *An Introduction to American Archaeology*. Vol. 1, *North and Middle America*. Englewood Cliffs, N.J.: Prentice Hall.

———. 1971. *An Introduction to American Archaeology*. Vol. 2, *South America*. Englewood Cliffs, N.J.: Prentice Hall.

———. 1984. "A Summary of the Archaeology of Lower Central America." In *The Archaeology of Lower Central America*, ed. Frederick W. Lange and Doris Z. Stone, 339–78. School of American Research Advanced Seminar Series. Albuquerque: University of New Mexico Press.

———. 1988. *Portraits in American Archaeology: Remembrances of Some Distinguished Americanists*. Albuquerque: University of New Mexico Press.

Willey, Gordon R., and Charles R. McGimsey. 1952. "Archaeology in Western Panama." *Archaeology* 5:173–81.

———. 1954. *The Monagrillo Culture of Panama*. Papers of the Peabody Museum of Archaeology and Ethnology, vol. 49, no. 2. Cambridge, Mass.: Harvard University.

Willey, Gordon R., and Philip Phillips. 1958. *Method and Theory in American Archaeology*. Chicago: University of Chicago Press.

Willey, Gordon R., and Jeremy A. Sabloff. 1993. *A History of American Archaeology*. 3rd ed. New York: W. H. Freeman.

Chapter Seven

Serendipity at Seibal:
Gordon Willey in the Pasión Valley

Gair Tourtellot and Norman Hammond

In 1754 the great English aesthete and connoisseur Horace Walpole coined the term "serendipity" in a letter to a friend. He had been reading the folktale "The Three Princes of Serendip"—Serendip being an old name for Sri Lanka—and remarked that these heroes "were always making discoveries, by accidents and sagacity, of things they were not in quest of"; hence Walpole said of his own current finding, "This discovery, indeed, is of the kind which I call serendipity." The dictionary now defines it as "the faculty of making happy and unexpected discoveries by accident"—and serendipity was a powerful factor in Gordon Willey's project at Seibal, Guatemala.

It struck first in his even thinking of the site: from 1953 to 1956, he had been working in the Belize River valley, principally at Barton Ramie, on the project that effectively launched settlement pattern studies as part of mainstream Maya archaeology (Ashmore, this volume). At the end of that period, he tells us, "I wanted to continue work in the Maya lowlands, and Harry Pollock suggested that I look at Altar de Sacrificios. Most previous work had been concentrated in the eastern Petén, because of ease of access through Belize, but Tikal now had an airstrip for the Penn project and similar dirt strips at places like Sayaxché had suddenly made the Pasión valley accessible" (Willey 1991).

Gordon's excavations at Altar from 1958 to 1964, the first extensive excavations upstream of the Usumacinta confluence, were intended to fill an immense gap in archaeological knowledge of the southern Petén, at a time when Uaxactun was still the primary comparison for the entire Southern Lowlands (see Willey 1973, 3–6, for summary). The region was still lightly populated and largely forested. Altar was an important Maya Lowland site in a riparian swamp, with a few big structures and the earliest hieroglyphic texts in the south (Maler 1908; Morley 1937–38, 2:309–14). It is situated at the confluence of the Pasión and Chixoy rivers, promising easy access to the edge of the highlands both for tracing origins and for cross-dating regional sequences through trade items. Besides a source of serendipitous data, Gordon viewed Altar as a potential crossroads of trade, where highland-lowland interaction could be observed. But, as Gordon said, "I don't think it ever turned out that way: Altar proved to be a typical Lowland Classic center, although with an earlier beginning to its Preclassic sequence in the Xe phase than had been found elsewhere" (Willey 1991). Nor did it include the Mexican—specifically, Teotihuacan—influences on the Maya that he sought (the first inkling of the conquest hypotheses later developed at Altar and Seibal). Instead, "the possibility of other Mexican impacts on the Maya, namely those of Toltec inspiration" (Willey 1973, 6), was confirmed in spades, for Altar had an unusual endgame. The Boca phase of typical Terminal Classic Tepeu 3, spanning 9.17.0.0.0–10.3.0.0.0, A.D. 771–889, was followed by Jimba as a functionally complete and "foreign" Fine Paste ceramic complex with stylistic attributes of allegedly Toltec design. Interestingly, the settlement pattern study was the least important rationale for investigating Altar (Willey 1973, 6), where William R. Bullard, Jr., found only forty-one mounds outside the three major plazas.

At this point Gordon wanted to do some more work in the region (Willey 1991), and A. Ledyard Smith, his field director, was enthusiastic about Seibal, pointing out that their logistics were already in place. Seibal was known mainly from Teobert Maler's report on his visit in 1895, which spoke of "stelae of extraordinary beauty" (1908, 11), many of which had what Tatiana Proskouriakoff later designated (1950, 152–53) as foreign traits (see fig. 7.1). These monuments were carved late in Maya history, dating to the second half of the ninth century, when many centers had already been abandoned. With Altar dedicating monuments until 9.17.0.0.0 and Seibal beginning only in 9.16.0.0.0, "the complementary pattern of the stelae dates argues for a west-to-east shift in authority and power" (Smith and Willey 1964, 5). John Graham, Dick Adams, and Timothy Fiske made an expedition upriver to Seibal and found that it was much larger than Maler, or Sylvanus Morley (1937–38, 2:249–89), had reported: these three discovered *sacbeob* linking the known Group A to two other hilltops, and they dug six test pits that, ironically, recovered no late Fine Paste pottery (Adams 1963).

So there was a conundrum: Altar had Fine Paste ceramics of apparently foreign origin in the Jimba phase but no late or non–Classic Maya monuments, whereas Seibal had plenty of late, weird stelae but no documented Fine Paste occupation. Resolving the issue of strong non–Classic Maya elements in the Pasión valley during the Terminal Late Classic period (as the Terminal Classic was then called) was very much the chief initial aim at Seibal (Smith and Willey 1964). Furthermore, Seibal seemed to offer abundant Early Classic pottery that might shed light on the mid-Classic weakness at Altar and on the Teotihuacan question. Adding to these concerns, "Altar de Sacrificios had revealed traces of very early farming and pottery making occupants of the Peten . . . [and] it was deemed wise to explore further on the Rio Pasión to see if further evidences of these people could be found" (Willey et al. 1968, 3). Thus, Gordon Willey had the rationale for a new project, following in the footsteps of two earlier explorers also associated with Harvard. A complete settlement study was not one of the initial rationales for Seibal but emerged during Ian Graham's mapping of the central area of the site, which found a great many highly visible small structures.

In the 1960s the forest was nearly unbroken, and the Seibal project had to import workers from as far away as La Libertad and even Baja Verapaz. The regular staff of the Seibal project, in the field from 1964 to 1968, consisted of Gordon as director, Ledyard Smith as field director (see fig. 7.2), artist José Antonio Oliveros, and four graduate students, recruited mainly from Gordon's fall Middle America or South America seminar. Two students were there throughout the project: Jerry Sabloff as ceramicist and Gair Tourtellot for settlement. Will Andrews V, Kent Day, Arthur Miller, Mark Leone, Bob Schuyler, Richard Rose, and Norman Hammond each attended for a season.

Figure 7.1. Seibal Stela 1, 10.2.0.0.0. 3 Ahau 3 Ceh (A.D. 869), one of the spectacular Terminal Classic monuments discovered by Teobert Maler in 1895. Photograph by Norman Hammond.

Figure 7.2. A. Ledyard Smith, Gordon Willey, visitor Henri Lehmann (in background), and Jeremy Sabloff, in the South Plaza of Group A at Seibal, February 13, 1968. Photograph by Norman Hammond.

Specialists were there for shorter periods, like Ian Graham for mapping, John Graham as epigrapher, and Rudi Kuylen for resetting stelae. Gordon had an extraordinary facility for engaging others in his work, eventually involving Ronald Bishop, Lawrence Feldman, Edwin Littmann, Peter Mathews, Stanley Olson, Mary Pohl, Robert Rands, Frank Saul, Raymond Sidrys, and Richard Wilk in various further analyses of human and animal bones, ceramics, obsidian, mollusca, and plaster floors and in historical interpretation.

At his station in the field lab, Gordon had the first look at all the ceramics and artifacts sent in daily for analysis right on-site. He and Jerry related finds from different places and suggested further digging. Gordon visited excavations from time to time but gave no formal instruction or academic credit. In all, eleven major buildings were excavated, two were substantially restored (see fig. 7.3), fifteen carved monuments were reset in place, and sixty-two house groups were tested. How do the initial aims for Gordon's investigations at Seibal match up against the data acquired, his conclusions, and evidence that has emerged subsequently? The following sections will address this question.

Figure 7.3. Seibal Structure A-3 after restoration in 1968, seen from the west. Photo by Gair Tourtellot.

Preclassic Discoveries

At Seibal, Gordon's and Jerry's ceramic analyses (Sabloff 1975; Willey 1970) identified the Real complex, or early Middle Preclassic, an extension of Dick Adams's Xe complex at Altar. At the time, this was the earliest pottery complex defined in the Southern Lowlands, and it was located surprisingly deep in the interior of the peninsula. The discovery stimulated Dennis and Olga Puleston's "riverine model" (1971) for the initial settlement of the Southern Lowlands. The extraordinary thing about the tiny first settlement in Real Xe times is that it attracted a cruciform cache containing an Olmec jade bloodletter (Smith 1982, 243; see fig. 7.4). We can only suppose that the Seibal hill, at the great bend of the Pasión River, was in a strategic position for trading. The location of that cache, on the highest ground, marks the ritual center of Seibal for 1,700 years.

The settlement area yielded a possible late Middle Preclassic temple mound, one of the earliest known. By the Late Preclassic, a regular network of these temple mounds marched across the landscape, suggesting a

Figure 7.4. Jadeite celts and blue jade "stiletto" bloodletter from Cache 7 at Seibal. Charcoal from an accompanying Real Xe vessel yielded a calibrated radiocarbon date of 900 B.C. The bloodletter, 7.4 centimeters long, may have been imported from the Olmec region of the Gulf Coast to the west, although the source of the jade is probably in the Motagua Valley of southern Guatemala. Photograph by Gordon R. Willey.

then-decentralized populace. Randomized excavations and 229 treefall collections were used to plot the progressive settlement of Seibal, from a tiny pioneer hamlet on the future site of Group A to a Late Preclassic community as extensive as Seibal ever became (Tourtellot 1988, maps 5–13). Although at the time of the Seibal project the Late Preclassic was still largely thought of as an era of small farming villages, Ledyard Smith's meticulous stratigraphic records later allowed Seibal to be recognized as a major Preclassic city (Hammond 1984).

Early Classic Disappointment

In a sense, Early Classic discoveries were the biggest disappointment at Seibal, for they were meager. In 1961 Dick Adams by chance had put a pit down in what turned out to be the only significant Early Classic deposit that was ever found. Sitewide, however, barely a thousand Early Classic Junco-phase potsherds were ever found, and little else.

Gordon found that both Altar and Seibal were actually weak in the middle of their occupation spans, around A.D. 500–600, eventually spawning his hiatus paper (Willey 1974; see Freidel, Escobedo, and Guenter, this volume). Neither community attracted significant attention from Teotihuacan, which implies Teotihuacanos were not primarily interested in trade—or anything else—along the Pasión. Seibal also provided one of the first demonstrations that Maya cities had highly particularized histories— site-specific trajectories or even oscillations between growth and decline (the "Nohmul/Seibal" pattern, in Hammond 1991, fig. 11.3)—rather than smooth growth to a Late Classic climax.

Late Classic Growth

The Late Classic Tepeu 2 at Seibal was just such an expected climax, but our understanding of it has changed greatly. This Tepejilote phase looked to us like a time of growth, a new occupation rapidly reoccupying the full extent of the abandoned Preclassic settlement. We thought that maybe Seibal was recolonized from mighty Tikal, that archetypal touchstone of 1960s Maya comparative archaeology. In fact, aside from Altar de Sacrificios, Tikal was the nearest available site that had been excavated to any significant degree. Nevertheless, Gordon continued his effort to expand knowledge within the

Pasión region. Downriver we recorded Itzán (Tourtellot, Hammond, and Rose 1978), the first major site north of the lower Pasión, and visited Aguateca. Upriver we briefly investigated Cancuén, quadrupling the known site area and recording a large, well-preserved palace complex, including the first standing architecture seen along the Pasión (Tourtellot, Sabloff, and Sharick 1978). Overall, it appears that the major sites on the Pasión River developed about one day's journey apart: Gordon's most magisterial review of the Pasión basin evidence is to be found in an article written with Peter Mathews (Mathews and Willey 1991). Gordon's explorations were fundamental to a series of later projects conducted by others, including Kevin Johnston at Itzán and Stephen Houston and Arthur Demarest in the Laguna Petexbatún at Dos Pilas, which were followed by Takeshi Inomata and Daniela Triadan at Aguateca and, most recently, by Arthur Demarest at Cancuén. These subsequent projects are rewriting our views and perspectives on the southern Petén.

We now know that Tepejilote at Seibal was a much more dynamic period than we thought, based on this greatly expanded regional context and the recent decipherment of monument texts (Willey 1990, 255–56; Houston 1993; Demarest 1997). Sometime during Tepejilote, Group D was built into the most impressive fortress of the time in the Pasión region: it was a shock to learn later that our great Seibal had been conquered and reduced to vassalage by Dos Pilas precisely during this time of growth. The historical substance of the Tepejilote-to-Bayal transition may turn out to correspond to the conquest of Seibal in A.D. 735, the destruction of its conqueror Dos Pilas in A.D. 761, and the collapse of the Petexbatún kingdom.

Terminal Classic Florescence

The striking Bayal innovations that first attracted Gordon may have been produced by elite intrusion. Features new to Seibal in the Terminal Classic Bayal phase appear not only in the bizarre Tenth Cycle monuments, but also in the radially planned Temple A-3—with elaborate, polychrome stucco decoration commemorating the "Maya millennium" at 10.0.0.0.0. and five stelae from a *k'atun* later—as well as in the texts and the iconography of other stelae, Fine Paste ceramics, the cruciform causeway system, a very dense and stratified settlement around it, and different house types. Pottery identified as Bayal may form a limited enclave around Group A, a densely packed settlement similar to Tecep-phase Nohmul in Belize (Hammond et al. 1988).

The most famous early product of the Seibal project was the hypothesis of ninth-century invasion and its possible role in the Classic Maya collapse. Conceived by Gordon and Jerry Sabloff, the hypothesis was founded on analysis of the so-called Mexicanoid iconographic elements on the Tenth Cycle monuments, and on distributional studies of the characteristic Fine Paste ceramics (Sabloff and Willey 1967). Many elements pointed northwestward, toward sites nearer the Gulf of Mexico, as Proskouriakoff pointed out (1950). These were reasonable constructions for the time, before we could read the glyphs. The only excavated sites in the Pasión basin were Altar and Seibal, so any comparisons were necessarily made to sites separated from Seibal by long distances: long distances were subtly conducive to thinking that Seibal was settled by migrants—as it certainly was in the Preclassic and probably in the Late Classic—or invaded by organized forces.

The invasion hypothesis has three components: invasion, conquest, and a foreign source to the northwest. Subsequent investigations in the region and continuing sourcing of pottery by Ron Bishop and his colleagues (Sabloff et al. 1982; Foias and Bishop 1997) now indicate that the "intrusive" Fine Paste wares actually may have been produced locally (Willey 1990, 257). New analyses of texts and iconography find a wider dispersion of possible sources for Bayal, including to the north and northeast (see, e.g., Stuart 1993; Tourtellot and González 2004). They name a man from Ucanal as ruler and provide a fuller Classic Maya ambit (see Schele and Mathews 1998, 175–96).

Gordon was correct in seeing evidence of conquest but was perhaps too modest in seeing only one conquest at Seibal. In a speculative mood, we could now imagine as many as *five* conquests: the first to finish off the vast Preclassic settlement—perhaps part of a broader Terminal Preclassic "collapse" now known from the Mirador Basin of northern Petén and elsewhere—and a second to account for the Late Classic resettlement after the quasi abandonment of the Junco phase. Third was the documented conquest by Dos Pilas within the Late Classic, and then the last conquests were the two waves Gordon and Jerry proposed as defining the Terminal Classic florescence. While war was one of the factors we considered relevant to the siting of Seibal—along with trade and subsistence—we never imagined the possibility of so many invasions or the shocking descent into endemic warfare suggested by subsequent investigators (Demarest et al. 1997). Terminal Classic Seibal stands out in stark splendor in a rapidly emptying landscape (Willey 1990, 260).

Conclusion

In conclusion, let us mention that Gordon's "yoke was easy and his burden was light." He let people be independent and responsible for their own work. There was no "party line"; he asked a question from time to time but specified neither the method a person should use nor the answer to be expected. Indeed, he often implied his questions merely by tilting his head back and cocking his eyebrow at you (see fig. 7.5). Gordon did not insist on certain topics nor that he approve your results. Then again, three of his researchers on the Seibal project took their own sweet time finishing their parts of the investigation.

Gordon had great *dignitas*. Even sitting in a dugout canoe in his crumpled and sweat-stained hat, he was a figure of commanding presence. It never occurred to us that we were being exploited to work ten-hour days for six days a week for three months at a stretch, all for just an airplane ticket, a cot, and two fingers of rum a day.

If Gordon had begun with predefined hypothetico-deductive nomothetic paradigm-seeking tests of his initial ideas for Seibal, as became de rigueur during the 1960s, he might have quit early and moved on. Some of his objectives were attained, some were not, and others were serendipitously modified as work proceeded. The Early Classic proved weak or nonexistent, the Preclassic deeply buried. Nothing like the Postclassic Jimba phase at Altar appeared. Instead, he persevered, encouraged the expansion of the investigation, and accepted the fortunate accidents of serendipity. As a consequence, he drove Lowland Maya history earlier into the Middle Preclassic and showed how a pioneer hamlet developed into a high-density Late Preclassic center. He showed that the trajectory of individual Maya site development was not always onward and upward. The splendid, if still enigmatic, florescence of Terminal Classic Seibal remains the apogee of the Pasión region and is still provoking debate over its true role. He and Jerry were able to develop a provocative explanation for the

Figure 7.5. Gordon Willey at
Seibal, 1965. Photograph by
Ian Graham.

Maya collapse—warfare and invasion—anticipating the breakthroughs in
hieroglyphic decipherment yet to come. Those decipherments were to
show that Seibal had indeed been conquered, although earlier than we ever
supposed, and confirmed a central role for warfare in the Late Classic, even
though long-distance conquest and hegemonic alliances were not demonstrated until the mid-1990s.

In sum, Gordon found Seibal to be unexpectedly rich. The ideas he generated or fomented continue to provoke investigation, household and settlement investigations proliferate, regional interests continue to expand,
and warfare has become a key theme, although migrations haven't received
much attention. Gordon Willey's Seibal project was a vital early component of, and still plays an important part in, our understanding of the
dynamics of ancient Maya civilization.

References

Adams, Richard E. W. 1963. "Seibal, Peten: Una sequencia ceramica preliminar y un nuevo mapa." *Estudios de Cultura Maya* 3:85–96.

Demarest, Arthur A. 1997. "The Vanderbilt Petexbatun Regional Archaeological Project 1989–1994: Overview, History, and Major Results of a Multidisciplinary Study of the Classic Maya Collapse." *Ancient Mesoamerica* 8:209–27.

Demarest, Arthur A., Matt O'Mansky, Claudia Wolley, Dirk Van Tuerenhout, Takeshi Inomata, Joel Palka, and Héctor Escobedo. 1997. "Classic Maya Defensive Systems and Warfare in the Petexbatun Region: Archaeological Evidence and Interpretations." *Ancient Mesoamerica* 8:229–53.

Foias, Antonia E., and Ronald L. Bishop. 1997. "Changing Ceramic Production and Exchange in the Petexbatun Region, Guatemala." *Ancient Mesoamerica* 8:275–91.

Hammond, Norman. 1984. Review of *Excavations at Seibal, Department of Peten, Guatemala*, ed. Gordon R. Willey, Memoirs of the Peabody Museum of Archaeology and Ethnology, vol. 15, nos. 1 and 2. *Antiquaries Journal* 64:119–21.

———. 1991. "Inside the Black Box: Defining Maya Polity." In *Classic Maya Political History: Hieroglyphic and Archaeological Evidence*, ed. T. Patrick Culbert, 253–84. Cambridge: Cambridge University Press.

Hammond, Norman, Laura J. Kosakowsky, Anne Pyburn, John Rose, J. C. Staneko, Sara Donaghey, Mark Horton, Catherine Clark, Colleen Gleason, Deborah Muyskens, and Thomas Addyman. 1988. "The Evolution of an Ancient Maya City: Nohmul." *National Geographic Research and Exploration* 4:474–95.

Houston, Stephen. 1993. *Hieroglyphs and History at Dos Pilas: Dynastic Politics of the Classic Maya*. Austin: University of Texas Press.

Maler, Teobert. 1908. *Exploration of the Upper Usumacintla and Adjacent Regions*. Memoirs of the Peabody Museum of Archaeology and Ethnology, vol. 4, no. 1. Cambridge, Mass.: Harvard University.

Mathews, Peter, and Gordon R. Willey. 1991. "Prehistoric Polities of the Pasion Region: Hieroglyphic Texts and Their Archaeological Settings." In *Classic Maya Political History: Hieroglyphic and Archaeological Evidence*, ed. T. Patrick Culbert, 30–71. Cambridge: Cambridge University Press.

Morley, Sylvanus G. 1937–38. *The Inscriptions of Peten*. 5 vols. Carnegie Institution of Washington Publication 437. Washington, D.C.: Carnegie Institution of Washington.

Proskouriakoff, Tatiana. 1950. *A Study of Classic Maya Sculpture*. Carnegie Institution of Washington Publication 593. Washington, D.C.: Carnegie Institution of Washington.

Puleston, Dennis E., and Olga S. Puleston. 1971. "An Ecological Approach to the Origins of Maya Civilization." *Archaeology* 24:330–37.

Sabloff, Jeremy A. 1975. "Ceramics." In *Excavations at Seibal, Department of Peten, Guatemala*. Memoirs of the Peabody Museum of Archaeology and Ethnology, vol. 13, no. 2. Cambridge, Mass.: Harvard University.

Sabloff, Jeremy A., Ronald L. Bishop, Graham Harbottle, Robert L. Rands, and Edward V. Sayre. 1982. "Analyses of Fine Paste Ceramics." In *Excavations at Seibal, Department of Peten, Guatemala*. Memoirs of the Peabody Museum of Archaeology and Ethnology, vol. 15, no. 2. Cambridge, Mass.: Harvard University.

Sabloff, Jeremy A., and Gordon R. Willey. 1967. "The Collapse of Maya Civilization in the Southern Lowlands: A Consideration of History and Process." *Southwestern Journal of Anthropology* 23 (4):311–36.

Schele, Linda, and Peter Mathews. 1998. *The Code of Kings: The Language of Seven Sacred Maya Temples and Tombs*. New York: Scribner.

Smith, A. Ledyard. 1982. "Major Architecture and Caches." In *Excavations at Seibal, Department of Peten, Guatemala*. Memoirs of the Peabody Museum of Archaeology and Ethnology, vol. 15, no. 1. Cambridge, Mass.: Harvard University.

Smith, A. Ledyard, and Gordon R. Willey. 1964. "Seibal 1964: First Preliminary Report of the Peabody Museum Harvard University Expedition." Mimeograph, Peabody Museum of Archaeology and Ethnology, Harvard University.

Stuart, David. 1993. "Historical Inscriptions and the Maya Collapse." In *Lowland Maya Civilization in the Eighth Century A.D.*, ed. Jeremy A. Sabloff and John S. Henderson, 321–54. Washington, D.C.: Dumbarton Oaks.

Tourtellot, Gair, III. 1988. *Excavations at Seibal, Department of Peten, Guatemala: Peripheral Survey and Excavation, Settlement and Community Patterns*. Memoirs of the Peabody Museum of Archaeology and Ethnology, vol. 16. Cambridge, Mass.: Harvard University.

Tourtellot, Gair, and Jason J. González. 2004. "The Last Hurrah: Continuity and Transformation at Seibal." In *The Terminal Classic in the Maya Lowlands: Collapse, Transition, and Transformation*, ed. Arthur A. Demarest, Prudence M. Rice, and Don S. Rice, 60–82. Boulder: University Press of Colorado.

Tourtellot, Gair, III, Norman Hammond, and Richard M. Rose. 1978. "A Brief Reconnaissance of Itzan." In *Excavations at Seibal, Department of Peten, Guatemala*. Memoirs of the Peabody Museum of Archaeology and Ethnology, vol. 14, no. 3. Cambridge, Mass.: Harvard University.

Tourtellot, Gair, III, Jeremy A. Sabloff, and Robert Sharick. 1978. "A Reconnaissance of Cancuen." In *Excavations at Seibal, Department of Peten, Guatemala*. Memoirs of the Peabody Museum of Archaeology and Ethnology, vol. 14, no. 2. Cambridge, Mass.: Harvard University.

Willey, Gordon R. 1970. "Type Descriptions of the Ceramics of the Real Xe Complex, Seibal, Peten, Guatemala." In *Monographs and Papers in Maya Archaeology*, ed. William R. Bullard, Jr., 313–55. Papers of the Peabody Museum of Archaeology and Ethnology, vol. 61. Cambridge, Mass.: Harvard University.

———. 1973. *The Altar de Sacrificios Excavations: General Summary and Conclusions*. Papers of the Peabody Museum of Archaeology and Ethnology, vol. 64, no. 3. Cambridge, Mass.: Harvard University.

———. 1974. "The Classic Maya Hiatus: A 'Rehearsal' for the Collapse?" In *Mesoamerican Archaeology: New Approaches*, ed. Norman Hammond, 417–30. Austin: University of Texas Press.

———. 1990. "General Summary and Conclusions." In *Excavations at Seibal, Department of Peten, Guatemala*. Memoirs of the Peabody Museum of Archaeology and Ethnology, vol. 17, no. 4. Cambridge, Mass.: Harvard University.

———. 1991. "Conversations with Gordon Willey: South America, Panama, and the Maya." Interviews by Norman Hammond. Videotaped by Katherine Jones. Tozzer Library, Harvard University, Cambridge, Mass.

Willey, Gordon R., A. Ledyard Smith, Gair Tourtellot III, and Jeremy A. Sabloff. 1968. "Seibal 1968: Fifth and Terminal Preliminary Report." Mimeograph, Peabody Museum of Archaeology and Ethnology, Harvard University.

Chapter Eight

The Classic Maya "Collapse" and Its Causes:
The Role of Warfare?

Prudence M. Rice

T he earliest effort to address comprehensively the perplexing problem of the end of Classic Lowland Maya civilization—its "collapse"—and its causes was an advanced seminar held in 1970 at
the School of American Research in Santa Fe, New Mexico. The publication of the seminar presentations, entitled *The Classic Maya Collapse* (Culbert 1973), concluded with a summary by Gordon R. Willey and coauthor
Demitri B. Shimkin (Willey and Shimkin 1973), who heroically attempted
to integrate all the possible causes, social and environmental, discussed by
the seminar participants into a single descriptive model. A model so all-
encompassing cannot be useful in a hypothesis-testing sense, but a singular
accomplishment of their chapter was that its breadth and depth effectively
laid to rest simplistic unicausal theories about the complex set of events
taking place in the late eighth through tenth centuries A.D. A less-heralded
aspect of their chapter, rather curious in light of today's perspectives, is
their minimal discussion of the role of warfare and militarism in the collapse—despite some enduring insights in what they *did* say. In this contribution to honoring Gordon Willey's great legacy in the archaeology of the
Americas, I examine the intellectual history of the role of warfare in the

Classic Maya collapse, situating the Willey-Shimkin chapter in this context, and I discuss changes in data and interpretations in the three decades since the chapter's publication.

Introduction: Ideas about Collapse

The "mysterious Maya collapse" and its causes have captured the hearts and minds of archaeologists and of the public for more than a century. The abrupt cessation of hallmark activities of the Classic Maya civilization (circa A.D. 250–950)—construction of monumental architecture and erection of carved, dated stelae and altars—indicated to early explorers that the elite occupation of the great cities of the Southern Lowlands had ceased and that the civilization had experienced transformations so dramatic as to be called "collapse."

The 1970 advanced seminar on the lowland collapse was the earliest effort to synthesize the many strands of data and theories on the collapse process. The seminar and, particularly, the resultant publication were pioneering efforts—classics in their own right—to compare field data and evaluate various contributory causes. The conference's reach was limited, however, because data were available from only a small number of sites, particularly sites in the Pasión and Usumacinta regions of the Western Lowlands, that had been extensively excavated by that time. Nonetheless, Willey and Shimkin's conclusion shows that a broad range of causal mechanisms was discussed. They organized their summary around two themes of stressors: descriptive, socio-"structural" considerations and more interrelated and "dynamic" causal mechanisms. The former included subsistence, population density, political organization, religion, militarism, urbanism, and economy (trade and markets), while the latter incorporated the changing roles of the burgeoning elite, social distinctions, intersite competition, agricultural problems, demographic pressures, disease burdens—especially malnutrition—and external trade (Willey and Shimkin 1973, 474–89).

Despite many decades of archaeological field research, conferences, and publications devoted to the topic, both before and after the 1970 seminar, the complex events and processes occurring at the end of the Classic period—known as the Terminal Classic period, variously dated from around A.D. 750/800 to 1000/1100 (see Demarest, Rice, and Rice 2004)—continue to defy easy explanation. As discussed elsewhere (Rice, Demarest, and Rice

2004), part of the problem is that while we have begun asking new questions about the Maya collapse, our attempts to answer them are often limited by outmoded concepts that no longer yield useful insights and explanations.

One such problematic concept is that of the Lowland Maya Terminal Classic itself, which was formally introduced at the 1965 Guatemala City Maya Lowland Ceramic Conference. This conference was held to allow archaeologists to compare excavated ceramic collections and discuss comparative chronologies, as published ceramic data were not widely available. The purpose of introducing the Terminal Classic concept was to create a temporal interval that separated the Classic tradition from the Postclassic cultures in the lowlands, as defined by ceramic content. The Terminal Classic was also characterized as an archaeological "horizon," not by the common standard of wide geographical distribution of a distinctive artifact style, but rather by an inference of process: that the cultural characteristics defining the Classic period ceased at roughly the same time throughout the Maya Lowlands, thereby constituting a societal collapse.

"Collapse" is another problematic term because it can mean different things, and as Norman Yoffee explains, these meanings can be grouped into two categories. One consists of words like "fall, collapse, fragmentation, and death," which imply that something important no longer exists; the second category uses words like "decline, decay, and decadence" to imply a devolution to something "morally or aesthetically inferior" (Yoffee 1988, 14). Related to this distinction is George Cowgill's observation of the need for careful consideration of the kinds of entities that are in transition. He distinguished between types of *political* organizations, such as states, which "fragment" or break apart (unless they "collapse" through conquest or experience reductions in complexity), and types of *cultural* organizations, such as civilizations. The collapse of a civilization—for example, that of the Maya—would then refer to "the end of a great cultural tradition" (Cowgill 1988, 256).

In the thirty-plus years since the 1970 Santa Fe seminar on collapse, an enormous amount of research in the Maya Lowlands has provided a wealth of new data, which stimulated a need for a fresh look at the changes that took place in the lowlands in the late eighth through tenth centuries (Demarest, Rice, and Rice 2004). In addition, the entire archaeological research enterprise has evolved conceptually, theoretically, and methodologically, with major shifts in approaches to culture history and causality.

Growing interest in settlement surveys (Ashmore 1981), combined with interpretations of massive depopulations in the ninth and tenth centuries, prompted closer attention to regional demographics and more realistic population estimates (Culbert and Rice 1990). Computerized studies capable of analyzing massive quantities of data have begun to be used; these include simulations (Hosler, Sabloff, and Runge 1977; Lowe 1985; Webster, Sanders, and Van Rossum 1992), general systems theory (Culbert 1977), catastrophe theory (Renfrew 1978), and trend-surface analysis (Bove 1981). Continuing studies link the collapse to ecological stresses, particularly to severe drought in the ninth century (Hodell, Curtis, and Brenner 1995; Gill 2000; Dahlin 2002; Robichaux 2002; Haug et al. 2003).

Research has revealed considerable variability in the timing of the processes and causes implicated in the political transitions, or "collapse," and in the extent to which they actually occurred. Rather than being an abrupt fifty- to one-hundred-year catastrophe in the south, the Terminal Classic is now identified as a series of politico-economic transitions and transformations evolving over as much as three to four hundred years over the entire lowlands (Demarest, Rice, and Rice 2004). An early analysis of available Long Count and radiocarbon dates provided hints at the sequential processes: a "rapid demise of kings, a somewhat later disappearance of associated nobles, and a protracted survival of Maya commoners [that is] inconsistent with pervasive conceptions of an extremely catastrophic demographic collapse" (Sidrys and Berger 1979, quoted in Webster, Freter, and Storey 2004, 231). Recent research indicates that this sequence is valid and seems to be applicable to the Petexbatún region (O'Mansky and Dunning 2004; Demarest 2004) and Copán (Webster, Freter, and Storey 2004; Fash, Andrews, and Manahan 2004), and there is good evidence for continuities of "commoner" settlement in the vicinity of Xunantunich, in western Belize (Ashmore, Yaeger, and Robin 2004).

The whole notion of civilizational collapse as the defining event of the ninth and tenth centuries in the Maya Lowlands is being rethought, in part because this concept has evoked enormous disagreement among Mayanists. The reevaluation also partly stems from acknowledgment that such an event did not occur simultaneously in the north, where cities flourished through the Terminal Classic and into the Postclassic (Andrews 1973). Moreover, postmodernist perspectives raised awareness that the notion of a collapse of Maya civilization is viewed as offensive by some scholars and Maya activists, given the vigor of the Maya cultural traditions of millions of speakers of Maya languages in Mexico and Guatemala today (see, e.g., Cojtí Cuxil 1994).

In addition, archaeological research in the Southern Lowlands, long focused on the large Late Classic sites once considered to be the principal topic of Maya history worthy of study, began to broaden in the late twentieth century. A new focus emerged—the Postclassic period (see, e.g., Chase and Rice 1985; Sabloff and Andrews 1986; Masson 2000)—and this has resulted in distinctly different perspectives on the Classic collapse. Instead of viewing the ninth and tenth centuries as simply the sudden *ending* of something Mayan (that is, Classic civilization, especially divine or sacred kingship and its sumptuous pageantry and paraphernalia), archaeologists have begun to realize that these centuries simultaneously represented a transition and, possibly, the *beginnings* of something else (for example, *multepal*, or "council government") that was of comparable culture-historical significance. Perhaps most important in our early twenty-first-century reconstruction of the Maya Terminal Classic are the accelerating advances in glyphic decipherments. These have brought about new interpretations of events of the Late Classic period, which have led, in turn, to an emphasis on militarism and intense intersite warfare as factors in the collapse of some regions (Demarest 1993, 1997, 2004; Demarest et al. 1997; Schele and Grube 1995).

In retrospect, then, it is of no little interest that in their summary chapter on the lowland collapse, Willey and Shimkin diminished the role of militarism of all types: both internal revolt and external ("foreign") invasion and conquest. The reasons for this de-emphasis are complex, as is the history of scholarly thinking on Maya warfare.

A Brief Intellectual History of Maya Collapse, Militarism, and Warfare

Through the mid-twentieth century, the Classic Maya world was romanticized as a peaceful, verdant, tropical garden occupied by farmers and astrologers, as scholars applied a familiar analogy of the philosophical Old World Greeks versus the militaristic Romans to the New World Maya as compared to the Aztecs, respectively (Spinden 1917). As early as the nineteenth century, however, explorers (see, e.g., Stephens 1841) and archaeologists who studied the empty ruined cities and the dates and scenes on carved stelae were aware that the cessation of dated monuments around the end of the four-hundred-year calendrical period known as B'aktun 9 (in A.D. 830) had implications for their benignly pastoral view of lowland civilization. These writers referred to this phenomenon as representing a "decline" of Maya civilization, and their attention focused principally on the human desertion of the region and the presumed northward migration of the population. It is not entirely clear how they envisioned cause and effect in this relationship: if abandonment occurred because of the decline, or if the decline occurred because of depopulation.

Possibly the first reference to this decline and abandonment as representing a collapse of the Maya civilization—or collapse of the "Old Empire" (followed by the rise of the northern "New Empire," in the prevailing language of the day)—came from Sylvanus G. Morley. While acknowledging that the causes of the depopulation were unknown, Morley proceeded to advance two possibilities: "The Maya were driven from their southern homes by stronger peoples pushing in from further south and from the west, or . . . the Maya civilization, having run its natural course, *collapsed* through sheer lack of inherent power to advance" (1915, 3, emphasis added).

Peculiarly, perhaps, at least in early twenty-first-century hindsight, the apocalyptic notion that the Maya Old Empire collapsed did not immediately fire archaeologists' imaginations. Herbert J. Spinden, in the first edition of *Ancient Civilizations of Mexico and Central America*, simply referred to a "Transition Period," characterized by the end of occupation of the southern cities followed by a shift to the north, and did not discuss possible causes of this change (1917, 132). In the later edition of this volume, however, he referred to the "collapse of the First Empire" (Spinden 1928, 148).

Thomas Gann and J. Eric Thompson, writing in 1935, continued to focus on the issue of depopulation and did not mention collapse. They noted that between A.D. 530 and 629 (using, as did Spinden, the now-disavowed 12.9.0.0.0 correlation of Maya to modern calendars),

> there occurred in the Old Empire perhaps one of the most remarkable events ever recorded in the history of any nation.
>
> The entire population of all the cities deserted their homes in the south . . . and migrated into the peninsula of Yucatan. . . . The abandonment of the area as a whole was a gradual one, and occupied approximately a century. It commenced in the extreme south, at Copan, and in the extreme west at Palenque, extending thence eastward and northward. (Gann and Thompson 1935, 60)

The causes they advanced for this regional depopulation included epidemic disease, earthquakes, warfare (internecine or foreign), climate change, soil exhaustion, "religious or superstitious reasons," and "national decadence" (Gann and Thompson 1935, 61–66; cf. Ricketson and Ricketson 1937). Concerning warfare in particular, they opined that the Maya seemed to have been "one of the least warlike nations who ever existed" and that "the only enemies at all likely to have attacked the Maya were Nahua tribes coming in from the northwest." At the same time, however, they also acknowledged the possibility that "internecine warfare, say between the eastern and western cities" might have contributed to the "break-up of the Old Empire" (Gann and Thompson 1935, 63).

By the 1950s, the two most influential Maya archaeologists of the time, Eric Thompson and Sylvanus Morley, had incorporated the collapse interpretation into their syntheses of Maya civilization (Morley 1946; Thompson [1954] 1966), but they continued to devote their attention to the puzzling problem of depopulation. Both favored the peaceable-kingdom model for the Maya, stoutly maintaining that the scenes carved on stelae provided no evidence of warfare and that images of bound captives represented ritual activity. In addition, they seemed to agree on a cause for the abandonment of the lowland cities: peasant uprising. Morley saw no archaeological evidence to suggest that the Southern Lowlands region was depopulated as a result of conquest by outsiders, but he did note "possible evidence of an anticlerical revolt at Piedras Negras," concluding from this that the "lower classes must have revolted, and word must have traveled" (Morley and Brainerd 1956, 70–71).

Considerably earlier, Thompson had advanced the idea that the depopulation of the southern ceremonial centers occurred after overthrow of the ruling hierarchy, with population loss accelerated by attendant warfare and spread of disease (1931, 230; for intellectual context, see Becker 1979). He subsequently expanded this idea in *The Rise and Fall of Maya Civilization*, in a section headed "Collapse of the City States" (Thompson [1954] 1966, 100–109).

> It is not illogical to suppose that there was a series of peasant revolts against the theocratic minority of priests . . . and nobles. This may have been caused by the ever growing demands for service in construction work and in the production of food for an increasing number of nonproducers. Exotic religious developments, such as the cult of the planet Venus, adopted by the hierarchy may have driven a wedge between the two groups, making the peasants feel that the hierarchy was no longer performing its main

function, that of propitiating the gods of the soils. . . . I am rather dubious of physical invasion and conquest of the Central area. . . .

In my opinion, . . . in city after city the ruling group was driven out or, more probably, massacred by the dependent peasants, and power then passed to peasant leaders and small-town witch doctors. (Thompson [1954] 1966, 105)

Two hundred pages later, however, Thompson seemed less confident about internal uprising bringing about the downfall of his peaceful Classic Maya, and in his telegraphic capsule summary of this period in Maya history, he shifted blame to the warlike Mexicans.

Collapse (A.D. 800–A.D. 925). One by one ceremonial centers of Central area abandoned, possibly because of revolt against hierarchy, perhaps an indirect result of chain reaction to barbarian pressure north of Mexico City. Mexican influences infiltrate west side of peninsula of Yucatán, and affect some Puuc cities, many of which are abandoned at end of period or shortly afterwards. (Thompson [1954] 1966, 309–10)

By the 1960s, then, the concept of a Classic Maya collapse was firmly entrenched in archaeologists' thinking, with ostensible support provided by new demographic and environmental analyses purporting to show that the Maya civilization should never have developed in the tropical lowlands in the first place (Meggers 1954; cf. Heckenberger et al. 2003). There were also ongoing debates about internal revolt versus external invasion as causes. George Cowgill, in a paper discussing "the end of Maya culture," revived the possibility of Mexican invasions, which he hypothesized might have lasted over a period of years or even generations and resulted in "substantial decline, but not extermination" of Southern Lowland populations owing to death in warfare, starvation through famine, and enslavement (1964, 155). Remaining populations were forcibly resettled in the Northern Lowlands, in a process analogous to later Spanish-colonial policies of *reducción*, in order for them to be closer to—and hence better controlled by—the newly established Mexican capital of Chichén Itzá. (Note that a major problem in this interpretation is the dating of the Chichén Itzá florescence.)

In 1967 Jeremy Sabloff and Gordon Willey, armed with data from their recent fieldwork at the site of Seibal, on the Río Pasión in southwestern Petén, Guatemala, provided additional support for the foreign—that is, Mexican—invasion theory of the Maya collapse (see also Graham 1973, 1990; cf. Tourtellot and González 2004). They hypothesized that a group of "Mexicans or people who had been thoroughly acculturated to their ways"—probably from the Gulf Coast area—invaded the Usumacinta valley and pushed up the Río Pasión at the end of B'aktun 9. The interlopers established a base at Seibal by approximately 10.0.0.0.0 (A.D. 830) and from there interfered in the rest of southern Petén and in central Petén for the next sixty years or so, raiding agricultural fields, forcing starvation and depopulation, and killing rulers and their dynasties. The Mexicans' success was credited to their superior weapons (darts and atlatls) and, possibly, to different "rules," or behaviors, for waging war. Richard E. W. Adams largely agreed with this point of view but suggested two phases of invasion, an earlier one from the Northern Lowlands and a later one at Altar de Sacrificios (1973, 32; see also Sabloff 1973b, 131n10). In 1970 Thompson gave a name to the intruders: the "Putun," seafaring Chontal-Maya speakers who lived in the coastal area of Tabasco and southern Campeche.

These debates—peasant revolt versus Putun invasion as the cause of the abandonment-cum-collapse of the Southern Lowlands—were subsequently entertained in the Maya collapse seminar in 1970 and in the resultant publication (Culbert 1973). The basic outline for discussion of these and the many other theories relating to the causes of collapse was established by Jeremy Sabloff, who organized them into a framework of external and internal causes (1973a), each with environmental and sociopolitical (that is, warfare) subdivisions. The sociopolitical causes of particular interest here can, in turn, be identified as "internal" (peasant revolt, intersite warfare) or "external" (invasion with or without resettlement).

Regarding internal causes, Sabloff commented that peasant-uprising theories suggested that Maya sovereigns might have gone "too far in suppressing the peasantry without the institutional means of enforcing their policies" and that "the nature of the lowland environment may not have permitted the development of more coercive polities" in the Southern Lowlands (1973a, 38). With respect to intersite fighting, Sabloff remarked that such civil wars could have resulted in the elimination of the ruling hierarchy of kings and other nobles or disrupted the agricultural system by burning fields or forcibly conscripting farmers into "standing armies" (1973a, 38). Turning to external military causes, such as foreign invasion, Sabloff observed that outside intervention might have brought about the Southern Lowland population loss because the Maya were unable to "battle a well-developed power over any extended period of time, or because the invaders toppled a fragile sociopolitical structure, or because the intruders could not effectively deal with a new agricultural situation, and so on. . . . [although] an invasion could have wiped out the Maya hierarchy and caused some population loss without causing widespread depopulation" (1973a, 39).

Following hot on the heels of two field projects (at Altar de Sacrificios and Seibal) that ostensibly provided evidence for intrusions into the Western Lowlands, and coming after an article suggesting who those intruders might be, the 1970 Maya collapse seminar might be expected to have devoted considerable discussion to the idea of foreign intervention and conquest. And so it did. But as T. Patrick Culbert, the seminar organizer and volume editor, later remarked,

> The idea of invasion has suffered a curious fate in Maya studies. . . . The issue was hotly debated at the 1970 collapse seminar and the majority of the participants seemed to favor the hypothesis. In the summary paper, however, Willey and Shimkin (1973) *downplayed the role of invasion, seemingly convinced that it had been a result rather than a cause of Maya disintegration* [see also Willey 1977, 70]. Since then, the theme of invasion has been almost completely absent from treatments of the collapse. (Culbert 1988, 79, emphasis added)

So what *did* Willey and Shimkin actually say about warfare and militarism in their summary chapter? True, they gave the issue relatively short shrift, particularly the idea of external invasion, yet in retrospect, the direction of their comments is oddly prescient.

> Portrayals of warfare, on wall paintings and in monumental carvings, in which Maya are obviously fighting other Maya, imply a degree of rivalry [regionally or locally]. . . . The widespread popularity of the ball game in the Maya Lowlands in Late Classic times may have served the function of mitigating intercity strife. (Willey and Shimkin 1973, 461)

> Late Classic stelae representations of brutal treatment of prisoners or captives are quite common, and it is likely that these depict the military and political subjugation of one group by another. Battle scenes also occur in Maya art, as in the murals of Bonampak. (Willey and Shimkin 1973, 479)

> Still, there is little in Maya art, or elsewhere in the archaeological record, to indicate that there was anything resembling the professional military orders of Central Mexico, or that Maya governments, in either their internal or external policies, depended upon the services of "standing armies." (Willey and Shimkin 1973, 480)

There was undoubtedly considerable competition between ceremonial centers or cities in the Southern Lowlands. Overt signs of this competition are to be seen in pictures of captives. . . . The competition is to be seen more covertly in the magnificence of the ceremonial centers themselves [which] represent great numbers of man-hours in both unskilled labor and skilled craftsmanship. . . . The *priestly leaders of these great centers*, in their efforts to outdo each other, to draw more wealth and prestige to themselves, and to bring more worshippers and taxpayers into their particular orbits, *must have diverted all possible labor and capital to their aggrandizement.* (Willey and Shimkin 1973, 485, emphasis added)

This summary is prescient because today, some thirty years later, discussions of warfare focus neither on peasant revolt nor on external invasion, but rather on internal competition and status rivalry (Webster 2000, 2002). (Current perspectives are reviewed in the following section of this chapter.)

Shortly after publication of the collapse seminar papers, Willey's thoughts turned to the possibility of cyclical rises and falls of the Maya civilization (1974; see also Freidel, Escobedo, and Guenter, this volume). In an imaginative turn of phrase, he suggested that the late Early Classic hiatus in monument erection in the Southern Lowlands might have been a foreshadowing, or "rehearsal," of the Late Classic collapse (I return later to the role of temporal cycling).[1] Here again, however, Willey avoided attributing the collapse to warfare, whether external or internal; rather, he proposed failure of external economic relations, specifically with central Mexico. Still later, Willey cautiously returned to the possible role of Mexicans in the collapse but referred to the contacts as "impingement" or "influence," rather than warfare and invasion, and mentioned the possibility of interference with trade routes (1977, 68–70; see also Webb 1964, 1973; Sabloff 1977; Kowalski 1989).

More-Recent Perspectives on Late Classic Maya Warfare

Since the 1970 Maya collapse seminar, considerable attention has been given to the nature and role of Classic Maya warfare and intersite conflict, especially as these activities relate to the origins of Maya civilization (Webster 1975, 1977) and, more relevant to this discussion, as they are delineated in Late Classic inscriptions. Inscriptions reveal competition among

Lowland Maya polities, competition often interpreted as warfare, but the causes of such bellicosity are unclear.

One important issue is simply to define "war" and "warfare" (see Stanton and Brown 2003, 2–3; essays in Brown and Stanton 2003). David Webster defines war as "planned confrontations between organized groups of combatants who share, or believe they share, common interests. Such groups represent political communities or factions that are prepared to pursue these interests through armed and violent confrontations that might involve deliberate killing of opponents" (2000, 72). This definition incorporates terms such as "political," "violent," and "armed," which themselves need to be defined. Jonathan Haas offers a simpler definition of war as "organized violence between political units" (2001, 17), but this too invokes the terms "political" and "violence." Dictionary definitions similarly emphasize "political" units and the condition of being "armed" with "weapons." I raise these definitional issues not because I intend to resolve them but because I suspect, and discuss in greater detail later, that much of what has been interpreted as hostile and conquest-oriented warfare among the Maya might actually be various forms of ritualized competition, such as ball games. Such competitions and rivalries, presumably carried out between polities, are described in the same terminology employed in modern sports: "contest," "conflict," "combat," "fight," and "battle" against an "opponent." Being "armed" with "weapons" in modern dictionaries (see, e.g., *Webster's New Universal Unabridged Dictionary*) includes "instruments of offensive or defensive combat," which, in the case of the ball game, could reference the protective gear worn by the players.

In addition to these issues, the term "warfare" carries a heavy interpretive load, implying infrastructural investment and organization such as standing armies, elaborate weaponry systems, defensive fortifications, large-scale offensive operations (often over long distances, thus requiring supply systems), territorial expansion and forcible conquest, destruction of enemies and property, especially land, and tribute collection (Webster 1976, 815; 1977, 363–64; 1993; 1998).

Ross Hassig's overview of Lowland Maya data suggests that true warfare of the sort described above would have been limited by numerous factors: the tropical forest environment hindering massive troop movements, rainfall cycles making trails impassable in the rainy season, and the lack of easily portable foodstuffs such as tortillas. He believes conflicts were a matter of quick raids and highly symbolic combat geared toward "internal political purposes, such as validating rulers" through acquisition of captives, rather than the kinds of territorial conquests envisioned or implied by many archaeologists. As such, war was primarily an "aristocratic" endeavor, with small numbers of nobles, typically richly attired, engaged in individual, or one-on-one, combat, as indicated by handheld weapons (Hassig 1992, 70–81, 94–99).

Recent interpretations of the causes of Classic Maya "warfare," explored in the following sections, range from highly materialist (population pressure, lack of resources) to highly ideological (celestial activity).

Materialist Interpretations and Evidence

Many materialist-oriented scholars argue, on the basis of population size as indicated by large cities with substantial surrounding residential settlement, that good agricultural land and labor to sustain such populations were in decreasing supply, and this would have led to increasing competition and enmity between cities over scarce resources (see Webster 1977, 1985, 1993, 1998). William Fash contends that, with reference to the southeastern lowland zone, "evidence from Copán and Quiriguá argues strongly that material incentives, rather than just some form of ritual jousting between rival rulers, were the cause of Late Classic Maya warfare" (1991, 151). Ethnohistoric data suggest that taxation and tribute demands, "boundary disputes, real or imagined insults, and acts of treachery or disloyalty" frequently led to conflict (Marcus 1992, 415).

In addition, second-order Maya sites may have carried out "wars of independence" against regional capitals, such as Quiriguá's claimed "victory" over Copán, and Caracol's over Tikal (Marcus 1992, 428–30). However, a contrary view comes from Arlen and Diane Chase, who suggest that Terminal Classic warfare represented new efforts at political integration rather than disintegration (2004; see also Chase, Grube, and Chase 1991). They propose that certain large sites such as Caracol might have been waging expansionist wars to bind "the latest Maya elites of the southern lowlands into larger, but highly competitive, political units. . . . or 'empires'" (Chase and Chase 2004, 365).

One popular interpretation of Late Classic warfare sees it as a matter of "status rivalry"; this view is grounded in reconstructions of Maya political organization based on a segmentary state model (see Sanders 1989). David Webster envisions the Late Classic Maya Lowlands as occupied by several million people in "scores of independent kingdoms, many with long histories of animosities" and all suffering the long-term consequences of agricultural mismanagement, including intensified land use, environmental degradation, and nutritional stress (2002, 338). These crises and vulnerabilities gave rise to competition between individuals, factions, and kingdoms, manifest in what Webster calls "status rivalry warfare," over limited "access to offices, titles, and alliances that bestow prestige, authority, leadership, and political security [which] . . . are keys to control over more fundamental resources such as land, labor, and political power" (2002, 338; see also Fash, Andrews, and Manahan 2004).

Perhaps one of the best illustrations of this kind of status rivalry warfare in the Late Classic Southern Lowlands comes from the Petexbatún region of southwestern Petén, where evidence of fortifications—including walls (often multiple), palisades, hilltop refuges, baffle gates, killing alleys, moats, burning, murder (a cache of decapitated heads of adult males, presumably warriors), and abandonment—abounds in the early eighth century (Demarest et al. 1997; Demarest 2004; O'Mansky and Dunning 2004). The site of Dos Pilas, which Arthur Demarest sees as the center of a "predatory tribute state," was one of the key players in this endemic warfare, but he cautions that the growth of elites and status rivalry were not causes of the collapse in the west but rather "structural vulnerabilities" (2004, 102, 109).

In an intriguing variant of the status rivalry hypothesis—and a turnabout on the early peasant-revolt theory—William Fash suggested a "nobles' revolt" as the cause of the collapse of divine rule at Copán (1983, 1988, 1991; see also Fash, Andrews, and Manahan 2004). Recognizing the evidence for growing Late Classic settlement and ecological data indicating the population exceeded the land's carrying capacity, he proposed that the nobles of the realm may have begun withholding tribute to the Copán lord, thereby disrupting the economy and the economic foundations of both kingdom and king.

What kinds of material, archaeologically recognizable evidence—or lack thereof—attest to Classic warfare? Maya kings were not buried with weaponry, suggesting that neither their royal identity nor their journey into the afterlife was tied to the role of successful warrior (McAnany 2001,

138). Mass burials indicate violence, such as the mass secondary burial at Chaa Creek (Ashmore, Yaeger, and Robin 2004) and the Colha "skull pit" containing thirty skeletons (Steele, Eaton, and Taylor 1980), but these might be sacrifices rather than evidence of warfare. Periodic destruction of monuments or architectural complexes was relatively widespread (see, e.g., Ambrosino, Ardren, and Stanton 2003; Suhler et al. 2004) but can be explained as the kind of competition or termination ritual associated with the end of calendrical periods as occurred in the Postclassic Northern Lowlands (see discussion in the following sections; Edmonson 1979; Rice 2004, 258–65). Especially important among these intervals are the *k'atun*, consisting of twenty 360-day *tuns*, or nearly twenty Gregorian years, and the thirteen-k'atun *may* (260 tuns, approximately 256 years). Such termination rituals do not necessarily indicate warfare.

Encircling walls around monumental construction are typically viewed as strong evidence of warfare. Although walls were constructed at a few Southern Lowland sites in the Late Preclassic and Early Classic periods, they are rare enough that they do not seem to confirm endemic conflict. One area where walls are particularly common in the Late Classic is the Petexbatún region (Demarest et al. 1997; Demarest 2004; O'Mansky and Dunning 2004, 94), where rapid construction of dry-laid defensive walls, using stone removed from civic-ceremonial structures, accompanied resettlement on easily defended islands and peninsulas and introduction of new weapons, such as atlatls and arrow or dart points. However, walls were not constructed in the region until after A.D. 761, the time of the fall of the Dos Pilas dynasty, and some sites, like Tamarindito, did not build such fortifications at all (Demarest 1997).

Walls are also present at sites in the Northern Lowlands. At Chichén Itzá, murals in the Upper Temple of the Jaguars and Las Monjas depict a siege tower and attacks on defensive walls. Well-built, paired, concentric walls are found at Cuca, Chacchob (Webster 1979), Muna, Tulum, and Ek' Balam (Ringle et al. 2004, 507), and single walls are known from Chunchucmil (Dahlin 2000), Uxmal, and Mayapán, but such enclosures are not present at Cobá or at most of the Puuc sites, such as Kabah, Labná, Sayil, and Oxkintok. Moreover, William Ringle and colleagues note that in the vicinity of Ek' Balam, walls occurred only at that major center and not in the rural areas beyond, even at the large and prosperous secondary site of Ichmul de Morley (Ringle et al. 2004, 510). However, it is not always clear that these walls in Yucatán were fortifications for the purpose of military defense. Ringle provides a different—an ideological—interpretation, suggesting that walls "were in equal measure marks of civic prestige, intended to segregate and restrict access to that space associated with the highest administrative and ritual activities . . . part of a general construction trend formalizing the relationship between center and periphery . . . designed to present the *image* of a powerful center, a type of construction permitted only the most powerful of regional centers" (Ringle et al. 2004, 510).

Ideological Interpretations

Ideological interpretations of Maya warfare have been shaped by the last twenty years of epigraphic advancements and iconographic study and by the consequent elevated awareness of the role of conflict in the Late Classic. Many newly deciphered glyphs have been read as indicating aggressive relations, combat, and other similar activities, but only a few refer to events that can be specifically interpreted in terms of war or warfare (see table 8.1). In fact, David Stuart has observed that "no event glyph is known that literally reads 'to wage war,'" and textual references do not exist until after the sixth century A.D. (1995, 293, 329; but see Flannery and Marcus 2003 [Archaic-period Mesoamerican raiding and warfare]; Brown and Garber 2003 and Reilly and Garber 2003 [Middle Formative warfare]). Maya images and other representations of "warfare" have generally emphasized its "'single-combat' nature . . . the many one-on-one struggles within the larger context of the battle itself" (Schele and Mathews 1991, 246). The problem is that we do not know exactly what that "larger battle context" really was.

Table 8.2 presents dates of known "war"-related events in the (primarily Late) Classic Southern Lowlands, taken from inscriptions. This table reveals that the conflicts are partly between large cities, but large sites also claim to attack small, relatively obscure satellites. It also reveals episodic bursts of hostilities at certain sites or in certain regions throughout the Late Classic, for example, at Tortuguero from 644 to 652 (see also Hruby and Child 2004), at Naranjo from 680 to 716, and at Yaxchilán in the very late Late Classic, from 796 to 808.

Tables 8.2 and 8.3, which tabulate 144 "warfare"-related events during a period of more than two and a half centuries, indicate that the primary purpose or result of the raiding seems to have been the taking of captives (for sacrifice and perhaps for slavery, as in the Postclassic period) rather than

Table 8.1. "Warfare"—related Maya words

Term	Definition
Bak (n.)	Bone, captive (T111/570, wavy bone)
Baksaj (n., v.)	Captive, to capture
B'ate'el/b'ate'il (n., v.)	Fighter, warrior, to fight, make war
Ch'ak (v.)	To chop, to cut or chop with a knife or ax, decapitate
Ch'akaj (n.)	"Axe" event, chop (either decapitation or damage to a place)
Ch'am (v.)	To grasp, seize, take (sometimes followed by toponym)
Chuk (v.)	To tie up, capture in war
Chuk (v.)	To capture, seize, apprehend. Also to collect or catch animals in the hunt or by trapping
Jatz' (n., v.)	**Beat, wound, hit, whip**
Jub' (n.)	**Discord, dissension, agitation, rebellion**
Jub'uy (v.)	To bring down, to tear down (as walls or monuments)
Kalomte' (n.)	Warrior title (T1030)
K'atun (n.)	Fight, fighter, war, warrior, combat, combatant, soldier, battle, battalion
K'atuntaj (v.)	To fight with someone (apparently one-on-one)
Kuy (n.)	**Owl associated with war or warriors**
Lok (v.)	To leave, flee, drive out
Lok' (v.)	To walk step by step (*andar paso a paso*), come out, emerge
Mach (v.)	To flatten
Mach (v.)	To grasp by the hand, to clasp hands
Nup (n.)	**Enemy, enmity**
Nupankil (n.)	Discord, war, enmity
P'entak (n.)	Slave, captive
P'isb'aj (n., v.)	War, to fight
Tok' pakal (n.)	Flint shield. War banner that is "thrown down"; possibly a symbol for, or general reference to, war or "royal duty of warfare"
U kanul (n.)	**Captor of (his captor)**
Yah (v.)	To wound (Early Classic)
Yaltanba (n., v.)	**War, struggle**

Sources: Schele and Grube 1995; Stuart 1995; Barrera Vásquez 1991; Montgomery 2001b; Andy Hofling, pers. comm., 2001; Phil Wanyerka, pers. comm., 2001.

Note: Words in boldface indicate definitions given in the *Diccionario Maya* (Barrera Vásquez 1991); those with definitions followed by a *T* plus a number appear in hieroglyphic texts.

Table 8.2. Dated "warfare"-related events in the southern Maya lowlands.

Victor	Opponent	Long Count Date	Date[a]	Type[b]
Yaxchilán	Calakmul		537	H
Tikal/Calakmul	Caracol			A
Tikal	Caracol	9.6.2.1.11 6 Chuwen 19 Pop	Apr 9 556	A
Caracol/Calakmul	Tikal	9.6.8.4.2 7 Ik' 0 Sip	Apr 29 562	C, S
Yaxchilán	Lacanjá	9.6.10.14.15 4 Men 3 Mak	Nov 17 564	H
Chinikihá			Dec 573	H
Yaxchilán			Jul 594	H
Altun Ha			May 596	A
Calakmul	Palenque		Apr 599	
Bonampak	Palenque	9.8.9.15.11 7 Chuwen 4 Sotz'	May 14 603	F
Calakmul	Palenque		Apr 611	
Caracol	Naranjo satellite	9.9.13.4.4 9 Kan 2 Sek	May 26 626	C, J
Caracol	Naranjo satellite	9.9.14.3.5 12 Chikchan 18 Sip	May 2 627	C, J
Caracol	Tzam		627	
Calakmul/Caracol	Naranjo	9.9.18.16.3 7 Ak'b'al 16 Muwan	Dec 25 631	S
Caracol	Naranjo	9.10.3.2.12 2 Eb' 0 Pop	Mar 2 636	C, S
Tortuguero		9.10.11.9.6 13 Kimi 14 Sek	Jun 2 644	C, A, S
Tortuguero			Feb 645	A
Yaxchilán	Hix Witz		Aug 647	H
Tortuguero			Jul 649	A
Tortuguero			Nov 649	H
Tortuguero			Nov 649	A
Tortuguero		9.10.17.2.14 13 Ix 17 Muwan	Dec 21 649	H, C
Tortuguero		9.10.19.8.4 11 Kan 12 Wo	Mar 30 652	C
Palenque	Calakmul		Aug 654	H, A
Palenque	Site Q	9.11.1.16.3 6 Ak'b'al 1 Yax	Aug 26 654	H, A
Calakmul	Tikal		Jan 657	
Palenque	Yaxchilán	9.11.6.16.11 7 Chuwen 4 Ch'en	Aug 8 659	
Piedras Negras		9.11.9.8.12 5 Eb' 15 Kumku'	Feb 14 662	C
Dos Pilas	Machaquilá	9.11.11.9.17 9 Kab'an 5 Pop	Feb 29 664	H
Dos Pilas			Mar 665	H
Piedras Negras		9.11.16.11.6 5 Kimi 9 Pop	Mar 3 669	C
Dos Pilas	Tikal	9.11.17.8.19 6 Kawak 2 Kayab'	Jan 10 670	S, H, C
Tikal		9.11.19.4.3 6 Ak'b'al 16 Zak	Sep 26 671	C
Palenque		9.12.0.0.0 10 Ajaw 8 Yaxk'in	Jun 29 672	S
Tikal	Dos Pilas	9.12.0.8.3 4 Ak'b'al 11 Muwan	Dec 9 672	C, S
Dos Pilas/Calakmul	Tikal	9.12.5.9.14 2 Ix 17 Muwan	Dec 14 677	C
Site Q	Tikal	9.12.5.10.1 9 Imix 4 Pax	Dec 21 677	S
Dos Pilas/Calakmul	Tikal	9.12.6.16.17 11 Kab'an 10 Sotz'	May 1 679	F
Naranjo	Caracol	9.12.7.14.1 3 Imix 9 Pop	Feb 29 680	S
Yaxchilán			Feb 681	H
Yaxchilán			Nov 689	H
Naranjo	Ucanal	9.13.1.4.19 12 Kawak 2 Yaxk'in	Jun 15 693	C, J
Naranjo	Tuub'al	9.13.1.9.5 7 Chikchan 8 Sak	Sep 12 693	B
Naranjo	B'ital	9.13.1.13.14 5 Ix 17 Muwan	Dec 10 693	B

(continued)

Table 8.2. (*Continued*)

Victor	Opponent	Long Count Date	Date[a]	Type[b]
Naranjo	Tikal/Ucanal?	9.13.2.16.10 5 Ok 8 Kumku'	Jan 30 695	H, J
Tikal	Calakmul/Site Q?	9.13.3.7.18 11 Etznab' 11 Ch'en	Aug 6 695	H, P, J
Tikal	Calakmul	9.13.3.13.15 11 Men 8 Muwan	Dec 1 695	H, F
Naranjo	Dotted Ko	9.13.4.1.13 12 B'en 1 Sip	Mar 28 696	B
Dos Pilas		9.13.4.17.14 8 Ix 2 Wayeb'	Feb 12 697	C
Naranjo	Eared Sk.	9.13.5.4.13 3 B'en 16 Sek	May 22 697	B
Naranjo	Kin. Kab'	9.13.6.4.17 3 Kab'an 15 Sek	May 21 698	B
Naranjo	Ucanal	9.13.6.10.4 6 Kan 2 Sak	Sep 5 698	H, B
Naranjo	Ucanal	9.13.7.3.8 9 Lamat 1 Sotz'	Apr 17 699	H
Yaxchilán			Nov 701	H
Dos Pilas	Tikal	9.13.13.7.2 7 Ik' 5 Xul	May 30 705	S, H, J
Naranjo	Yootz	9.13.14.4.2 8 Ik' 0 Sip	Mar 26 706	H
Naranjo	Yaxhá	9.13.18.4.18 8 Etznab' 16 Wo	Mar 21 710	H, B
Toniná	Palenque	9.13.19.6.3 3 Ak'b'al 16 Sip	Apr 10 711	H
Toniná	Palenque	9.13.19.13.3 13 Ak'b'al 16 Yax	Aug 28 711	S
Yaxchilán	B'uktuun		Nov 713	H
Altar de Sacrificios		9.14.2.0.14 12 Ix 17 Muwan	Dec 6 713	C
Naranjo	Sakha'	9.14.2.15.7 6 Manik' 5 Kej	Sep 25 714	B
Naranjo		9.14.4.7.5 5 Chikchan 13 Sip	Apr 5 716	B
Dos Pilas			717	V
Dos Pilas			721	V
Palenque			Sep 723	H
Piedras Negras	Yaxchilán		726	H
Yaxchilán			Jul 727	H
Yaxchilán			Sep 727	H
Palenque			May 729	A
Yaxchilán	Lacanha	9.14.17.15.11 2 Chuwen 14 Mol	Jul 12 729	H, C
Yaxchilán	Hix Witz		Apr 732	H
Tikal	Calakmul		733–6?	H
		9.15.3.8.8 4 Lamat 6 Kumku'	Jan 19 735	
Dos Pilas	Seibal	9.15.4.6.4 8 Kan 17 Muwan	Dec 1 735	C, S
Dos Pilas	Seibal	9.15.4.6.5 9 Chikchan 18 Muwan	Dec 2 735	A
Quiriguá	Copán	9.15.6.14.6 6 Kimi 4 Sek	May 1 738	H, A
Bonampak		9.15.9.3.14 3 Ix 2 Kej	Sep 15 740	H
Dos Pilas	Ahkul		pre-741	H, C?
Aguateca	Cancuen	>9.15.9.17.17		
Machaquilá	Motul de SJ	>9.15.10.0.0		
Tikal	Yaxhá/El Perú?	9.15.12.2.2 11 Ik' 15 Ch'en	Jul 30 743	S, P
Dos Pilas	El Chorro		743	H
Dos Pilas	Yaxchilán	c. 9.15.10–9.16.10.0.0		
Tikal	Naranjo/ Motul de SJ?	9.15.12.11.13 7 B'en 1 Pop	Feb 6 744	H, S, P
Dos Pilas	Motul de SJ		745	
Dos Pilas	Yaxchilán	ca. 9.16.0.0.0?	751	H
Copán		9.15.15.12.16 5 Kib' 9 Pop	Feb 13 747	S

(*continued*)

Table 8.2. *(Continued)*

Victor	Opponent	Long Count Date	Date[a]	Type[b]
Tikal	Naranjo		748	H
Yaxchilán	Wak'ab		Feb 752	H
Yaxchilán	Sanab' H.	9.16.4.1.1 7 Imix 14 Sek	May 7 755	H, C
Yaxchilán	Piedras Negras?		759	H
Dos Pilas	Tamarindito		761	A
Aguateca	El Chorro	9.17.0.0.0 13 Ajaw 18 Kumku'	Jan 22 771	
La Mar	Pomoná	9.17.3.5.19 3 Kawak 17 Sek	May 5 774	C
Naranjo	B'ital		775	B
Naranjo			777	B
Ixkun	Sacul	9.17.9.0.13 3 B'en 6 Kayab'	Dec 19 779	A
Ixkun	Ucanal	9.17.9.5.11 10 Chuwen 19 Sip	Mar 26 780	C
Piedras Negras		9.17.10.6.1 3 Imix 4 Sotz'	Mar 31 781	S
	Yaxchilán	9.17.11.6.10 8 Ok 8 Sotz'	Apr 4 782	C
			Aug 783	H
Bonampak			Jan 787	H
Bonampak			Jan 787	H
Piedras Negras	Pomoná	9.17.16.14.19 1 Kawak 12 Sak	Aug 25 787	H
La Mar			Apr 792	A
		9.18.1.15.5 13 Chikchan 13 Yax	Aug 4 792	
Copán			Mar 793	H
Piedras Negras	Pomoná	9.18.3.9.12 9 Eb' 10 Sotz'	Apr 3 794	C
La Mar			Nov 794	H
Yaxhá	[Bat Jaguar]		Aug 796	H
Yaxchilán			Dec 796	H
Yaxchilán			Dec 796	H
Yaxchilán			Jan 798	H
Yaxchilán			Jul 798	H
Yaxchilán			Nov 798	H
Naranjo	Yaxhá satellite	9.18.8.8.16 12 Kib' 9 Wo	Feb 20 799	C?
Najanjo	Yaxhá		Jul 799	C
Naranjo	Yaxhá	9.18.9.0.13 1 B'en 6 Kej	Sep 5 799	H, C
Naranjo??		9.18.9.4.4 7 Kan 17 Muwan	Nov 15 799	
Yaxchilán			Dec 799	H
Yaxchilán			Jan 800	H
Yaxchilán			Mar 800	H
Yaxchilán			Mar 800	H
Naranjo		9.18.9.13.15 3 Men 3 Yaxk'in	May 24 800	H
Caracol	Ucanal, B'ital	pre-19.18.10.0.0		H
Yaxchilán			Mar 808	H, C
Caracol	Tikal	post-9.19.9.9.15		A

Sources: Chase and Chase 2003:Table 10.1; Schele and Mathews 1991:Table 10.4,
1998:52–58; Justeson 1989:Table 8.8; Hassig 1992:219–222; Martin and Grube 2000. See
also Marcus 1992:Table 11.1.

[a] Gregorian dates according to the modified GMT 584,283 correlation.

[b] Event types are as follows: H, human capture; C, conquest; V, victory; A, "axe event"; S,
"star war"; B, burning; F, flint shield thrown down; J, *jubuy*; P, palanquin capture.

Table 8.3. Occurrence of dated Classic-period "warfare"-related events by month in the Gregorian calendar and type.

Gregorian Month	Event Type									
	H	C	A	S	B	F	J	P	TOTAL	(T-H)
Dec.	6	5	2	4	1	1			19	13
Jan.	6	1		1			1		9	3
Feb.	4	3	1	4				1	13	9
March	7	5		2	2				16	9
April	3	3	2	1	1				10	7
May	4	4	3	1	2	2	3		19	15
Subtot.	30	21	8	13	6	3	4	1	86	56
Jun		2	1	2			1		6	6
Jul	4	2	1	1				1	9	5
Aug	8		2	1				1	12	4
Sep	5	2			3				10	5
Oct										
Nov	7		1						8	1
Subtot.	24	6	5	4	3	0	1	2	45	21
TOTAL	54	27	13	17	9	3	5	3	131	77

Source: Data taken from Table 8.2.

Note: Column headings are as follows: H, human capture; C, conquest; V, victory; A, "axe event"; S, "star war"; B, burning; F, flint shield thrown down; J, *jubuy*; P, palanquin capture; T–H, total number of events minus human capture (H) events.

outright territorial conquest, as 54 of the events (37.5 percent) report that activity. These tables also suggest that the conflictive events exhibit seasonal patterns of occurrence (see Marcus 1992, 431–43; Milbrath 1999, 193), being twice as likely to have occurred during the dry-season months of December through May (96 events) in the Gregorian calendar than during the rainy-season months of June through November (48 events). This scheduling might reflect the difficulties of travel in the tropical forest during the rainy-season months.

Table 8.4 displays 82 dated warfare occurrences, broken down into eight individual types of events (plus unidentified events), as they occurred in the months of the Maya 365-day calendar. This table reveals that acts of intersite hostilities seemed to be particularly common at set times: in the middle-to-late dry season, especially the months of Pop, Sip, and Sek, and in the month of Muwan, which corresponds to the month of November in

Table 8.4. Occurrences of total numbers of dated "war-related" events and types of event by Maya months (365-day calendar), subdivided into dry and rainy season months of the Late Classic.

Month	No. events	Event Type									
		H	C	A	S	B	F	J	P	?	Total
Kayab'	2	1	1	1	1						4
Kumk'u	4	1	1					1		2	5
Wayeb'	1		1								1
Pop	7	2	2	1	4				1		10
Wo	3	1	2		1						4
Sip	7	2	3		1	2		1			9
Sotz'	6	1	2			1	2				6
Sek	7	2	4	2	1	2		1			12
Xul	1	1			1			1			3
Subtotal[a]	38	11	16	4	9	5	2	4	1	2	54
Yaxk'in	3	1	1		1			1			4
Mol	1	1	1								2
Ch'en	3	1			1				2	1	5
Yax	3	1		1	1					1	4
Zak	4	2	1		2						5
Kej	3	2	1		1						4
Subtotal[b]	17	8	4	1	3	3	0	1	2	2	24
Mak	1	1									1
K'ank'in	0										0
Muwan	10	2	5	1	3	1	1			1	14
Pax	1				1						1
Subtotal[c]	12	3	5	1	4	1	1	0	0	1	16
TOTAL	67	21	25	6	16	9	3	5	3	5	94

Source: Data taken from Table 2.

Note: The totals and subtotals for event types may exceed the totals for "numbers of events" (no. events) because many of the dated episodes record more than one kind of activity—for example, both human capture and sacrifice. Column headings are as follows: H, human capture; C, conquest; A, "axe event"; S, "star war"; B, burning; F, flint shield thrown down; J, *jubuy*; P, palanquin capture.

Specific correspondences of Maya months and months in the Gregorian calendar vary over the approximately 250 years of the Late Classic covered by this table. Here, dry season months roughly correspond to late December through May. Early rainy season months correspond to June through September. Late rainy season months are October through mid December; note the great activity in the month of Muwan and the virtual absence of activity in the months before and after.

[a] Dry-season subtotal.

[b] Early rainy-season subtotal.

[c] Late rainy-season subtotal.

the Gregorian calendar during most of the Late Classic period. Although not shown on table 8.4, but evident from the day numbers in table 8.2, these events tended to occur at the beginning or end of Sip, the middle of Sek, and the end of the month of Muwan (6 events occurred on a day 17 Muwan). Concerning Muwan, 2 events were recorded in the preceding month of Kank'in, and only 1 took place in the following month of Pax. I am unable to suggest, at present, why this might be the case, although it might relate to the owl (*muwan*) as a long-standing symbol of war, as derived from Teotihuacan symbolism (Stuart 2000). In any case, it seems clear that, over a period of two centuries, Maya augurers recognized the end of the late rainy-season month of Muwan as a propitious time for displays of strength.

As a final general note on ideological interpretations of Maya warfare, some of the Late Classic "wars" might be analogous to the "wars of proof" conducted by Aztec kings to demonstrate cosmic sanction for their rule through the taking and sacrifice of captives. As Simon Martin and Nikolai Grube remark about Maya kings, "Although blood[line] was their main claim to legitimacy, candidates still had to prove themselves in war. A bout of captive-taking often preceded elevation to office" (2000, 14). For example, raids carried out by Bonampak might have been undertaken to seize captives in preparation for royal accession (Justeson 1989, 106, citing Miller 1986).

"STAR WARS"

The planet Venus and its glyphic referents have played key roles in recent ideological interpretations of Maya warfare (see Aveni and Hotaling 1994; Milbrath 1999, 157–214). Among Mesoamericanists, Venus is known as the "war star" (Lounsbury 1982) because of certain references in Maya texts dating back to the Late Preclassic period. For example, the Epi-Olmec La Mojarra Stela, dated A.D. 159, depicts a leader, and the accompanying text may refer to the relationship between Venus, battles, and his accession (Kaufman and Justeson 2001). Venus-related warfare also has been linked to Early Classic Mexican interventions in the lowlands, contributing to the Late Classic "Tlaloc-Venus war complex," so-called because the central Mexican god Tlaloc was a "symbol of war and bloodletting" (Schele and Mathews 1998, 416). And it is known from the Dresden and Grolier Codices that the Maya carefully calculated the variable times and places of the appearance of Venus. Surely, they were well aware of disjunctions in correlations of solar and Venus calendars, as well as those between their calculations and visible sightings.

Venus's role in Maya warfare has been postulated on the basis of three kinds of Venus-star (also *ek'*, "star") glyphs appearing in Classic texts: star-over-earth, star-over-shell, and star-over-emblem-glyph (Stuart 1995, 304–15; Harris and Stearns 1997, 57; Montgomery 2002, 192–93). Apparent co-occurrences of these glyphs and "war events" with certain points of Venus's visibility (as determined through retrodiction), particularly its first appearance as evening star or morning star, have led to the attention-grabbing notion of "star wars" (Schele and Freidel 1990, 165–215). As Martin and Grube summarize, the key points of Venus's progression across the sky

> were seen as favourable for warfare and some battles were timed to exploit this supernatural advantage. The appropriate hieroglyph, a still undeciphered verb known as "star war", shows a star showering the earth with liquid—water or perhaps even blood. . . . It usually marks only the most decisive of actions, the conquest of cities and the fall of dynasties.
>
> It is curious, perhaps, that narratives about star-war defeats are usually recorded by the losing party. (Martin and Grube 2000, 16)

In any case, these kinds of interpretations have led some scholars to regard the "collapse" of Classic civilization in the Southern Lowlands as the outcome of centuries of protracted civil war.

However, Venus glyph occurrences do not always correspond to either wars or dates of significant positions of the planet, nor do Maya war events invariably correlate with significant positions of Venus (Harris and Stearns 1997, 131–33; Aldana 2005). John Justeson's survey (1989, 110, table 8.8) of twenty-five "shell-star" war events revealed that warfare commonly occurred within ten to twenty days of significant points in the cycles of not just Venus, but also of Saturn, Jupiter, and Mars. In addition, he observes that "there are contrasts of content between the rituals and battles associated with Venus events, and those not so associated. Among rituals, only accessions, bloodletting and *the ball game* are clearly associated with Venus dates" (Justeson 1989, 106, emphasis added). More recently, Gerardo Aldana also challenged (2005) the association between the planet Venus and warfare. He notes that many of the Maya dates purporting to corroborate this association are wrong, suggests that "ek'" refers to celestial bodies in general rather than specifically to Venus, and claims that the "star war verb" can be read as describing descent.

Linda Schele and David Freidel (1990, 444–46n7) compiled forty-two occurrences of the star war–related iconographic complex (particularly the ruler in "war costume") and associated astronomical (Venus/Jupiter/Saturn stations) and historical events, from A.D. 378 to 849. Only two of these forty-two occurrences are supposed wars, a shell-star event in 662 recorded on Piedras Negras Stela 35 and a star-over-Seibal war recorded on Aguateca Stela 2 and Dos Pilas Stela 16, in 735. In a larger tabulation of ninety-eight dated references to Venus (Aveni and Hotaling 1994, table 1), only twenty-five include references to battle or war. Among the war-related events recorded herein in tables 8.2 through 8.4, only 17 of 110 (or 15.4 percent) are star wars. In other words, a maximum of 25 percent of recorded events, and usually far fewer, represent real Venus-war correlations.

The glyph showing the Venus star showering the earth with what has been interpreted as drops of liquid (water or blood) more strongly suggests a meteor shower (Montgomery 2002, 193, citing David Stuart; Aldana 2005, 313–14)[2] or the more intense meteor "storms." Meteor showers are now known to occur nearly every month of the year, the three most visible today being the Perseids (appearing to emanate from the constellation Westerners know as Perseus) in late July through late August, the Leonids (apparently from Leo, but actually originating in the Tempel-Tuttle comet) in mid-November, and the Geminids (from Gemini) in early-to-mid-December. There is also a meteor shower called the Quadrantids in early January and a less impressive showing of the Eta-Aquarids in late April through May.

How might these (and other) meteor showers have appeared to the Classic Maya? Meteor showers occurring in the rainy-season months (June–December) might have had limited visibility because of the high cloud cover that remains after the daily afternoon and evening storms. However, rainy-season skies in Petén frequently clear well before sunrise, and because of the earth's rotation, meteors tend to be more visible in the early morning (Kronk a), thus suggesting the Maya could have observed them. Worldwide, many meteor showers and storms were recorded in prehistoric and early historical times, with some, such as the late-April Lyrids, noted as early as 687 B.C. (Kronk b). The Eta-Aquarids were recorded in A.D. 401, 839, 927, 934, and 1009 and are best viewed from farther south than the United States (Kronk c). Best known from ancient history are the Leonid meteor showers, which produce storms every thirty-three years or so. Leonid meteor showers were recorded by Chinese, Japanese, and Korean astronomers as early as the tenth century, and these accounts reveal that the month of occurrence has advanced from mid-October in the tenth century to mid-November in the twentieth (Kronk d).

Certainly, the Classic Maya, with their advanced skills in astronomy, could hardly have failed to notice the occurrence of meteor showers at regular times throughout the year. Yet there is no clear evidence that these celestial star showers played any more of a regular part in the timing of warfare than did the phases of Venus. In fact, there might have been a negative association of warfare with meteor showers, as might be seen in the relative lack of warfare events in the month of Mak (which probably corresponded to the appearance of the Leonids in the Late Classic).

BALL GAME RITUAL

Much of the vocabulary read as describing intersite warfare could instead refer to ball game ritual, as hinted by Willey and Shimkin (1973, 461). That is, textual references to combat, battle, and conquest could be interpreted in the context of symbolic and ritualized ball game contests between structurally mandated "opponents," rather than as literal warfare. Here, the obvious analogy is to the K'iche' origin myth, *Popol Vuh*, in which the Hero Twins overcame the evil lords of the underworld in a ball game contest. Among the Late Classic Maya, the texts of Yaxchilán's ball game panels identify associated sacrifices as "conquests" (Freidel, Schele, and Parker 1993, 361), and the bound captives displayed on monuments and in ball game scenes could have been the actual or symbolic vanquished opponent in a ball game contest, bound prior to sacrifice. These captives sometimes included the governing elites of important cities, and the permanent and public display of their "defeated" status on stone monuments seems to be of paramount significance (Miller and Houston 1987).

Throughout Mesoamerica the ball game was increasingly politicized and tied to warfare in the Classic period (Santley, Berman, and Alexander 1991; Taladoire and Colsenet 1991; Fox 1991), and this certainly appears to hold true in the central Maya area: "The ballgame was used as a substitute and a symbol for war. . . . If the ballgame had acquired a war-like and political meaning, it may have been restricted to prominent sites and capitals. Ballcourts would then be built only at major sites or in communities where political or military activities were especially important" (Taladoire and Colsenet 1991, 174).

In light of these findings, I propose that many of the "combat" and "warfare" events recorded in the Classic inscriptions refer to the taking of captives before, during, or after the ball game for purposes of sacrifice in association with other pivotal events in the geopolitical sphere. Representations of bound, prone captives seem to be particularly associated with monuments celebrating period endings—that is, commemorating the completion of calendrical periods such as k'atuns or half-k'atuns (see Rice 2004, 262–64).

K'atun- and *May*-Based Conflict

A direct-historical approach, yielding insights into calendrical cycling based on observations drawn from Late Postclassic and Early Colonial northern Yucatán, provides additional perspectives on intersite conflict in the Classic-period Southern Lowlands (see Rice 2004, 259–61). Spanish chroniclers inform us that conflict between towns in the region was relatively constant and pervasive: Bishop Diego de Landa reported "great strifes and enmities" among the major ruling lineages, and Antonio de Herrera y Tordesillas reported that "for any little cause [the Maya] fought. . . . And so they never had peace, especially when the cultivation was over" (Tozzer 1941, 40–41, 217). (While it is not exactly clear what Herrera meant by "cultivation" being "over," this observation does not seem to be supported by the dates of Late Classic warfare, as seen in table 8.4.) Wars were led by the *nakom*s, war captains elected to office for three years, during which time they were treated almost as gods and largely withdrew from normal life, having no contact with women (Tozzer 1941, 113, 122n562). Alfred Tozzer concluded (1941, 123n563) that all of this reflects "the religious significance placed on warfare" by the Maya.

Numerous causes besides long-standing enmities can be identified for the conflicts in postconquest Yucatán, and many are specific to the wretched circumstances of the Maya under Spanish colonial control: forced conversion to Christianity, demands of tithes to the Catholic Church, labor and tribute payments to both native rulers and new Spanish overlords, forced resettlements (*reducción* or *congregación*) and crowding, elimination of traditional social and political authority structures, and so on (see Farriss 1987; Restall 1997; Roys 1972, 65–70). The Early Colonial–period "prophetic histories" known as the books of the *chilam b'alam* (speaker of the jaguar priest) reveal the presence of numerous military orders among both nobles and the peasantry, which were given various nicknames: Flags, Possums, Many Skunks, Hanging Rabbits, and Foxes (Edmonson 1986, 209–14); Snakes, Ants, Jaguars, Silent Leopards, Locusts, Monsters, and Chiggers (Edmonson 1982, 37, 113–14); and Strong Skunks, Masked Deer, and Rabbits, who were described as being "usurpers in the land" in a K'atun 7 Ajaw[3] (ending A.D. 1342 or 1599) (Edmonson 1982, 62–63).

More subtle causes of Postclassic conflict are long-standing antagonisms between ruling lineages about certain calendrical matters, and these could date back to the Classic period. One issue that has received little attention from archaeologists is that in the Late Classic period, two new calendars were introduced into the Usumacinta region and Campeche (Edmonson 1988, 126–27; Bricker 1989, 235; cf. Stuart 2004). Both calendars changed the counting system and introduced terminal dating of the 365-day year. The latter practice is characterized as distinctively non-Mayan: Munro Edmonson calls it an "intrusive foreign idea" (1988, 103), attributing it to Ch'olan speakers and calendars used in the Gulf Coast ("Putun"?) and/or Oaxaca regions. Terminal dating came to be used in the Western Lowlands at Palenque, Yaxchilán, Bonampak, and Piedras Negras in the Usumacinta region, and at Uxmal, Edzná, Jaina, and Holactún in the Puuc area of Campeche, but was not adopted elsewhere in the Eastern or Central Lowlands (except perhaps at Naranjo). Conflict over the traditional "Classic" calendar and associated practices versus the new Campeche calendar continued through the Postclassic period, with the Xiw favoring the former and the Itzá the latter (see Edmonson 1982, 1986).

Classic-Period K'atun Conflict

K'atun-related conflict has not been ignored in the literature to date on Classic warfare, but neither has its possible significance been fully explored. As noted, bound captives frequently appear on period-ending (k'atun-ending) monuments, and this might refer to ball game contests occurring as part of period-ending celebrations. Returning to the idea of

Venus as war star, we can see that at every third k'atun ending—that is, at intervals of fifty-nine years—during the Late Classic, Venus is evening star near maximum elongation: these occurrences are evident in A.D. 613, 672, 731, 790, and 849. If these fifty-nine-year Late Classic intervals are projected back in time (allowing for a small correction factor in the Early and Middle Classic), we find the k'atun endings shown in table 8.5. Unfortunately, it remains unclear from these relatively limited data whether these co-occurrences are meaningful or merely coincidental. The latter is likely, however. Only sixteen period endings coincide with war-star (Venus) iconography (see Schele and Freidel 1990, 444–46n47; Aveni and Hotaling 1994, table 1), but none of the associated texts incorporate references to warlike activity.

It has been conjectured that after the completion of the K'atun 8 Ajaw of A.D. 692, "both the pace of warfare and the status of the captives increased" (Schele and Miller 1986, 209). Famously, in central Petén the year 692 was the date of accession of Tikal ruler Jasaw Kan K'awil, who expanded the site's program of constructing twin-pyramid groups that was begun by his father. Stela 16, in Tikal's twin-pyramid Group N, depicts the ruler in a mask with Venus symbols (but the date, A.D. 711, is not in the three-k'atun sequence of table 8.5). On Tikal Stela 16, Jasaw Kan K'awil is shown celebrating the k'atun ending that occurred four days before the first appearance of Venus as evening star. Monuments at three other sites—Naranjo Stela 1, Piedras Negras Stela 7, and Copán Stela C—also celebrate that period ending with references to Venus. Tikal Stela 22 (A.D. 771) shows ruler Kitam celebrating a k'atun ending occurring ten days before the first appearance of Venus as evening star; this timing was also noted on Quiriguá Stela E and Copán Temple 11. The accompanying Tikal Altar 10 shows a prone, bound captive.

Evidence of site and monument destruction has been interpreted as indication of pervasive warfare, but this could instead represent the "reverential" termination rituals (see Pagliaro, Garber, and Stanton 2003) that accompanied the end of calendrical cycles and the geopolitical "seatings" of an important calendrical period such as the k'atun (about 20 Gregorian years) or the *may* (about 256 years) in a city. As Edmonson comments about the Postclassic Maya in northern Yucatán (1979, 11), they "destroyed the primate city and its road at the end of the *may*. There are indications that this 'destruction' may have been largely ritual and symbolic, and that the

Table 8.5. K'atun endings on 59-year intervals and maximum elongation of Venus as eveningstar.

Maya date		Julian date	No. of stelae[a]	No. of days from max. elongation
10.4.0.0.0	12 Ajaw	Jan. 18, 909	1	
10.3.0.0.0				
10.2.0.0.0				
10.1.0.0.0	5 Ajaw	Nov. 30, 849	5	20 before
10.0.0.0.0				
9.19.0.0.0				
9.18.0.0.0	11 Ajaw	October 11, 790	15	19 before
9.17.0.0.0				
9.16.0.0.0				
9.15.0.0.0	4 Ajaw	August 22, 731	14	9 before
9.14.0.0.0				
9.13.0.0.0				
9.12.0.0.0	10 Ajaw	July 1, 672	8	2 before
9.11.0.0.0				
9.10.0.0.0				
9.9.0.0.0	3 Ajaw	May 10, 613	5	3 after
9.8.0.0.0				
9.7.0.0.0				
9.6.0.0.0	9 Ajaw	March 20, 554	2	
9.5.0.0.0				
9.4.0.0.0				
9.3.0.0.0	2 Ajaw	January 28, 495		
9.2.0.0.0				
9.1.0.0.0				
9.0.0.0.0	8 Ajaw	December 6, 435		
8.19.0.0.0				
8.18.0.0.0				
8.17.0.0.0	1 Ajaw	October 19, 376		

Source: Aveni and Hotaling 1994, table 1; Puleston 1979, fig. 5–1.

[a] Total number of stelae erected on period ending.

'abandonment of the city' was an evacuation by the ruling dynasty rather than total depopulation. But since the dynasties (e.g., the Xiu and the Itzá) did not necessarily agree on the ending date of the cycle, there was room for maneuver in politics, ideology and warfare."

So, for example, the intentional destruction and burial of ball court ring stones at Oxkintok, Uxmal, and Edzná in the Terminal Classic (Carmean, Dunning, and Kowalski 2004) could represent such *may*-related termination rituals. This is particularly intriguing given that I have elsewhere suggested

(Rice 2004, 230–31) that ball courts represent the particular architectural "signature" of the *may* seating at Chichén Itzá in the Terminal Classic.

K'atuns of Conflict, Postclassic and Classic

Besides clashing over the different calendars, Postclassic Yucatán peoples also engaged in conflict over the rights to seat the politically and ritually important calendrical intervals of the k'atun and the *may*, a 256-year (or 260-tun) interval encompassing thirteen k'atuns (Edmonson 1986; Rice 2004, 259–61). Here it is useful to recall that the Maya word "k'atun" not only refers to a period of 20 tuns, or 7,200 days, but also means "fight, combat, battle, war, warrior" (Barrera Vásquez 1991). The so-called k'atun wars (*u k'atun k'atunob*) of Yucatán were waged over competing calendars (Edmonson 1982, xvi–xvii), as "katuns not only chronicled the wars of Yucatan but actually caused them" (Edmonson 1986, 99). Limited evidence suggests that future k'atun seats were selected at the midpoint of the k'atun in progress (Rice 2004, 111–12).

An example of the possible role of "k'atun wars" in the Late Classic period can be found in southeastern Petén (Laporte 2004), where Ixkun Stela 2 records a "war" against Sacul on December 19, 779, almost a year before the mid-k'atun of 9.17.10.0.0 (November 30, 780). This war was not recorded at Sacul, suggesting that Ixkun "won" in some sense. I take this to mean that Ixkun was successful in a mid-k'atun bid to seat the upcoming k'atun that would begin 10 years later, on 9.18.0.0.0 in 790, as the k'atun of 9.17.0.0.0 ended (Rice 2004, 113–14). On 9.18.0.0.0, both Ixkun and Sacul celebrated the k'atun ending by erecting stelae recording the previously "defeated" ruler Ch'iyel of Sacul's visit to Ixkun and the "victorious" lord Rabbit God K. Together, they celebrated the period ending and, according to my hypothesis, the new seating of the k'atun at Ixkun.

Another possible example comes from Tikal, where the Middle Classic hiatus in stelae erection has been correlated with the star-war "defeat" of that site by Calakmul in 562. The hiatus ended some 130 years later, when Tikal again began to erect stelae (692) and claimed "victory" over Calakmul in 695. This defeat and victory sequence roughly defines a half-*may* interval of 128 years. Within the *may* model, this can be interpreted as Calakmul ruler Sky Witness (Martin and Grube 2000, 104) undertaking a "war of proof" to validate the seating of the *may* for 128 years at his capital beginning in 562. This was followed by Tikal ruler Jasaw Kan K'awil's similar war of proof against Calakmul in 695, in order to seat or reseat the *may* at Tikal.

Apparently, during the Postclassic period, certain named k'atuns (see note 3 at the end of this chapter) had specific associations with warfare and conflict. K'atuns 11 Ajaw were nicknamed the "flower k'atuns," alluding to the "Flowery Wars" of Aztec central Mexico. K'atuns 7 Ajaw are described as k'atuns of chaos, usurpation, and "seven-day rule" (Edmonson 1982, 62–63). Finally, the day 1 Ajaw is also the preferred ending date of the idealized Venus cycle (Milbrath 1999, 170), with its association of "star wars." Could these k'atuns of conflict also have existed during the Classic period?[4]

With respect to conflict in K'atuns 7 Ajaw, it is important to note that K'atuns 8 Ajaw were the Maya k'atuns of change, at least in the calendar used during the Classic period and by the Xiw in the Postclassic (Edmonson 1982). Major political transitions were expected to take place during this k'atun (see Puleston 1979; Edmonson 1986; Chase 1991), such as changes in the location of cities seating the 256-year geopolitical cycle of the *may*. Elsewhere, I have hypothesized that the decisions about seatings of the *may*, like decisions about seating the k'atuns, took place in midcycle, or 128 years after the beginning of the cycle (Rice 2004, 111–15). Counting forward 128 years from the ending day of a K'atun 8 Ajaw brings us to the beginning day of a K'atun 7 Ajaw. If this *may* cycle midpoint marked the time of deciding upon new *may* seats, this could account for K'atuns 7 Ajaw being k'atuns of competition, conflict, and political chaos. In the Classic period, then, it might be significant that Caracol's "defeat" of Tikal in A.D. 562 occurred just before the midpoint of a K'atun 7 Ajaw. Similarly, the 20-year interval from 810 to 830, often considered the end of the Late Classic or Terminal Classic occupation and abandonment of the Southern Lowlands, is a K'atun 7 Ajaw.

The Venus-warfare associations of K'atun 1 Ajaw might relate to events in the Early Classic period. In particular, a K'atun 1 Ajaw ended in A.D. 376, two years before the arrival of Siyaj K'ak' and his entourage in Tikal. This group is presumed to be from central Mexico, and Venus-Tlaloc war imagery was likely introduced into the Maya Lowlands from Teotihuacan. Later, a star war involving Calakmul and Caracol against Naranjo is said to have occurred in A.D. 631, just before the ending of a K'atun 1 Ajaw, in 633. Significantly, perhaps, Venus's movements were tracked for 384 years, and this interval is also the duration of one and a half *may* cycles (256 plus 128 years).

In Colonial-period Yucatán, the half-*may* cycle sequence of odd-numbered k'atuns—K'atuns 13 Ajaw, 11 Ajaw, 9 Ajaw, 7 Ajaw, 5 Ajaw, 3 Ajaw, and 1 Ajaw—seems to have been a source of calendrical conflict (Edmonson 1982, 39n723). This might be because the Xiw counted the k'atun and the *may* on their terminal dates from 6 Ajaw through 8 Ajaw, as did the Classic Maya of Petén, while the Itzá counted them from their initial dates from 11 Ajaw through 13 Ajaw (Edmonson 1988, 202). Notably, Classic Tikal's traditional "enemy," Calakmul, and its allies, such as Caracol, seemed to gain power in K'atuns 2 Ajaw, the k'atun that precedes a K'atun 13 Ajaw in the system of naming k'atuns (Rice 2004, 201–202). For example, on a half-k'atun-ending day 2 Ajaw in A.D. 623, Calakmul ended a hiatus in stela erection, similar to that at Tikal, and began erecting large numbers of monuments through the K'atun 2 Ajaw ending in A.D. 751. Caracol also became active in monument erection as well as in warfare after 623.

What might have been the origin of this alternative system of calendrical reckoning? Although the central Mexican "arrival event" at Tikal in A.D. 378 has drawn considerable attention to subsequent Teotihuacan–Lowland Maya relations, central Mexican–style talud-tablero architecture began to appear at central Tikal as early as A.D. 250 or so (Laporte and Fialko 1990, 1995). In addition, Tikal's dynastic histories record three kings named Chak Tok Ich'ak, who ruled (or had significant life-cycle dates) approximately 128 years apart (Martin and Grube 2000, 27–28, 37). These include a possible Chak Tok Ich'ak who ruled in the late third century (perhaps as early as A.D. 250?), another who was apparently killed as part of the A.D. 378 event, and a third who died in A.D. 508. The years 250 and 508 fall in K'atuns 13 Ajaw if they are identified by their terminal day and in K'atuns 2 Ajaw if named by their initial day.

One conclusion to be drawn from these data is that two competitive groups, or factions, seem to have existed in Tikal in the middle-to-late fourth century A.D.: the long-lived Jaguar Paw dynasty and a faction favoring some sort of alliance with central Mexico (Rice 2004, 201–202, 264–65; see also Freidel, MacLeod, and Suhler 2003). The former observed traditional calendrical cycling based on K'atuns 8 Ajaw, while the other regarded K'atuns 13/2 Ajaw as the pivotal units of time's cycles. Subsequent dynastic histories at Tikal indicate that the names, symbols, and iconographic programs of the old Jaguar Paw dynasty, as well as the importance of K'atuns 8 Ajaw, continued to be publicly celebrated, while the faction favoring central Mexican ties and K'atuns 13/2 Ajaw suffered diminishing power and might eventually have been ousted from Tikal—and perhaps found a sympathetic home at Calakmul. Significantly, no further battles with Caracol or Calakmul occurred after Tikal "defeated" the latter site in A.D. 695, and the Tikal, or Classic, calendar continued in use through the Colonial period.

Conclusion

Scholarly study of the demise of the Classic Southern Lowland Maya civilization began in the early twentieth century in a search for causes of the apparent wholesale depopulation of the region at the end of the Old Empire. Scores of possibilities have been suggested over the past century of reflection on this phenomenon, including disaster, disease, environmental degradation, and warfare (see Demarest, Rice, and Rice 2004), but the concept that we embrace so uncritically today—that the abandonment signaled the "collapse" of Classic civilization—was relatively slow to take hold.

For the first half of the twentieth century, archaeologists agreed on the peaceful Maya model, but today, the Maya are widely perceived as having been wracked by conflict. A major contributing factor to this revisionist model has been recent decipherments of hieroglyphic texts, which have led some scholars to envision "endemic" warfare in the lowlands (see, e.g., Demarest 2004) and to discuss "total system collapse" (see, e.g., Webster 2002, 218). These readings of conflict-equals-warfare have been uncritically reified and unchallenged. But accumulations of data on the occurrences of warfare, together with data on the alleged celestial phenomena that supposedly motivated them, fail to demonstrate convincing correlations. Moreover, there is little to no evidence from the Classic or Postclassic period indicating that this "warfare" was expansionist territorial conquest. Instead, available evidence is consistent with an interpretation that competition was designed for the taking of captives (for sacrifice or maybe for slavery), frequently by means of ball game ritual, and that site destruction was termination ritual occasioned by the geopolitical cycling of ritual capitals. The encircling walls that are commonly interpreted as defensive constructions might instead be simply markers of high geopolitical status and regional prestige (Ringle et al. 2004), as might be associated with the privilege of seating the k'atun and the *may*.

In my view, and in that of my coeditors of and contributors to a data-rich volume on the Terminal Classic period (Demarest, Rice, and Rice 2004), there was not a single, monolithic civilizational collapse in the southern Maya Lowlands. Rather, we believe it is now clear that any "collapse," if such it was, involved the abandonment of only some of the large southern cities and, more precisely, constituted a failure of the institution of *k'ul ajaw*, or sacred kingship. In addition, considerable region-to-region variability clearly existed, resulting in a complex mosaic of transitions and transformations throughout the Southern and Central Lowlands during a period of as much as three hundred or more years (circa A.D. 750/800 to 1050/1100). Rapid abandonments as well as slow declines, sudden but also gradual economic changes, population dispersions, destruction, reorientation, and florescence—all are represented in this interpretation of change and transformation in regional lowland cultures during these centuries.

Recognition of substantial variability in Maya cultural responses during the three to four centuries spanning the Terminal Classic "collapse" period demands that archaeologists evaluate hypothesized causes more carefully. In particular, as I have argued here, interpretations of "warfare" are more complex than simple, unicausal models of peasant revolt, menacing Mexicans, or the positions of the stars. These factors might have played roles, yet broader sociopolitical contexts should be considered in explanatory frameworks. The idea of status rivalry warfare is one example of such a multicausal approach. Additionally, many glyph decipherments interpreted with a broad brush as describing intersite warfare might instead refer to smaller-scale competition, combat, or conquest in other arenas, such as that of the ball game or as kingly "wars of proof." In addition, the occasional destruction of sites and monuments, combined with the political importance of seating cyclical calendrical intervals and the intense competition to do so, as seen in the Postclassic period, supports the position that a similar calendar-based system of geopolitical organization (the *may*) operated in the Classic period.

During the decades leading up to the 1970 advanced seminar on the Maya collapse, archaeologists tended to zealously espouse one causal mechanism or another to explain the abandonment of the cities and the attendant cultural demise. Perhaps the most laudable feature of Willey and Shimkin's concluding chapter to the collapse seminar publication is its role as a watershed in putting to rest the previously dominant "single factor" hypotheses about the Classic decline. At the same time, however, the chapter's consensus model arguably masked some significant debates of the day—peasant revolt versus external invasion in particular, or militarism and warfare in general—that have reemerged as major topics of discussion in the last decade. While conflict and competition were likely constant undercurrents among the Lowland Maya from the civilization's earliest days (Webster 1977; Brown and Garber 2003), it is clear that in only some areas had conflict intensified by and during the Late and Terminal Classic (Demarest et al. 1997), as seen in resettlement of easily defended sites, widespread construction of fortifications, and other evidence.

Willey and Shimkin provided a more nuanced interpretation of warfare than did their contemporaries, tying it to dynastic rivalries and kingly aggrandizement, and possibly ball game ritual, as we can also read in more recent writings. In his coauthored conclusion to the 1973 collapse volume, as in his other writings, Gordon R. Willey took a far more cautious and catholic view of events and processes affecting the Maya than did some of his predecessors, and as a result, his scholarship continues to resonate with archaeologists into the twenty-first century.

Acknowledgments

I never had the privilege of working with or being taught by Gordon Willey, but as an archaeologist who has worked in the southeastern United States, the Maya Lowlands, and Andean Peru, I am certainly intellectually beholden to his broad scholarship and to that of his students. I am grateful to Bill Fash and Jerry Sabloff for their kind invitation to contribute to the Society for American Archaeology symposium that served as the basis for this volume. In addition, I would like to thank Jerry for bringing the Morley 1915 and Spinden 1928 quotations to my attention. Thanks also to Don Rice and Andy Hofling for their critical readings of this manuscript.

Notes

1. In a not-unrelated idea, Robert Sharer proposed (1977, 547–48) that an elite-led revitalization led to recovery after the hiatus and that a similar revitalization attempt in the Terminal Classic was nonelite led and thus failed.

2. Karl Taube also cites David Stuart on this point in his informative discussion (Taube 2000, 289–301) of the relations between warfare and meteors in Mesoamerica based on iconographic and linguistic evidence. Meteors and meteorites, he writes, were widely regarded as celestial fire and a rain of darts and have complex associations with the War (also Fire) Serpent god Xiuhcoatl, fire, and obsidian, the latter of which, in turn, was thought to be the earthly remains of such star fire, or "star excrement." Similarly, Barbara Tedlock comments that a "Colonial Quiché term for meteor was ch'olanic ch'umil, 'star that makes war'" (1992b, 28).

3. Maya k'atuns were "named" for the number and the day on which they ended, always a day named "Ajaw." There were thirteen k'atuns in a cycle, and the numbering proceeded in retrograde order, as K'atun 6 Ajaw, K'atun 4 Ajaw, 2 Ajaw, 13 Ajaw, 11 Ajaw, 9 Ajaw, 7 Ajaw, 5 Ajaw, 3 Ajaw, 1 Ajaw, 12 Ajaw, 10 Ajaw, and 8 Ajaw. During the Classic period, the k'atun cycle always ended with a K'atun 8 Ajaw.

4. The characteristics of specifically named and numbered k'atuns are of interest in light of an observation of practices of modern daykeepers in the Maya highlands. Here, the numbers used to identify days in the 260-day calendar have certain values: low numbers (1, 2, 3) are "gentle" because they are young or new, while high numbers (11, 12, 13) are powerful or even "violent" because they are older and more mature; numbers in the middle (7, 8, 9) are "indifferent" (Tedlock 1992a, 107–108). It is unknown if the Classic Maya might have used similar interpretations or if this system might have been extended to the qualities of k'atuns bearing these numbers.

References

Adams, Richard E. W. 1973. "Collapse of Maya Civilization: A Review of Previous Theories." In *The Classic Maya Collapse*, ed. T. Patrick Culbert, 21–34. School of American Research Advanced Seminar Series. Albuquerque: University of New Mexico Press.

Aldana, Gerardo. 2005. "Agency and the 'Star War' Glyph: A Historical Reassessment of Classic Maya Astrology and Warfare." *Ancient Mesoamerica* 16 (2):305–20.

Ambrosino, James N., Traci Ardren, and Travis W. Stanton. 2003. "The History of Warfare at Yaxuná." In *Ancient Mesoamerican Warfare*, ed. M. Kathryn Brown and Travis W. Stanton, 109–23. Walnut Creek, Calif.: AltaMira.

Andrews, E. Wyllys, IV. 1973. "The Development of Maya Civilization after Abandonment of the Southern Cities." In *The Classic Maya Collapse*, ed. T. Patrick Culbert, 243–65. School of American Research Advanced Seminar Series. Albuquerque: University of New Mexico Press.

Ashmore, Wendy, ed. 1981. *Lowland Maya Settlement Patterns*. Albuquerque: University of New Mexico Press.

Ashmore, Wendy, Jason Yaeger, and Cynthia Robin. 2004. "Commoner Sense: Late and Terminal Classic Social Strategies in the Xunantunich Area." In *The Terminal Classic in the Maya Lowlands: Collapse, Transition, and Transformation*, ed. Arthur A. Demarest, Prudence M. Rice, and Don S. Rice, 302–23. Boulder: University Press of Colorado.

Aveni, Anthony F., and Lorren D. Hotaling. 1994. "Monumental Inscriptions and the Observational Basis of Maya Planetary Astronomy." *Archaeoastronomy* (Supplement to *Journal for the History of Astronomy*) 19:S21–S54.

Barrera Vásquez, Alfredo. 1991. *Diccionario Maya: Maya-Español, Español-Maya*. 2nd ed. Mexico City: Editorial Porrúa.

Becker, Marshall Joseph. 1979. "Priests, Peasants, and Ceremonial Centers: The Intellectual History of a Model." In *Maya Archaeology and Ethnohistory*, ed. Norman Hammond and Gordon R. Willey, 3–20. Austin: University of Texas Press.

Bove, Frederick J. 1981. "Trend Surface Analysis and the Lowland Classic Maya Collapse." *American Antiquity* 46 (1):93–112.

Bricker, Victoria R. 1989. "The Calendrical Meaning of Ritual among the Maya." In *Ethnographic Encounters in Southern Mesoamerica*, ed. Victoria Bricker and Gary Gossen, 231–49. IMS Studies in Culture and History, no. 3. Albany: State University of New York at Albany.

Brown, M. Kathryn, and James F. Garber. 2003. "Evidence of Conflict during the Middle Formative in the Maya Lowlands: A View from Blackman Eddy, Belize." In *Ancient Mesoamerican Warfare*, ed. M. Kathryn Brown and Travis W. Stanton, 91–108. Walnut Creek, Calif.: AltaMira.

Brown, M. Kathryn, and Travis W. Stanton, eds. 2003. *Ancient Mesoamerican Warfare*. Walnut Creek, Calif.: AltaMira.

Carmean, Kelli, Nicholas Dunning, and Jeff Karl Kowalski. 2004. "High Times in the Hill Country: A Perspective from the Terminal Classic Puuc Region." In *The Terminal Classic in the Maya Lowlands: Collapse, Transition, and Transformation*, ed. Arthur A. Demarest, Prudence M. Rice, and Don S. Rice, 424–49. Boulder: University Press of Colorado.

Chase, Arlen F. 1991. "Cycles of Time: Caracol in the Maya Realm." In *Sixth Palenque Round Table, 1986*, ed. Merle Greene Robertson, 32–50. Norman: University of Oklahoma Press.

Chase, Arlen F., and Diane Z. Chase. 2003. "Texts and Contexts in Maya Warfare: A Brief Consideration of Epigraphy and Archaeology at Caracol, Belize." In *Ancient Mesoamerican Warfare*, ed. M. Kathryn Brown and Travis W. Stanton, 171–88. Walnut Creek, Calif.: AltaMira.

———. 2004. "Terminal Classic Status-Linked Ceramics and the Maya 'Collapse': De Facto Refuse at Caracol, Belize." In *The Terminal Classic in the Maya Lowlands: Collapse, Transition, and Transformation*, ed. Arthur A. Demarest, Prudence M. Rice, and Don S. Rice, 342–66. Boulder: University Press of Colorado.

Chase, Arlen F., Nikolai Grube, and Diane Chase. 1991. *Three Terminal Classic Monuments from Caracol, Belize*. Research Reports on Ancient Maya Writing, no. 36. Washington, D.C.: Center for Maya Research.

Chase, Arlen F., and Prudence M. Rice, eds. 1985. *The Lowland Maya Postclassic*. Austin: University of Texas Press.

Cojtí Cuxil, Demetrio. 1994. *Políticas para la revindicación de los Maya de hoy*. Guatemala City: Cholsamaj.

Cowgill, George L. 1964. "The End of Classic Maya Culture: A Review of Recent Evidence." *Southwestern Journal of Anthropology* 20 (2):145–59.

———. 1979. "Teotihuacan, Internal Militaristic Competition, and the Fall of the Classic Maya." In *Maya Archaeology and Ethnohistory*, ed. Norman Hammond and Gordon R. Willey, 51–62. Austin: University of Texas Press.

———. 1988. "Onward and Upward with Collapse." In *The Collapse of Ancient States and Civilizations*, ed. Norman Yoffee and George L. Cowgill, 244–76. Tucson: University of Arizona Press.

Culbert, T. Patrick, ed. 1973. *The Classic Maya Collapse*. School of American Research Advanced Seminar Series. Albuquerque: University of New Mexico Press.

———. 1977. "Maya Development and Collapse: An Economic Perspective." In *Social Process in Maya Prehistory: Studies in Honour of Sir Eric Thompson*, ed. Norman Hammond, 509–30. London: Academic Press.

———. 1988. "The Collapse of Classic Maya Civilization." In *The Collapse of Ancient States and Civilizations*, ed. Norman Yoffee and George L. Cowgill, 69–101. Tucson: University of Arizona Press.

Culbert, T. Patrick, and Don S. Rice, eds. 1990. *Precolumbian Population History in the Maya Lowlands*. Albuquerque: University of New Mexico Press.

Dahlin, Bruce H. 2000. "The Barricade and Abandonment of Chunchucmil: Implications for Northern Maya Warfare." *Latin American Antiquity* 11 (3):283–98.

———. 2002. "Climate Change and the End of the Classic Period in Yucatan: Resolving a Paradox." *Ancient Mesoamerica* 13 (2):327–40.

Demarest, Arthur A. 1993. "The Violent Saga of a Maya Kingdom." *National Geographic*, February, 94–111.

———. 1997. "The Vanderbilt Petexbatun Regional Archaeological Project 1989–1994: Overview, History, and Major Results of a Multidisciplinary Study of the Classic Maya Collapse." *Ancient Mesoamerica* 8 (2):209–27.

———. 2004. "After the Maelstrom: Collapse of the Classic Maya Kingdoms and the Terminal Classic in Western Petén." In *The Terminal Classic in the Maya Lowlands: Collapse, Transition, and Transformation*, ed. Arthur A. Demarest, Prudence M. Rice, and Don S. Rice, 102–24. Boulder: University Press of Colorado.

Demarest, Arthur A., Matt O'Mansky, Claudia Wolley, Dirk van Tuerenhout, Takeshi Inomata, Joel Palka, and Hector Escobedo. 1997. "Classic Maya Defensive Systems and Warfare in the Petexbatun Region." *Ancient Mesoamerica* 8 (2):229–53.

Demarest, Arthur A., Prudence M. Rice, and Don S. Rice, eds. 2004. *The Terminal Classic in the Maya Lowlands: Collapse, Transition, and Transformation*. Boulder: University Press of Colorado.

Edmonson, Munro S. 1979. "Some Postclassic Questions about the Classic Maya." In *Tercera mesa redonda de Palenque*, ed. Merle Greene Robertson and Donnan Call Jeffers, 4:9–18. Palenque, Mexico: Pre-Columbian Art Research Center.

———. 1982. *The Ancient Future of the Itza: The Book of Chilam Balam of Tizimin*. Austin: University of Texas Press.

———. 1986. *Heaven Born Merida and Its Destiny: The Book of Chilam Balam of Chumayel*. Austin: University of Texas Press.

———. 1988. *The Book of the Year: Middle American Calendrical Systems*. Salt Lake City: University of Utah Press.

Farriss, Nancy. 1987. "Remembering the Future, Anticipating the Past: History, Time, and Cosmology among the Maya of Yucatan." *Comparative Studies in Society and History* 29:566–93.

Fash, William L., Jr. 1983. "Maya State Formation: A Case Study and Its Implications." PhD diss., Harvard University.

———. 1988. "A New Look at Maya Statecraft from Copan, Honduras." *Antiquity* 62:157–69.

———. 1991. *Scribes, Warriors and Kings: The City of Copan and the Ancient Maya*. London: Thames & Hudson.

Fash, William L., Jr., E. Wyllys Andrews V, and T. Kam Manahan. 2004. "Political Decentralization, Dynastic Collapse, and the Early Postclassic in the Urban Center of Copán, Honduras." In *The Terminal Classic in the Maya Lowlands: Collapse, Transition, and Transformation*, ed. Arthur A. Demarest, Prudence M. Rice, and Don S. Rice, 260–87. Boulder: University Press of Colorado.

Flannery, Kent V., and Joyce Marcus. 2003. "The Origin of War: New ^{14}C Dates from Ancient Mexico." *Proceedings of the National Academy of Sciences* 100 (20):11801–805.

Fox, John W. 1991. "The Lords of Light versus the Lords of Dark: The Postclassic Highland Maya Ballgame." In *The Mesoamerican Ballgame*, ed. Vernon L. Scarborough and David R. Wilcox, 213–38. Tucson: University of Arizona Press.

Freidel, David A., Barbara MacLeod, and Charles K. Suhler. 2003. "Early Classic Maya Conquest in Words and Deeds." In *Ancient Mesoamerican Warfare*, ed. M. Kathryn Brown and Travis W. Stanton, 189–215. Walnut Creek, Calif.: AltaMira.

Freidel, David A., Linda Schele, and Joy Parker. 1993. *Maya Cosmos: Three Thousand Years on the Shaman's Path*. New York: William Morrow.

Gann, Thomas, and J. Eric Thompson. 1935. *History of the Maya: From the Earliest Times to the Present Day*. New York: Scribner's.

Gill, Richardson B. 2000. *The Great Maya Droughts: Water, Life, and Death*. Albuquerque: University of New Mexico Press.

Graham, John A. 1973. "Aspects of Non-Classic Presences in the Inscriptions and Sculptural Art of Seibal." In *The Classic Maya Collapse*, ed. T. Patrick Culbert, 207–19. School of American Research Advanced Seminar Series. Albuquerque: University of New Mexico Press.

———. 1990. "Monumental Sculpture and Hieroglyphic Inscriptions." In *Excavations at Seibal, Department of Peten, Guatemala*. Memoirs of the Peabody Museum of Archaeology and Ethnology, vol. 17, no. 1. Cambridge, Mass.: Harvard University.

Haas, Jonathan. 2001. "Cultural Evolution and Political Centralization." In *From Leaders to Rulers*, ed. Jonathan Haas, 3–18. New York: Kluwer Academic / Plenum Press.

Harris, John F., and Stephen K. Stearns. 1997. *Understanding Maya Inscriptions: A Hieroglyph Handbook*. 2nd ed. Philadelphia: University Museum, University of Pennsylvania.

Hassig, Ross. 1992. *War and Society in Ancient Mesoamerica*. Berkeley and Los Angeles: University of California Press.

Haug, Gerald H., Detlef Günther, Larry C. Peterson, Daniel M. Sigman, Konrad A. Hughen, and Beat Aeschlimann. 2003. "Climate and the Collapse of Classic Maya Civilization." *Science*, March 14, 1731–35.

Heckenberger, Michael J., Afukaka Kuikuro, Urissapá Tabata Kuikuro, J. Christian Russell, Morgan Schmidt, Carlos Fausto, and Bruna Franchetto. 2003. "Amazonia 1492: Pristine Forest or Cultural Parkland?" *Science*, September 19, 1710–14.

Hodell, David A., Jason H. Curtis, and Mark Brenner. 1995. "Possible Role of Climate in the Collapse of Classic Maya Civilization." *Nature* 375:391–94.

Hosler, Dorothy, Jeremy A. Sabloff, and Dale Runge. 1977. "Simulation Model Development: A Case Study of the Maya Collapse." In *Social Process in Maya Prehistory: Studies in Honour of Sir Eric Thompson*, ed. Norman Hammond, 553–90. London: Academic Press.

Hruby, Zachary X., and Mark B. Child. 2004. "Chontal Linguistic Influence in Ancient Maya Writing: Intransitive Positional Verbal Affixation." In *The Linguistics of Maya Writing*, ed. Søren Wichmann. Salt Lake City: University of Utah Press.

Justeson, John. 1989. "Ancient Maya Ethnoastronomy: An Overview of Hieroglyphic Sources." In *World Archaeoastronomy*, ed. Anthony Aveni, 76–129. Cambridge: Cambridge University Press.

Kaufman, Terrence, and John Justeson. 2001. "Epi-Olmec Hieroglyphic Writing and Texts." *Mesoamerican Languages Documentation Project*. http://www.albany.edu/anthro/maldp/papers.htm.

Kowalski, Jeff Karl. 1989. "Who Am I among the Itza?: Links between Northern Yucatan and the Western Maya Lowlands and Highlands." In *Mesoamerica after the Decline of Teotihuacan: A.D. 700–900*, ed. Richard A. Diehl and Janet C. Berlo, 173–85. Washington, D.C.: Dumbarton Oaks.

Kronk, Gary W. a. "Frequently Asked Questions about Meteors and Meteor Showers." *The American Meteor Society*. http://www.amsmeteors.org/faqm.html.

———. b. "Lyriad History." *Comets and Meteor Showers*. http://comets.amsmeteors.org/meteors/showers/lyridhistory.html.

———. c. "Eta Aquarid History." *Comets and Meteor Showers*. http://comets.amsmeteors.org/meteors/showers/eta_aquaridhistory.html.

———. d. "Leonid History: Ancient and Medieval." *Comets and Meteor Showers*. http://comets.amsmeteors.org/meteors/showers/leonidancient.html.

Laporte, Juan Pedro. 2004. "Terminal Classic Settlement and Polity in the Mopan Valley, Petén, Guatemala." In *The Terminal Classic in the Maya Lowlands: Collapse, Transition, and Transformation*, ed. Arthur A. Demarest, Prudence M. Rice, and Don S. Rice, 195–230. Boulder: University Press of Colorado.

Laporte, Juan Pedro, and Vilma Fialko. 1990. "New Perspectives on Old Problems: Dynastic References for the Early Classic at Tikal." In *Vision and Revision in Maya Studies*, ed. Flora S. Clancy and Peter D. Harrison, 33–66. Albuquerque: University of New Mexico Press.

———. 1995. "Un reëncuentro con Mundo Perdido, Tikal, Guatemala." *Ancient Mesoamerica* 6:41–94.

Lounsbury, Floyd. 1982. "Astronomical Knowledge and Its Uses at Bonampak." In *Archaeoastronomy in the New World*, ed. Anthony F. Aveni, 143–68. Cambridge: Cambridge University Press.

Lowe, John G. W. 1985. *The Dynamics of Apocalypse: A Systems Simulation of the Classic Maya Collapse*. Albuquerque: University of New Mexico Press.

Marcus, Joyce. 1992. *Mesoamerican Writing Systems: Propaganda, Myth, and History in Four Ancient Civilizations*. Princeton, N.J.: Princeton University Press.

Martin, Simon, and Nikolai Grube. 2000. *Chronicle of the Maya Kings and Queens: Deciphering the Dynasties of the Ancient Maya*. London: Thames & Hudson.

Masson, Marilyn A. 2000. *In the Realm of Nachan Kan: Postclassic Maya Archaeology at Laguna de On, Belize*. Boulder: University Press of Colorado.

McAnany, Patricia. 2001. "Cosmology and the Institutionalization of Hierarchy in the Maya Region." In *From Leaders to Rulers*, ed. Jonathan Haas, 125–48. New York: Kluwer Academic / Plenum Press.

Meggers, Betty J. 1954. "Environmental Limitation on the Development of Culture." *American Anthropologist* 56:801–24.

Milbrath, Susan. 1999. *Star Gods of the Maya: Astronomy in Art, Folklore, and Calendars*. Austin: University of Texas Press.

Miller, Mary Ellen. 1986. *The Murals of Bonampak*. Princeton, N.J.: Princeton University Press.

Miller, Mary Ellen, and Stephen D. Houston. 1987. "Stairways and Ballcourt Glyphs: New Perspectives on the Classic Maya Ballgame." *RES* 14:47–66.

Montgomery, John. 2002. *How to Read Maya Hieroglyphs*. New York: Hippocrene Books.

Morley, Sylvanus G. 1915. *An Introduction to the Study of the Maya Hieroglyphs*. Bureau of American Ethnology Bulletin 57. Washington, D.C.: Smithsonian Institution.

———. 1946. *The Ancient Maya*. Stanford, Calif.: Stanford University Press.

Morley, Sylvanus G., and George W. Brainerd. 1956. *The Ancient Maya*. 3rd ed. Stanford, Calif.: Stanford University Press.

O'Mansky, Matt, and Nicholas Dunning. 2004. "Settlement and Late Classic Political Disintegration in the Petexbatun Region, Guatemala." In *The Terminal Classic in the Maya Lowlands: Collapse, Transition, and Transformation*, ed. Arthur A. Demarest, Prudence M. Rice, and Don S. Rice, 83–101. Boulder: University Press of Colorado.

Pagliaro, Jonathan B., James F. Garber, and Travis W. Stanton. 2003. "Evaluating the Archaeological Signatures of Maya Ritual and Conflict." In *Ancient Mesoamerican Warfare*, ed. M. Kathryn Brown and Travis W. Stanton, 75–89. Walnut Creek, Calif.: AltaMira.

Palka, Joel. 2001. "Ancient Maya Defensive Barricades, Warfare, and Site Abandonment." *Latin American Antiquity* 12 (4):427–30.

Puleston, Dennis E. 1979. "An Epistemological Pathology and the Collapse, or Why the Maya Kept the Short Count." In *Maya Archaeology and Ethnohistory*, ed. Norman Hammond and Gordon R. Willey, 63–74. Austin: University of Texas Press.

Reilly, F. Kent, III, and James F. Garber. 2003. "The Symbolic Representation of Warfare in Formative Period Mesoamerica." In *Ancient Mesoamerican Warfare*, ed. M. Kathryn Brown and Travis W. Stanton, 127–48. Walnut Creek, Calif.: AltaMira.

Renfrew, Colin. 1978. "Trajectory Discontinuity and Morphogenesis: The Implications of Catastrophe Theory for Archaeology." *American Antiquity* 43:203–22.

Restall, Matthew. 1997. *The Maya World: Yucatec Culture and Society, 1550–1850*. Stanford, Calif.: Stanford University Press.

Rice, Prudence M. 2004. *Maya Political Science: Time, Astronomy, and the Cosmos*. Austin: University of Texas Press.

Rice, Prudence M., Arthur A. Demarest, and Don S. Rice. 2004. "The Terminal Classic and the 'Classic Maya Collapse' in Perspective." In *The Terminal Classic in the Maya Lowlands:*

Collapse, Transition, and Transformation, ed. Arthur A. Demarest, Prudence M. Rice, and Don S. Rice, 1–11. Boulder: University Press of Colorado.

Ricketson, Oliver G., and Edith B. Ricketson. 1937. *Uaxactun, Guatemala, Group E, 1926–1937*. Carnegie Institution of Washington Publication 477. Washington, D.C.: Carnegie Institution of Washington.

Ringle, William M., George J. Bey III, Tara Bond Freeman, Craig A. Hanson, Charles W. Houck, and J. Gregory Smith. 2004. "The Decline of the East: The Classic to Postclassic Transition at Ek Balam, Yucatán." In *The Terminal Classic in the Maya Lowlands: Collapse, Transition, and Transformation*, ed. Arthur A. Demarest, Prudence M. Rice, and Don S. Rice, 485–516. Boulder: University Press of Colorado.

Robichaux, Hubert R. 2002. "On the Compatibility of Epigraphic, Geographic, and Archaeological Data, with a Drought-Based Explanation for the Classic Maya Collapse." *Ancient Mesoamerica* 13 (2):341–45.

Roys, Ralph L. 1972. *The Indian Background of Colonial Yucatan*. Norman: University of Oklahoma Press.

Sabloff, Jeremy A. 1973a. "Major Themes in the Past Hypotheses of the Maya Collapse." In *The Classic Maya Collapse*, ed. T. Patrick Culbert, 35–40. School of American Research Advanced Seminar Series. Albuquerque: University of New Mexico Press.

———. 1973b. "Continuity and Disruption during Terminal Late Classic Times at Seibal: Ceramic and Other Evidence." In *The Classic Maya Collapse*, ed. T. Patrick Culbert, 107–31. School of American Research Advanced Seminar Series. Albuquerque: University of New Mexico Press.

———. 1977. "Old Myths, New Myths: The Role of Sea Traders in the Development of Ancient Maya Civilization." In *The Sea in the Pre-Columbian World*, ed. Elizabeth P. Benson, 67–88. Washington, D.C.: Dumbarton Oaks.

Sabloff, Jeremy A., and E. Wyllys Andrews V, eds. 1986. *Late Lowland Maya Civilization: Classic to Postclassic*. School of American Research Advanced Seminar Series. Albuquerque: University of New Mexico Press.

Sabloff, Jeremy A., and Gordon R. Willey. 1979. "The Collapse of Maya Civilization in the Southern Lowlands: A Consideration of History and Process." *Southwestern Journal of Anthropology* 23 (4):311–36.

Sanders, William T. 1989. "Household, Lineage, and State at Eighth-Century Copan, Honduras." In *The House of the Bacabs, Copan, Honduras*, ed. David L. Webster, 89–105. Studies in Pre-Columbian Art and Archaeology, no. 29. Washington, D.C.: Dumbarton Oaks.

Santley, Robert S., Michael J. Berman, and Rani T. Alexander. 1991. "The Politicization of the Mesoamerican Ballgame and Its Implications for the Interpretation of the Distribution of Ballcourts in Central Mexico." In *The Mesoamerican Ballgame*, ed. Vernon L. Scarborough and David R. Wilcox, 3–44. Tucson: University of Arizona Press.

Schele, Linda, and David A. Freidel. 1990. *A Forest of Kings: The Untold Story of the Ancient Maya*. New York: William Morrow.

Schele, Linda, and Nikolai Grube. 1995. *Notebook for the XIX Maya Hieroglyphic Workshop at Texas: Late Classic and Terminal Classic Warfare*. Austin: Department of Art, University of Texas.

Schele, Linda, and Peter Mathews. 1991. "Royal Visits and Other Intersite Relationships among the Classic Maya." In *Classic Maya Political History: Hieroglyphic and Archaeological*

Evidence, ed. T. Patrick Culbert, 226–52. School of American Research Advanced Seminar Series. Cambridge: Cambridge University Press.

———. 1998. *The Code of Kings: The Language of Seven Sacred Maya Temples and Tombs*. New York: Scribner's.

Schele, Linda, and Mary Miller. 1986. *The Blood of Kings: Dynasty and Ritual in Maya Art*. Fort Worth, Tex.: Kimbell Art Museum.

Sharer, Robert J. 1977. "The Maya Collapse Revisited: Internal and External Perspectives." In *Social Process in Maya Prehistory: Studies in Honour of Sir Eric Thompson*, ed. Norman Hammond, 531–52. London: Academic Press.

Spinden, Herbert J. 1917. *Ancient Civilizations of Mexico and Central America*. American Museum of Natural History Handbook Series, no. 3. New York: American Museum of Natural History.

———. 1928. *Ancient Civilizations of Mexico and Central America*. 2nd ed. New York: American Museum of Natural History.

Stanton, Travis W., and M. Kathryn Brown. 2003. "Studying Warfare in Ancient Mesoamerica." In *Ancient Mesoamerican Warfare*, ed. M. Kathryn Brown and Travis W. Stanton, 1–16. Walnut Creek, Calif.: AltaMira.

Steele, Gentry, Jack D. Eaton, and A. J. Taylor. 1980. "The Skulls from Operation 2011 at Colha: A Preliminary Examination." In *The Colha Project: Second Season 1980 Interim Report*, ed. Thomas R. Hester, Jack D. Eaton, and Harry J. Shafer, 163–72. San Antonio: Center for Archaeological Research, University of Texas.

Stephens, John Lloyd. 1841. *Incidents of Travel in Central America, Chiapas and Yucatan*. 2 vols. New York: Harper.

Stuart, David. 1995. "A Study of Maya Inscriptions." PhD diss., Vanderbilt University.

———. 2000. "'The Arrival of Strangers': Teotihuacan and Tollan in Classic Maya History." In *Mesoamerica's Classic Heritage: From Teotihuacan to the Aztecs*, ed. Davíd Carrasco, Lindsay Jones, and Scott Sessions, 465–513. Boulder: University Press of Colorado.

———. 2004. "The Entering of the Day: An Unusual Date from Northern Campeche." *Mesoweb*. http://www.mesoweb.com/stuart/notes/enteringday.html.

Suhler, Charles, Traci Ardren, David Freidel, and Dave Johnstone. 2004. "The Rise and Fall of Terminal Classic Yaxuna, Yucatán, Mexico." In *The Terminal Classic in the Maya Lowlands: Collapse, Transition, and Transformation*, ed. Arthur A. Demarest, Prudence M. Rice, and Don S. Rice, 450–84. Boulder: University Press of Colorado.

Taladoire, Eric, and Benoit Colsenet. 1991. "'Bois Ton Sang, Beaumanoir': The Political and Conflictual Aspects of the Ballgame in the Northern Chiapas Area." In *The Mesoamerican Ballgame*, ed. Vernon L. Scarborough and David R. Wilcox, 161–74. Tucson: University of Arizona Press.

Taube, Karl. 2000. "The Turquoise Hearth: Fire, Self Sacrifice, and the Central Mexican Cult of War." In *Mesoamerica's Classic Heritage: From Teotihuacan to the Aztecs*, ed. Davíd Carrasco, Lindsay Jones, and Scott Sessions, 269–340. Boulder: University Press of Colorado.

Tedlock, Barbara. 1992a. *Time and the Highland Maya*. Rev. ed. Albuquerque: University of New Mexico Press.

———. 1992b. "The Road of Light: Theory and Practice of Maya Skywatching." In *The Sky in Mayan Literature*, ed. Anthony Aveni, 18–42. Oxford: Oxford University Press.

Thompson, J. Eric S. 1931. *Archaeological Investigations in the Southern Cayo District, British Honduras*. Field Museum of Natural History Anthropological Series, vol. 17, no. 2. Chicago: Field Museum of Natural History.

———. [1954] 1966. *The Rise and Fall of Maya Civilization*. 2nd ed. Norman: University of Oklahoma Press.

———. 1970. "Putun (Chontal Maya) Expansion in Yucatan and the Pasión Drainage." In *Maya History and Religion*, 3–47. Norman: University of Oklahoma Press.

Tourtellot, Gair, and Jason J. González. 2004. "The Last Hurrah: Continuity and Transformation at Seibal." In *The Terminal Classic in the Maya Lowlands: Collapse, Transition, and Transformations*, ed. Arthur A. Demarest, Prudence M. Rice, and Don S. Rice, 60–82. Boulder: University Press of Colorado.

Tozzer, Alfred M., ed. 1941. *Landa's relación de las cosas de Yucatan*. Papers of the Peabody Museum of Archaeology and Ethnology, no. 28. Cambridge, Mass.: Harvard University. Repr., New York: Kraus Reprint Co., 1966.

Webb, Malcolm C. 1964. "The Post-Classic Decline of the Peten Maya: An Interpretation in the Light of a General Theory of State Society." PhD diss., University of Michigan.

———. 1973. "The Peten Maya Decline Viewed in the Perspective of State Formation." In *The Classic Maya Collapse*, ed. T. Patrick Culbert, 367–404. School of American Research Advanced Seminar Series. Albuquerque: University of New Mexico Press.

Webster, David. 1975. "Warfare and the Origin of the State." *American Antiquity* 40 (4):464–71.

———. 1976. "On Theocracies." *American Anthropologist* 78 (4):812–27.

———. 1977. "Warfare and the Evolution of Maya Civilization." In *The Origins of Maya Civilization*, ed. Richard E. W. Adams, 335–72. Albuquerque: University of New Mexico Press.

———. 1979. "Three Walled Sites of the Northern Maya Lowlands." *Journal of Field Archaeology* 5:375–90.

———. 1985. "Surplus, Labor and Stress in Late Classic Maya Society." *Journal of Anthropological Research* 41:375–99.

———. 1993. "Study of Maya Warfare: What It Tells Us about the Maya and What It Tells Us about Maya Archaeology." In *Lowland Maya Civilization in the Eighth Century A.D.*, ed. Jeremy A. Sabloff and John S. Henderson, 415–44. Washington, D.C.: Dumbarton Oaks.

———. 1998. "Warfare and Status Rivalry: Lowland Maya and Polynesian Comparisons." In *Archaic States*, ed. Gary M. Feinman and Joyce Marcus, 311–51. Santa Fe, N.Mex.: School of American Research Press.

———. 2000. "The Not So Peaceful Civilization: A Review of Maya War." *Journal of World Prehistory* 14 (1):65–117.

———. 2002. *The Fall of the Ancient Maya: Solving the Mystery of the Maya Collapse*. London: Thames & Hudson.

Webster, David, AnnCorinne Freter, and Rebecca Storey. 2004. "Dating Copán Culture-History: Implications for the Terminal Classic and the Collapse." In *The Terminal Classic in the Maya Lowlands: Collapse, Transition, and Transformation*, ed. Arthur A. Demarest, Prudence M. Rice, and Don S. Rice, 231–59. Boulder: University Press of Colorado.

Webster, David, William T. Sanders, and Peter van Rossum. 1992. "A Simulation of Copan Population History and Its Implications." *Ancient Mesoamerica* 3 (1):185–97.

Willey, Gordon R. 1974. "The Classic Maya Hiatus: A Rehearsal for the Collapse?" In *Mesoamerican Archaeology: New Approaches*, ed. Norman Hammond, 417–44. Austin: University of Texas Press.

———. 1977. "External Influences on the Lowland Maya: 1940 and 1975 Perspectives." In *Social Process in Maya Prehistory: Studies in Honour of Sir Eric Thompson*, 57–75. London: Academic Press.

Willey, Gordon R., and Demitri B. Shimkin. 1973. "The Maya Collapse: A Summary View." In *The Classic Maya Collapse*, ed. T. Patrick Culbert, 457–501. School of American Research Advanced Seminar Series. Albuquerque: University of New Mexico Press.

Yoffee, Norman. 1988. "Orienting Collapse." In *The Collapse of Ancient States and Civilizations*, ed. Norman Yoffee and George L. Cowgill, 1–19. Tucson: University of Arizona Press.

Chapter Nine

A Crossroads of Conquerors:
Waka' and Gordon Willey's "Rehearsal for the Collapse" Hypothesis

David A. Freidel, Hector L. Escobedo, and Stanley P. Guenter

Introduction

The site of El Perú, ancient Waka', in northwestern Petén, perches on a one-hundred-meter-high escarpment overlooking the San Juan River six kilometers north of its confluence with the San Pedro Mártir—the name means "centipede place with water," and there was a pond in the center at one time. Defensible and with a water supply, Waka' was suited to be a citadel or a fort. A natural harbor on the San Juan next to Waka' evidently made it a good location for a center maintaining a naval installation capable of sending protected convoys of trade canoes along the eighty-kilometer stretch of calm river linking the interior of Petén to the Usumacinta region (see fig. 9.1). Settlement patterns and geological patterns of north-south-trending ridges suggest that a second route overland through this water-rich zone linked the Petén with southeastern Campeche and the heartland of Calakmul. This route proved particularly important in the seventh century, when Yuknoom Ch'een the Great attempted to consolidate an empire in the Southern Lowlands (Martin and Grube 2000). At a strategic crossroads, Waka' was situated to be a participant in the political, military,

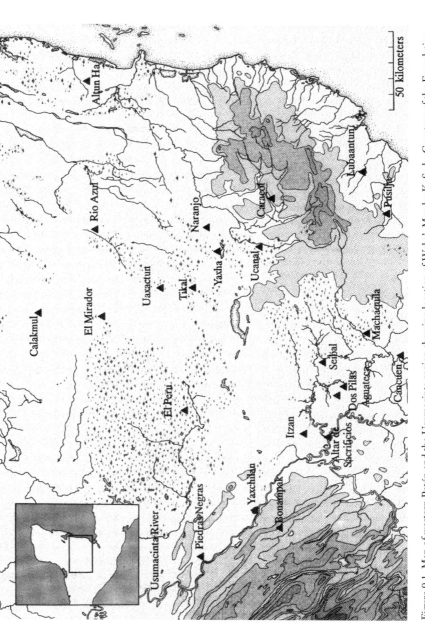

Figure 9.1. Map of western Petén and the Usumacinta region showing location of Waka'. Map by K. Sadr. Courtesy of the Foundation for Mesoamerican Studies, Inc.

and commercial dynamics of Southern Lowland Maya civilization. Preliminary research at the site supports this hypothesis and bears on Gordon Willey's seminal article about Teotihuacan-Maya relations in the Early Classic period.

Willey's Hiatus Model

"The Classic Maya Hiatus: A Rehearsal for the Collapse?" (Willey 1974) illustrates several important features of an influential and thought-provoking archaeology article: discussion of interesting patterns in evidence, timely theorizing, and bold conjecture. The essence of Willey's argument is that the historical record of public inscriptions in the Maya Lowlands registered a significant pause, or hiatus, in the middle of the Classic period, from about A.D. 534 to 593, as observed by Sylvanus G. Morley (1938–39). Tatiana Proskouriakoff noted (1950) significant changes in the style of stela portraiture after the hiatus. Robert E. Smith placed the ceramic dividing line between the Early Classic and Late Classic periods at about A.D. 600, or at the end of the hiatus (R. Smith 1955). For Willey, this pause between the Early Classic and Late Classic periods reflected real regional historical events that could be elucidated through archaeology.

Writing in 1972 during the height of the New Archaeology movement, Willey declared himself an "old archaeologist." But he based his argument on the cultural ecological core-buffer zone model (1972) of his student William Rathje, notably of the new school. And in keeping with the general aspirations of the New Archaeologists (Watson, Redman, and LeBlanc 1971), Willey tried to make his case both explicit and explanatory. Nevertheless, commensurate with his contributions to culture-historical reconstruction in the Maya case of Pre-Columbian civilization and throughout the New World, the article provides a history of the ancient Maya that combined data from carved and inscribed stone monuments with data from the archaeological record. Thirty years later that thread is gradually becoming the fabric of Classic-period archaeology in the southern Maya Lowlands.

Today, archaeological research and the revolution in the decipherment of Maya texts challenge several key features of Willey's argument. Indeed, some archaeologists now propose that the Middle Classic hiatus is a product of inscribed-monument destruction largely confined to Tikal (Harrison 1999, 119–24). We take the view that the hiatus, while not all that

Willey proposed, still exists as a regional cluster of pauses in stela dates at important royal centers between roughly A.D. 550 and 700, primarily in the central Southern Lowlands, and that this pattern registers important historical events and developmental dynamics in Maya civilization. But with the luxury of hindsight and in the wake of advances in the decipherment of texts on monuments, we have developed different explanations for these patterns. Willey thought that the production of Maya stelae was a prestige activity keyed to a general tempo of ceremonial life that was, in turn, driven by the relative prosperity or poverty of ruling elites. Pauses, in his view, registered economic hard times. He discerned related slowdowns in the construction of monumental architecture at Altar de Sacrificios, where he directed research, and at Uaxactun, following A. Ledyard Smith's publication (A. Smith 1950) on Group A. He speculated that the preliminary evidence for a slowdown at Tikal would hold up, although we now know that the hiatus-period rulers commissioned significant construction there (Jones 1991, 116).

We can point to an emerging consensus that the pauses in dated stelae of Maya sites register the deliberate destruction of monuments through warfare and sacking in the centers (see, e.g., Schele and Freidel 1990, chaps. 4–5; Sharer 1994, 210; Harrison 1999). Willey and Demitri Shimkin considered military competition as a factor in the collapse (1973, 485–86), following Robert Rands's contributions to the School of American Research seminar, but not as a factor in the hiatus. Indeed, warfare as a precollapse-period phenomenon began to gain credence only with the work of David Webster on the Becan battlements (1976, 1977), published a few years after Willey's hiatus article. Only subsequently—with the Vanderbilt research in the Petexbatún region directed by Arthur Demarest, Stephen Houston, and Juan Antonio Valdez (Demarest and Houston 1990; Demarest et al. 1997; O'Mansky and Dunning 2003); the work of Takeshi Inomata at Aguateca (2003); and the Selz Foundation Yaxuna project in Yucatán directed by David Freidel (Freidel, Suhler, and Cobos 1998; Suhler and Freidel 1998; Ambrosino, Ardren, and Stanton 2003)—did the archaeological termination patterns of war-related destruction in centers start to come into focus. However, war as a proximate cause behind the multiple hiatuses in dated stelae does not belie Willey's embrace of economy as a foundation for understanding the root causes of the varying fortunes of Maya rulers commissioning or destroying inscribed monuments.

Core-Buffer Zone Economics

As mentioned previously, Willey's views on Classic Maya economy in his article were inspired by Rathje's core-buffer zone model. Rathje's model explained the ninth-century collapse as at least partly the product of buffer zone Maya polities outcompeting core zone polities for access to outside markets for their comparable lowland products. Willey suggested that this would have happened earlier, in the Early Classic period, had it not been for a special relationship between the preeminent core area capital, Tikal, and the major highland Mexican city of the time, Teotihuacan. He conjectured that a sudden severing of Teotihuacan-related trade links may have drastically diminished Tikal's competitive edge over other Maya polities and precipitated an economic depression in the core that was analogous in some respects to the depression in the collapse period proposed by Rathje. That is why Willey saw the hiatus as a rehearsal for the collapse. But in contrast to Rathje, Willey underscored that the entire Southern Lowlands, core and periphery together, fell in the collapse period. He speculated that perhaps a new, outer buffer zone of non-Classic Mexicanized Maya might have cut off the lowland centers of the old core and buffer zones from their markets. At the very least, they were economically interdependent and went down together.

Rathje's ideas are the subject of a recent volume on Maya political economy (Masson and Freidel 2002), so we won't linger over a critique of them here. What we still agree with is the notion that the Maya elite in some significant ways managed the economic activities of their subjects. Moreover, we think that the transport of trade goods out of the core area centers of the lowlands through the peripheral polities to other parts of Mesoamerica assured the prosperity of the core polities. The movement of goods into the core capitals was equally important. But the interactions of the major lowland centers can now be understood as alliances, in some key instances forged by intermarriage, as proposed by Joyce Marcus and Clemency Coggins (Marcus 1973; Coggins 1975). And as Simon Martin and Nikolai Grube suggest (1994, 2000), these Classic-period regional alliances endured for centuries as two competing hegemonic spheres dominated by the lords of Kan, with their capital at Dzibanché and then at Calakmul, and those of Mutul, Tikal.

In the context of Willey and Rathje's political geography, one important feature of the currently discerned alliance patterns is that they integrated core area polities with those of the peripheries, usually along what appear to be critical communication and transportation routes into and out of the core area. We call these routes corridors, and they included both rivers and overland routes. While Dzibanché in southern Quintana Roo might be regarded as a site edging out onto the periphery, it was evidently a temporary sojourn of the Kan state originally centered on the vast Preclassic city of El Mirador in the core area, a position echoed by Calakmul some forty kilometers to the northwest of El Mirador. So we see the dominant states of the Classic-period alliances in the core, while vassals, clients, and some relatively independent polities were in the periphery. This domination had a fundamentally military character, as is evident from an emerging pattern of chronic warfare beginning well before the period of the hiatuses and continuing through the collapse period. Sadly, then, the artful persuasion of Rathje's advanced core states selling their periphery clients on high culture must be discarded in favor of the banalities of brute force. But armed coercion must have been linked to mutual interest in trade and commerce. It is hard to imagine trade caravans in Classic Mesoamerica moving securely without the kind of military backup implied for the Postclassic- and Contact-period professional traders, particularly in light of the clear evidence of endemic war in the Maya case. The whole matter of the Classic-period merchant organizations, and their relationships with nobility, is ripe for review, in our opinion.

The Teotihuacan Factor Today

Returning to Willey's model for the hiatus, we offer the following update. Teotihuacan allied with several key lowland sites throughout the region, not just with Tikal. Copán and Río Azul were among an emerging constellation of strategic participants in this long-distance relationship. Tres Islas, on the southern Río Pasión corridor, and El Perú/Waka', on the western San Pedro corridor, are coming into focus as other nodes in Teotihuacan's Lowland Maya alliances. So rather than shoring up the core state of Tikal, as Willey proposed, Teotihuacan was somehow involved in the alliance networks linking the core state of Tikal to key polities on the corridors and in the peripheries.

Teotihuacan's rulers had both military and commercial interests in the Maya Lowlands. One of this chapter's authors, Stanley Guenter, accepts

David Stuart's hypothesis (2000) that the Teotihuacan warrior Siyaj K'ak' conquered Tikal in A.D. 378 and placed a new king on the throne there, Yax Nuun Ayiin, the son of Spearthrower Owl. Stuart believes Spearthrower Owl to have been the king of Teotihuacan. This king apparently sired Yax Nuun Ayiin by a royal Maya woman from Tikal named Une Balam K'awil. The other two authors of this chapter find such an outright conquest logistically implausible. We favor the hypothesis of military and commercial alliances between factions of Maya nobility and Teotihuacan *pochteca*-like military leaders intent on commanding the trade between the Maya Lowlands and Mexico. This is not to diminish the drama or legendary impact of Siyaj K'ak's incursion into and subsequent military exploits in the Maya region.

We are trying to investigate this matter at Waka', dubbed El Perú in the modern literature, seventy-four kilometers west of Tikal and on a major western corridor to Mexico. Stela 15 at Waka', as noted by Stuart (2000), recounts the arrival of Siyaj K'ak' there, which occurred eight days before he arrived in Tikal. At Waka' we have reassembled the fragments of the all-glyphic Stela 15, on which Siyaj K'ak's arrival is recorded, and can advance the arguments somewhat beyond those given by Stuart based on the *Corpus of Maya Hieroglyphic Inscriptions* field drawings (see fig. 9.2). Like the famous Stela 31 at Tikal, Waka' Stela 15 displays an unusually long text. The history is retrospective and is written in 415 by a successor of the Waka' king who received Siyaj K'ak' in 378, some forty years after the event. From the discovery of new monument fragments, we can confirm Stuart's supposition that the primary event is indeed an arrival, with all of the implications of that kind of event as outlined by Martin and Grube (2000). But there are other, more obscure events that follow on the text, including some action by Siyaj K'ak' at a "*wi-te*'-place," perhaps accompanied by the king of Waka', K'inich B'alam. Given the distinctive nature of the wi-te' glyphs, we surmise that this is a reference to a Wite' Naah, a founder's house of the kind whose introduction into Maya royal rhetoric coincides with the establishment of the New Order (Martin and Grube 2000) and Teotihuacan political presence. Following this event is another featuring K'inich B'alam of Waka', clearly indicating that the Waka' king was acting in concert with Siyaj K'ak' as, we presume, a willing vassal and ally. The main text is framed on the sides by cartouched texts listing honored earlier kings of Waka', underscoring both the continuity of government in the city and the vital nature of the affiliation with Siyaj K'ak' to the succeeding ruler there.

Figure 9.2. Photograph of reassembled fragments of Stela 15 at Waka'. Photograph by Phillip Hofstetter.

From the text on Stela 15, we feel that K'inich B'alam of Waka' was quite likely acknowledged as an important ally by Siyaj K'ak' and that the latter's arrival at Waka' signaled formal and probably voluntary incorporation of this corridor kingdom into the New Order hegemony even before the fate of Tikal was sealed eight days later. That the descendant king of Waka' forty years later raised Stela 15 celebrating this arrival event—and the wi-te'-place event carried out by Siyaj K'ak' and K'inich B'alam—suggests how central the alliance was to the politics of his realm.

Other relevant inscriptions and artifacts suggest that Waka' continued as a participant in the Teotihuacan-affiliated hegemony for perhaps a century or more. One of these is the famous back-mirror from Costa Rica. The text, as deciphered by David Mora Marin, Marc Zender, and Stanley Guenter, describes a vital relationship between Waka' and the neighboring kingdom to the east, El Zodz. The text begins by describing the mirror itself as a *pujib'* (Toltec/Teotihuacan item). Indeed, back-mirrors such as this are items of regalia regularly found with images of Teotihuacan-affiliated individuals. The text continues by identifying the item's owner as one Siyaj Chan Ahk, a lord of the Pa' Chan (Split Sky) kingdom. This emblem glyph is one of the most common known from the Classic period, being held by the kings of Yaxchilán, El Zodz, and Uaxactun. While this mirror-back has previously been associated with Uaxactun, it almost certainly originally belonged to a king of El Zodz, as the name of the owner's father, Chak Chay Tz'i', is the same as that of a lord of El Zodz named upon a wooden lintel found at the site. This same lord is also named upon a beautiful blackware vessel currently in Australia. It should be noted, however, that the Chak Chay Tz'i' named upon the wooden lintel is not the same individual that owned the Costa Rican mirror-back, as the lintel dates stylistically to about a century and a half after the mirror-back.

The mirror-back text concludes by stating that the item was a *sih* (gift) of K'inich B'alam, the lord of Waka'. With this information we can see that in the wake of Siyaj K'ak's arrival at his city, K'inich B'alam was cementing his position in the New Order by gifting Teotihuacan-related regalia to his neighbors along the trade route between distant Teotihuacan and the hub of Teotihuacan's imperial alliance in the Maya region, Tikal. We see Teotihuacan's strategy, which unfolded through diplomatic alliances and conquests, as consisting of an attempt to control strong points along the major trade routes between the Maya region and central Mexico. The Costa Rican mirror-back indicates that El Zodz, between Tikal and Waka', was a member in this association.

To the west of Waka' was the Classic-period Wa-Bird kingdom that has recently been identified with the archaeological site of Santa Elena Balancán. While only the most cursory exploration of this large and important site has been carried out, it can hardly be coincidental that in texts at Palenque referring to this kingdom, its emblem glyph is once replaced by the face of the Teotihuacan storm god. Palenque itself abounds in

Teotihuacan iconography, and Simon Martin has located the name Siyaj K'ak' on a pier of the palace, which may tie this western gateway city into the Teotihuacan alliance. East of Tikal we see two major trade routes moving along major rivers to the Caribbean Sea. Directly east of Tikal, the city of Yaxhá is located on the lake of the same name, which was formed by the same fault line that gave rise to Lake Petén Itzá in the center of Petén, the San Pedro Martír river leading west, and the Belize River flowing east. Stela 11 of Yaxhá provides strong evidence of that city's inclusion within the same alliance as Tikal and Waka', as it depicts a Teotihuacan warrior complete with spear and shield, in central Mexican fashion, frontally.

Draining the *bajos* northeast of Tikal, the Río Azul/Río Hondo provided another major route of trade from central Petén to the Caribbean. Sitting astride the headwaters of this river, the site of Río Azul was another member of the Teotihuacan alliance. Stela 1 from that site bears the name of Siyaj K'ak' and carries the date of 396. Río Azul was one of the wealthiest kingdoms of the Early Classic period, and its pyramids tower over those of its contemporaries, including Tikal. While much of Río Azul's wealth came from the fertile farmlands of the northeast Petén, we believe much of it also derived from the trade route it controlled. Río Azul had extensive foreign contacts during its florescence in the fifth century, and a princess from the kingdom may have even married the king of Tikal. Río Azul's Sorcerer King is even mentioned on a contemporary monument at distant Copán, and the famous chocolate pot with the twist-off lid, from Río Azul's Tomb 19, may have originally held chocolate from that city. The glyphs on this vessel state that it was for holding *witik kakaw*—"witik" being the ancient name of Copán.

While this system of allied kingdoms was centered on Tikal, this city was not the capital of an Early Classic Maya "empire." Though Tikal does appear to have controlled extensive territory in the central Petén, none of the major kingdoms described previously record their subjection to Tikal. Instead, they all make clear their vassal status in relation to Siyaj K'ak' and the lord for whom he worked, the probable Teotihuacan ruler Spearthrower Owl. For example, on a set of looted earflares, Río Azul's Sorcerer King is said to have been the "vassal lord of" (*yajaw*) the western emperor Spearthrower Owl. He was not a subject of Tikal, to which the amount and the size of construction at Río Azul attest.

Siyaj K'ak' at Waka'

Returning to Waka', we note that this site also shows absolutely no evidence of subjection to Tikal. Not coincidentally, the contemporary monuments of Waka' are much larger than those of Tikal. In addition, the quality of monumental art at Waka' is in no way inferior to that of the major centers of the central Petén. Stela 9, the lower fragments of which were found in front of the Southeast Acropolis of Waka', provides one of the best examples of Early Classic art from the site. Apparently, the fifth century was one of the golden ages of Waka', a time when the site's relationship with Teotihuacan allowed its kings to present themselves as the political equals of the neighboring kings of Tikal.

At the time of its discovery, Waka' Stela 15 lay shattered in several large pieces on one of the plazas, with the base reset in Terminal Classic times. Nearby lay the fragments of Stela 16, another Early Classic monument. Unfortunately, this monument has suffered a lot of damage from both nature and humans. Nevertheless, we have managed to recover an accession date of 458 and the probable dedication date of the stela, 465. From Ian Graham's drawings and our own initial field inspection, we could see that the individual on Stela 16 was carrying a distinctive owl-headed scepter and wearing a Teotihuacan-style headdress (see fig. 9.3). Closer scrutiny of the monument reinforces the notion that this individual is dressed as a Teotihuacano. What the *Corpus* drawing shows as clusters of long beads or shells along the base of the collar, for example, we discern as pecten shells. The assembled regalia are almost identical to the collar worn by Yax Nuun Ayiin in his flanking portraits on Stela 31 at Tikal. The *Corpus* drawing hints at the presence of a mouth mask like that seen on Tikal Stela 32 and on the image decorating the shield carried by Yax Nuun Ayiin on Stela 31. Now that the stela fragments are reassembled, we can also report that the individual is wearing knee garters and sandal tassels typical of Teotihuacan apparel in the fourth century. The strange and eroded girdle ornament appears to consist of a kind of woven shield flanked by tassels extending out at angles, similar to Teotihuacan pectoral assemblages.

The most important differences between the *Corpus* drawing and our own field sketches and photographs lie in the disposition of the arms. We see a glovelike right hand holding the owl scepter, with a clear depiction of

Figure 9.3. Drawing of Stela 16 by Sarah Sage, after field drawings by David Freidel and photographs.

the upper arm and elbow preserved next to the slender waist of the individual. The left elbow and arm are also clear. Wrapping around the rectangular object on the left side is the badly eroded outline of the forearm and a hand in the crab-claw position. While the rendering is a bit awkward, we think that the individual is holding the long, rectangular object in question as a bundle. The nature of this bundle is central to our overall interpretation of Stela 16. At the top, the bundle is broken off, but it has a series of rectangular vertical elements rising from three large dots. The *Corpus* drawing showed these elements, along with striations along the body of the bundle that we can also see. We hypothesize that this bundle is of a particular kind depicted at Teotihuacan as carried by rulers or priests. Such bundles feature featherlike fire symbols on top and sometimes show water droplets coming off them below. Karl Taube has identified (2003) the striated, crossed bundles of the Wite' Naah glyph as torches, and the Wite' Naah itself as a fire shrine.

These fire shrines, the Wite' Naah structures, may have been built at a site after the arrival of Siyaj K'ak' or other Teotihuacan-related personages, and such buildings have been identified archaeologically and iconographically at Copán and other sites (Taube 2003, 278). We have yet to identify the Wite' Naah at Waka', but as this edifice is mentioned on at least two Early Classic monuments, we have every reason to believe one was built at the site. We believe that the Teotihuacan-garbed individual on Stela 16 is carrying a fiery torch-bundle to light the sacred fire at Waka's wi-te'-shrine.

This brings us back to the ceremony carried out by Siyaj K'ak' at the Waka' wi-te'-place, as declared on Stela 15. A recent reexamination of the text to the right of this figure on the face of the stela has revealed new details. A number of mentions of an individual named K'inich B'alam Chan Ahk appear in the text, although the only clear reference is in a parentage statement with K'inich B'alam being the father. It seems quite likely that this is the famous K'inich B'alam who received Siyaj K'ak' at Waka' in 378. We cannot yet pin down the name of the king who commissioned this monument, although a number of names do appear on the monument, including Dragon Jaguar, who may be the son of K'inich B'alam, as the latter name immediately follows that of Dragon Jaguar on the right side text, in a position that usually corresponds to parentage statements.

The text to the right of the face of the figure states that on a day 18 Uo or Sip *tz'apaj u lakamtuun Siyaj* . . . (was planted the stela of Siyaj . . .). The bottom part of the glyph containing "Siyaj" is badly damaged (see fig. 9.4). Guenter believes those parts remaining are quite consistent with a reading of "K'ak'." Freidel, as an iconographer, sees an alternative; namely, that what is preserved depicts the striated shaft and circle marking a burning dart such as that wielded by king K'inich Yax K'uk' Mo' on Altar Q at Copán (Taube 2003, fig. 13.1b). This unusual substitution for the fire glyph strengthens the argument for a Siyaj K'ak' connection, as does another rendering of Siyaj K'ak's name on Stela 15. In this case, it is clearly a reference to the great warrior, for he is declared *kaloomte'*, supreme warlord (see fig. 9.5). The glyph standing for fire in this case is quite clearly a Teotihuacan-style dart (see fig. 9.6; see also Taube 2003, fig. 13.1 for examples). We believe that the Stela 16 text suggests that this most Teotihuacano of portraits from Waka' is likely that of Siyaj K'ak' himself.

Significantly, Stela 16 dates to almost a century after Siyaj K'ak's arrival at Waka', and if our interpretation is correct, the portrait on this stela is posthumous. While such monuments are rare in the Maya record, they are not unheard of, and we find appealing the notion that this is a depiction of the great kaloomte'. To date, no definite portraits of this most important individual in Early Classic Maya history have been identified, making this identification all the more intriguing. Curiously, at the time that Stela 16 was carved, Tikal had already moved away from depicting Teotihuacan garb, and there is little evidence at that site for continued strong Teotihuacan cultural traditions into the late fifth century. Tikal appears to have been trying to assert its independence in the late fifth century and establish itself as the capital of its own miniempire in Petén. Tikal's 486 war against the kingdom of Masul, possibly present-day Naachtun, may be relevant in this respect. Living in the shadow of Tikal, the smaller centers along the major trade routes, such as Waka', likely highlighted their Teotihuacan connections for a longer period as a means of maintaining their independence from such an aggressive giant. For Waka' and the other small centers integrated into the Teotihuacan alliance, the period of the late fourth and early fifth centuries must have been a golden age of relative independence, when the imperial aspirations of larger centers such as Tikal were kept in check.

Stelae 15 and 16 at Waka' register the impact of the entrada of Siyaj K'ak' and the New Order on peripheral centers in the western region of the lowlands. The Proyecto Arqueológico Waka' is only in its second field season, but we already have evidence that the center was monumental in

Figure 9.4. Detail of Stela 16 showing
the name Siyaj K'ak'. The central fragment of K'ak' as a fire dart is preserved.

the Early Classic period. We have not found clear material documentation
of a Teotihuacan presence beyond some green obsidian and a new carved
stela, number 40, which has a base panel that seems to present a variant of
the butterfly war god of that city. A newly published photograph of a
looted vase in the Kerr corpus is apparently an Early Classic royal vessel
from Waka' with a new king's name and images of the butterfly war god.
There is one open tomb in a *plazuela* adjacent to the Southeastern Acropolis that might have held such offerings. In the meantime, we remain alert

Figure 9.5. Detail of Stela 15 showing glyphs Kaloomte' Siyaj K'ak'. K'ak' is written as a fire dart.

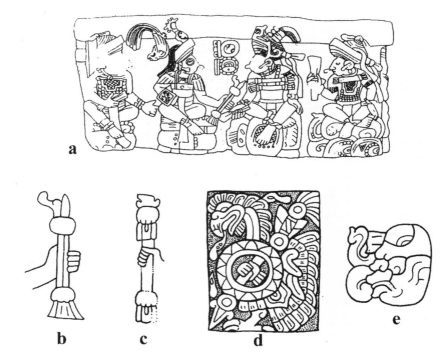

Figure 9.6. Examples of Teotihuacan-style fire darts from Copán. Drawings by Barbara Fash and Karl Taube. Reprinted by permission from Taube 2003.

to the prospect of finding the kind of evidence reported from Tikal, Copán, Río Azul, and other investigated participants in the Early Classic Teotihuacan alliance.

The Legacy of Teotihuacan in Hegemonic States

Whether or not the Teotihuacanos conquered Lowland Maya cities, they were certainly participants in the forging of major military hegemonies in the lowlands during the late fourth and fifth centuries A.D. We see such hegemonic alliances as dominated locally, at least, by Tikal in the Central Lowlands, by Copán in the southeastern periphery, by Río Azul in the northeastern corridor, and probably by Oxkintok in the far northwestern periphery. While Palenque is a logical candidate for another Teotihuacan-affiliated Maya capital because of its later alliance affiliations, we have no direct confirmation of this archaeologically. Other kingdoms, like Waka' on the western corridor and Tres Islas on the southern corridor, may have also played important roles, but that remains to be elucidated by the ongoing Vanderbilt work at Cancuén, the successor capital of Tres Islas, and by the Proyecto Arqueológico El Perú-Waka'.

The dynasts of Kan evidently both resisted and challenged this Teotihuacan alliance of Maya kingdoms (Martin and Grube 1994, 2000). The archaeological research at Dzibanché may help clarify this possibility. So far, the preliminary reports evince some Teotihuacan-style artifacts in precious materials but do not show the kind of influence in texts, architecture, and ceramic styles seen in the case of Tikal and Copán. At Calakmul, which became the later Classic capital of the Kan court, the relatively rich Early Classic tombs contain typically Lowland Maya materials rather than Teotihuacan-style ones. Perhaps as early as A.D. 510, and certainly by the mid-sixth century, the Kan state was building an alternative hegemonic alliance. The Tikal hiatus, we now know, was precipitated by the defeat of Tikal in A.D. 562 by the kingdom of Caracol in alliance with the lords of Kan. Subsequently, the Calakmul state under Yuhknoom Ch'een the Great would become the capital of a hegemonic alliance that dominated the seventh-century lowlands. The Kan kingdom of the Classic period appears to have been a continuation of the major Preclassic lowland kingdom of El Mirador, so its reemergence as a power was likely not simply a response to the Teotihuacan alliance, but also a recovery of traditional vassals and clients, particularly those interested in resisting incorporation into the new international order. So in contrast to the general view in the time Willey was writing, the consensus now is that there were minimally two great alliance networks in the Classic lowlands.

The military character of these alliances suggests to us that they served not only to move trade into and out of the lowlands, but also to extract wealth as tributes from vassals and clients and bring it into the courts of the dominant rulers. Some of the centers listed previously, Tikal and Copán in particular, have yielded some spectacularly rich royal tombs from the era of the Teotihuacan alliance. The Early Classic tombs of Río Azul, while mostly looted, were evidently just as well stocked. We have few examples of coeval tombs from vassals and clients, but if we encounter Early Classic tombs at Waka', we hope to test the idea that vassals paid heavy tributes. We would expect the tombs to be relatively modest in their furniture. Although the peripheral center of Altun Ha boasts a rich tomb from the Early Classic, Altun Ha's dynasts are not listed as clients, vassals, or allies of any core sites or of Teotihuacan—despite the notable Teotihuacan cache found there above a very early Early Classic royal tomb. Indeed, Altun Ha appears to have been one of the independent kingdoms of the periphery assiduously avoiding such relationships, for it raised no stelae, the common medium for publicly declaring relationships. On the Kan alliance side, Dzibanché has one quite elaborate Early Classic tomb, but its contents have not been reported in any detail. The Early Classic tombs of Calakmul are quite rich and show a particular propensity for finely wrought, precious stone mosaic funerary masks.

For the Late Classic period, we have some examples of the proposed pattern of wealth extraction by the hegemonic capitals. The tomb of Ruler 2 at Dos Pilas is rather impoverished considering that this king's father captured the king of Tikal and that Dos Pilas was a vital ally of Calakmul. The other tombs found by the Petexbatún project were equally unimpressive when compared to the Late Classic royal tombs of Tikal and Calakmul. One important test of our ideas would be the tomb of Balaj Chan K'awiil, the greatest Dos Pilas king. We predict that when it is found and recorded, its contents will pale in comparison to those of the tombs of Jasaw Chan K'awiil and Yik'in Chan K'awiil of Tikal. Dos Pilas commanded the Pasión River, part of what Arthur Demarest and Federico Fahsen recently declared (2003) was a jade trail to Mexico, and yet so far, the tombs do not evince this command. Farther down the posited river-based jade trail of the western periphery, the rulers of Piedras Negras were also clients of Calakmul in the Late Classic, and the tombs there are likewise surprisingly meager in their furniture. Caracol, despite an enormous abundance of tombs, royal and otherwise, has no exceptionally rich ones preserved in the record—although the extensive looting of tombs there makes this pattern somewhat problematic. As mentioned, at Waka' we hope to discover royal tombs to test this pattern further. We can say at this point that the stelae of the first Late Classic king to ally with Calakmul, K'inich B'alam the Long-Lived (portrayed on Stela 33), are not as impressive as the one well-preserved stela (number 34) portraying his wife, Lady K'ab'il, a princess of the Calakmul royal house. So if we are lucky enough to find the tomb of this woman and that of her husband or other Waka' kings, we would predict that her tomb will be the richest one since she would represent Calakmul there.

Thus, the alliances moved tribute as well as trade, warriors as well as merchants. The multiple hiatuses of the mid-sixth through seventh centuries were the product, we think, of repeated clashes between kingdoms struggling for control of trade and tribute flowing along the rivers and the footpaths of the Maya Lowlands. If we are right, then one way to measure the viability of the hypothesis of a Teotihuacan conquest of Maya capitals is to look at the tombs of the proposed vassals relative to those of Teotihuacan. As mentioned earlier, the lowland allies of Teotihuacan seemed to be enjoying the kind of wealth we might expect to flow out of their hands and into the buildings of Teotihuacan. This would support the notion of collaboration with Maya lords rather than their outright conquest. Contrast this prosperity with the impoverished tomb of K'inich Waaw, the twenty-second successor to the Tikal throne, who ruled after the A.D. 562 defeat of Tikal by Caracol and Kan, and who presided over much of the hiatus period there. Despite his successful efforts to commission new buildings and to project Tikal back into the southern corridor of the Petexbatún, his mourners still had meager access to the moveable wealth siphoned off by years of tribute to enemies.

Conclusion

The issues raised by Willey are still timely, controversial, and intriguing. Political economy, the foundation of Willey's arguments, must now be regarded through the statecraft of warfare. But it is still a foundation for our own views of Classic Maya history. In this brief consideration, we have had to pass over the critical linkages between the documented trade in precious materials and the more elusive trade in perishables like cotton textiles and cacao, lowland commodities highly prized in central Mexico. Moreover, projects like Arthur Demarest's at Cancuén, on the southern corridor, are documenting the vertical integration of court and commoner economies that characterized at least some Maya kingdoms. As we work at Waka', a node on the western corridor, we are alert to such possibilities. So far, we have found abundant evidence that the final, Terminal Classic occupants of Waka' both sacked and rebuilt there. They enjoyed access to far-flung trade still flowing on the San Pedro River in the wake of collapse of the royal court. Some of them even inscribed square-cartouche glyphs like those Willey saw at Seibal, harbingers of his barbarians from the outer buffer zone to the west. And yes, in the last analysis, the hiatuses of the Classic period were likely early acts in the same destructive tragedy that eventually culminated in the sacking of Tikal, Calakmul, and their clients in the lowlands. Willey never lost sight of the contingency of Maya development on ties to the rest of Mesoamerica, but we are presently convinced that the outside markets for lowland products persisted from the Classic into the Postclassic and that the collapse, along with its rehearsals, must be ultimately explained as a failure of the Southern Lowland Maya themselves to either unite by force of arms or to find alternatives in lasting peace.

References

Ambrosino, James N., Traci Ardren, and Travis W. Stanton. 2003. "The History of Warfare at Yaxuna." In *Ancient Mesoamerican Warfare*, ed. M. Kathyrn Brown and Travis W. Stanton, 109–23. Walnut Creek, Calif.: AltaMira.

Coggins, Clemency C. 1975. *Painting and Drawing Styles at Tikal: A Historical and Iconographic Reconstruction*. Ann Arbor, Mich.: University Microfilms.

Demarest, Arthur A., and Federico Fahsen F. 2003. "Nuevos datos e interpretaciones de los reinos occidentales del clasico tardio: Hacia una vision sintetica de la historia Pasion/Usumacinta." In *XVI simposio de investigaciones arqueológicas en Guatemala, 2002*, ed. Juan Pedro LaPorte, Héctor Escobedo, and Bárbara Arroyo.

Demarest, Arthur A., and Stephen D. Houston. 1990. *Proyecto arqueológico regional Petexbatun: Informe preliminar no. 2, segunda temporada 1990*. Nashville, Tenn.: Vanderbilt University / Guatemala City: IDAEH.

Demarest, Arthur A., Matt O'Mansky, Claudia Woolley, Dirk van Tuerenhout, Takeshi Inomata, Joel Palka, and Héctor Escobedo. 1997. "Classic Maya Defensive Systems and Warfare in the Petexbatun Region: Archaeological Evidence and Interpretations." *Ancient Mesoamerica* 8:229–54.

Fahsen, Federico. 1988. *A New Early Classic Text from Tikal.* Research Reports on Ancient Maya Writing, no. 17. Washington, D.C.: Center for Maya Research.

Freidel, David A., Charles K. Suhler, and Rafael Cobos Palma. 1998. "Termination Deposits at Yauxna: Detecting the Historical in Archaeological Contexts." In *The Sowing and the Dawning: Termination, Dedication, and Transformation in the Archaeological and Ethnographic Record of Mesoamerica,* ed. Shirley B. Mock, 135–44. Albuquerque: University of New Mexico Press.

Grube, Nikolai, and Simon Martin. 2000. *Notebook for the XXIV Maya Hieroglyphic Workshop at Texas: Tikal and Its Neighbors,* ed. Phil Wanyerka, 1–178. Austin: Department of Art, University of Texas.

Hansen, Richard D. 2004. "El Mirador Guatemala: El apogeo del Preclasico en el area Maya." *Arqueología Mexicana* 11 (66):28–33.

Harrison, Peter D. 1999. *The Lords of Tikal: Rulers of an Ancient Maya City.* London: Thames & Hudson.

Inomata, Takeshi. 2003. "Warfare, Destruction, and Abandonment: The Fall of the Classic Maya Center of Aguateca, Guatemala." In *The Archaeology of Settlement Abandonment in Middle America,* ed. Takeshi Inomata and Ronald W. Webb, 43–60. Salt Lake City: University of Utah Press.

Jones, Christopher. 1991. "Cycles of Growth at Tikal." In *Classic Maya Political History: Hieroglyphic and Archaeological Evidence,* ed. T. Patrick Culbert, 102–27. School of American Research Advanced Seminar Series. Cambridge: Cambridge University Press.

Marcus, Joyce. 1973. "Territorial Organization of the Lowland Classic Maya." *Science,* June 1, 911–16.

Martin, Simon, and Nikolai Grube. 1994. "Evidence for Macro-Political Organization amongst the Classic Maya Lowland States." London and Bonn.

———. 2000. *Chronicle of the Maya Kings and Queens: Deciphering the Dynasties of the Ancient Maya.* London: Thames & Hudson.

Masson, Marilyn A., and David A. Freidel, eds. 2002. *Ancient Maya Political Economies.* Walnut Creek, Calif.: AltaMira.

Morley, Sylvanus G. 1938–39. *The Inscriptions of Peten.* 5 vols. Carnegie Institution of Washington Publication 437. Washington, D.C.: Carnegie Institution of Washington.

O'Mansky, Matt, and Nicholas P. Dunning. 2003. "Settlement and Late Classic Political Disintegration in the Petexbatun Region, Guatemala." In *The Terminal Classic in the Maya Lowlands: Collapse, Transition, and Transformation,* ed. Arthur A. Demarest, Prudence M. Rice, and Don S. Rice, 83–101. Boulder: University Press of Colorado.

Proskouriakoff, Tatiana. 1950. *A Study of Classic Maya Sculpture.* Carnegie Institution of Washington Publication 593. Washington, D.C.: Carnegie Institution of Washington.

Rathje, William L. 1972. "Praise the Gods and Pass the Metates: A Hypothesis of the Development of Lowland Rainforest Civilizations in Mesoamerica." In *Contemporary Archaeology: A Guide to Theory and Contributions,* ed. Mark P. Leone. Carbondale: Southern Illinois University Press.

Satterthwaite, Linton. 1958. "Problem of Abnormal Stela Placements at Tikal and Else-where." In *Tikal Reports Numbers 1–4*, 61–83. Philadelphia: University Museum, University of Pennsylvania.

Satterthwaite, Linton, Vivian L. Broman, and William A. Haviland. 1961. "Miscellaneous Investigations: Excavations near Fragment 1 of Stela 17, with Observations on Stela P34 and Miscellaneous Stone 25; Excavation of Stela 25, Fragment 1; Excavation of Stela 27; Excavation of Stela 28, Fragment 1." In *Tikal Reports 5–10*, 149–70. Philadelphia: University Museum, University of Pennsylvania.

Schele, Linda, and David A. Freidel. 1990. *A Forest of Kings: The Untold Story of the Ancient Maya*. New York: William Morrow.

Smith, A. Ledyard. 1950. *Uaxactun, Guatemala: Excavations of 1931–1937*. Carnegie Institution of Washington Publication 588. Washington, D.C.: Carnegie Institution of Washington.

Smith, Robert E. 1955. *Ceramic Sequence at Uaxactun, Guatemala*. 2 vols. Middle American Research Institute Publication 20. New Orleans: Tulane University.

Stuart, David. 2000. "'The Arrival of Strangers': Teotihuacan and Tollan in Classic Maya History." In *Mesoamerica's Classic Heritage: From Teotihuacan to the Aztecs*, ed. Davíd Carrasco, Lindsay Jones, and Scott Sessions, 465–514. Boulder: University Press of Colorado.

Suhler, Charles K., and David A. Freidel. 1998. "Life and Death in a Maya War Zone." *Archaeology* 51 (3):28–34.

Taube, Karl. 2003. "Structure 1-L-16 and Its Early Classic Antecedents: Fire and the Evocation and Resurrection of K'inich Yax K'uk' Mo.'" In *Understanding Early Classic Copan*, ed. Ellen E. Bell, Marcello A. Canuto, and Robert J. Sharer, 265–95. Philadephia: University of Pennsylvania Press.

Watson, Patty Jo, Steven A. LeBlanc, and Charles L. Redman. 1971. *Explanation in Archaeology: An Explicitly Scientific Approach*. New York: Columbia University Press.

Webster, David. 1976. *Defensive Earthworks at Becan, Campeche, Mexico: Implications for Maya Warfare*. Middle American Research Institute Publication 41. New Orleans: Tulane University.

———. 1977. "Warfare and the Evolution of Maya Civilization." In *The Origins of Maya Civilization*, ed. Richard E. W. Adams, 335–72. School of American Research Advanced Seminar Series. Albuquerque: University of New Mexico Press.

Willey, Gordon R. 1974. "The Classic Maya Hiatus: A 'Rehearsal' for the Collapse?" In *Mesoamerican Archaeology: New Approaches*, ed. Norman Hammond, 417–30. London: Duckworth.

Willey, Gordon R., and Demitri B. Shimkin. 1973. "The Maya Collapse: A Summary View." In *The Classic Maya Collapse*, ed. T. Patrick Culbert, 457–500. School of American Research Advanced Seminar Series. Albuquerque: University of New Mexico Press.

Chapter Ten

Culture Heroes and Feathered Serpents:
The Contribution of Gordon R. Willey
to the Study of Ideology

Patricia A. McAnany

I cannot be satisfied to believe that we have all of the worthwhile answers about human cultural behavior in the data of subsistence, demography, war, trade, or the processes of social class differentiation" (Willey 1976, 213). With these words, Gordon R. Willey summed up his ambitious foray into the ideological underpinnings of the mythico-historical figure of Ce Acatl Topiltzin Quetzalcoatl (One Reed, Our Prince, Green-Feathered Serpent). For a scholar who generally stayed close to his data and prided himself on having published his findings on every site that he ever excavated, Willey was making a decided departure from business as usual with his 1976 article entitled "Mesoamerican Civilization and the Idea of Transcendence." In this essay published in the journal *Antiquity*, Professor Willey synthesized information from disparate ethnohistorical sources to evaluate the significance of the historical personage Topiltzin Quetzalcoatl—a legendary ruler of the Early Postclassic highland capital of Tula— in light of the concept of ideological transcendence. As in many of his other writings, in this article, Willey sought to place Mesoamerica on par with Old World civilizations and, in this case, the widely acknowledged transcendent movements of Judaism, Buddhism, and Jainism, among others.

Rather than hold his ideas close to his vest, Gordon Willey boldly proposed that the antiwar and anti–human sacrifice ethic embraced by Topiltzin Quetzalcoatl (TQ) transcended the aggressive religious-political charters espoused by most Mesoamerican states in the wake of the dissolution of Teotihuacan. According to various ethnohistorical accounts (see Nicholson 2001 for a comprehensive treatment of sources), TQ's transcendent ethos ultimately was defeated by darker forces. Even after TQ was vanquished, however, his impact on later Mesoamericans can hardly be underestimated, as his putative reappearance as a deified ruler has been cited as a factor in the military success of the Spanish conquistador Hernán Cortés. Noting comparable cases of transcendent movements in other parts of the world (particularly those presented in Schwartz 1975), Willey emphasized (1976, 206) that transcendent movements tend to appear during times of civilizational crisis. He further suggested that the transcendent ideology of TQ was incorporated into an ethos of mercantile activity and initially may have spread throughout Mesoamerica by what Willey referred to as "peaceful processes of penetration" (1976, 209).

Three decades later, what can be said of this thought-provoking essay? Written during the heyday of processual archaeology, the essay placed ideology and historical contingency front and center and, in doing so, did not win accolades for Willey beyond his core of Harvard graduate students. This fact was highlighted by Glyn Daniel (editor of *Antiquity* in 1976), who introduced Willey's article with the epithet "courageous." To further place this contribution in temporal perspective, consider that Kent Flannery's immensely popular *Early Mesoamerican Village* also was published in 1976. Flannery's classic parable of three archaeological personalities—Skeptical Graduate Student, Real Mesoamerican Archaeologist, and Great Synthesizer (1976, 2–4)—aptly characterized the tension between traditional culture-historians and "counter-culture" processualists that was prevalent within Americanist archaeology during the 1970s. Ideology was not exactly on the archaeological radar screen during the first half of an era that has been characterized as the "Modern Period" in archaeological research (Willey and Sabloff 1993, 214–41). Given the precocious nature of this essay on transcendence, a historical exegesis of the larger intellectual milieu is warranted in order to place Gordon Willey's contribution in perspective. Following a discussion of temporal trends in the study of ideology, I shift focus to Mesoamerica, Topiltzin Quetzalcoatl, and the feathered serpent deity. One can legitimately ask whether, given the accumulation of new data from both the Mexican Highlands and the Maya Lowlands, we are now in a better position to evaluate the impact of this cultural icon on the post-Teotihuacan Mesoamerican world. In order to achieve fine-grained focus, I include a case study from the Sibun River valley of the Terminal Classic Maya Lowlands, where the feathered serpent deity appears to have played an influential role.

Study of Ideology as a Courageous Enterprise

Willey opens his essay on transcendence with a soft critique of the reluctance of archaeologists to consider ideology as anything but derivative of a "first cause" materialist matrix (1976, 205). This same critique later would be presented in a hardened form by Geoffrey Conrad and Arthur Demarest in *Religion and Empire* (1984, 3) and crystallize into a programmatic condemnation of processual archaeology by Ian Hodder and followers (see, e.g., Hodder 1982). Ironically, one of the first manifestos of processual archaeology introduced a conceptual category of artifacts explicitly labeled as ideologically charged, or "ideotechnic" (Binford 1962, 219); however, the study of ideotechnic artifacts did not become one of the major platform planks of the New Archaeology of the 1960s and 1970s. Most processualists avoided the ideational basis of culture and instead embraced quantifiable and material factors such as diet, settlement location, technology, and assemblage composition. This materialist trend was not restricted to archaeology but was present in anthropology as well.

Support for this assertion is provided by a longitudinal study of the content of the eight anthropology journals: *American Anthropologist*, *American Antiquity*, *American Ethnologist*, *Ethnohistory*, *Journal of American Folklore*, *Journal of Field Archaeology*, *Man*, and *World Archaeology*. Each journal was queried for the presence of the word "ideology" in either the title or the abstract of articles, essays, reports, and book reviews. Two computerized search engines were utilized: JSTOR and ISI Web of Knowledge. Within JSTOR, journals are searchable from the date of their inception until the mid-1990s (varies by journal title). The ISI Web of Knowledge is the digital version of the Social Science Citation Index and references only the last five years of journal publications. These tools affected the selection of journals included within this study. For instance, *Antiquity*—where Gordon Willey's seminal article was published—is not available on JSTOR and, lamentably, could not be included within this study. Also, there is a perceptible gap in data retrieval between 1995 and 1997; these years are too recent for inclusion in JSTOR and not recent enough to be included in ISI. Regardless of these limitations, the changing frequency over time of the occurrence of the term "ideology" provides food for thought (see table 10.1).

Between the years of 1966 and 2002 (this analysis was conducted during the summer of 2003), the word "ideology" appears in seventy discrete publications across the eight journals. Despite the significant reach of the JSTOR searches (back to 1888 for *American Anthropologist* and 1935 for *American Antiquity*), the term "ideology" does not appear before 1966, after which it does not occur again until 1978, and then only once or twice per year until 1991. Since Willey did not deem it necessary to define the term in his 1976 publication, we can assume that the term was in common academic usage, although not generally the subject of anthropology journal articles. Prior to 1994, all titular references to ideology occurred in anthropology journals such as *American Anthropologist, American Ethnologist, Ethnohistory, Journal of American Folklore,* and *Man* (as opposed to journals devoted exclusively to archaeology). *American Antiquity* appears suddenly to become enamored of the term "ideology" in 1994, when it appears four times, although three of the four citations represent reviews of books that contained the word "ideology" in the title. The low incidence of this key term during the years 1995–97 reflects the data gap described previously (see table 10.1). During and after 1998, the incidence of ideologically focused journal articles climbs more or less steadily, reaching a crescendo in 2001, with ten such pieces being published within the journals surveyed.

These results are startling for several reasons. The real surge in visibility of the concept in journal publications occurs fully two decades after Willey's publication. Given the popularity of notions like ideology and hegemony among postmodern scholars, the relatively infrequent appearance of "ideology" during the late 1990s and early 2000s is somewhat unexpected. Out of the seventy total occurrences, only fourteen were found in archaeology journals. The fact that three of the four original references to this term in the 1994 pages of *American Antiquity* occurred within book reviews probably indicates that students of ideology were receiving a more welcome reception among university press editors than among academic journal editors and peer reviewers.

Table 10.1. Frequency of the term "ideology" in contributions to anthropology and archaeology journals, 1966–2002

Year	American Anthropologist	American Antiquity	American Ethnologist	Ethnohistory	Journal of American Folklore	Journal of Field Archaeology	Man	World Archaeology	Total
1966	1								1
1978							1		1
1979							2		2
1980				1					1
1981				1					1
1982				1			1		2
1983			1						1
1984			1				1		2
1986							1		1
1987							1		1
1988					1		1		2
1989	1								1
1990	1								1
1991	1						1		2
1992	1		1		1		1		3
1993	1						1		3
1994		4	1						1
1995		1	1						5
1996						1			2
1997		1							1
1998	2	1	2						6
1999	2		1		1			1	4
2000	3	1	1		1	1			7
2001	5	1	2		1				10
2002	3		5		1			1	9
2003		1							1
Total	20	10	16	3	6	2	11	2	70

Within Mesoamerican archaeology of the 1960s and 1970s, the situation was somewhat different. The rich corpus of ancient iconography and written texts served to mitigate archaeologists' commitment to orthodox processualism and to draw them toward concerns with historical trajectories and ideology. This bent, particularly among Mayanists, made them vulnerable to critiques of historical particularism (Kluckhohn 1962; see also exchange between Binford 1968 and Sabloff and Willey 1967) but concomitantly "preadapted" to postprocessualism. The collegial rapport in research and publication between archaeologists and art historians in the Mesoamerican field also served to preemptively foreground the topic of ideology, as a few examples will show. Gordon Willey himself made an early foray into the world of art history with his 1962 publication of "The Early Great Styles and the Rise of the Pre-Columbian Civilizations" in *American Anthropologist* (see Marcus, this volume). Many Dumbarton Oaks publications, notably the 1981 treatise *Mesoamerican Sites and World-Views* (edited by Elizabeth Benson), were collaborative efforts between art historians and archaeologists. Art historians such as Clemency Coggins highlighted early on the importance of the Mesoamerican calendar as an ideological factor in cultural transformation (1979), while Maya archaeologist Dennis Puleston wove together aquatic iconography with evidence of hydraulic agriculture (1977). With art historian Barbara MacLeod, Dennis Puleston wrote persuasively (1980) of the overwhelming ritual significance of caves within Maya cosmology. This trend strengthened through the 1980s with the highly influential museum show catalog *The Blood of Kings*, coauthored by Maya art historians Linda Schele and Mary Miller (1986), and archaeologist David Freidel's advocacy (1986) of a ritual basis for Maya warfare. Meanwhile, in Oaxaca, the study of Zapotec religion was popularized by the work of archaeologist Joyce Marcus (1978, 1983), and Richard Blanton stirred controversy in 1976 by suggesting that the location of Monte Albán may have been determined by noneconomic factors (cf. Santley 1980).

This selective review of Mesoamerican literature focused on the topic of ideology indicates that, while Gordon Willey's concern with ideological transcendence placed him ahead of the curve, traffic soon picked up behind him and the flow was heavier than indicated by journal articles alone. If Willey was a trendsetter topically, was he also ahead of his time in the substance of his essay, that is, the contention that culture hero Topiltzin was a transcendent figure, a visionary idealist who changed the course of Mesoamerican history? To evaluate Willey's contribution to this area of research, we must turn to the complex and often contradictory accounts of the life and times of Topiltzin Quetzalcoatl and of his cultural entanglement with the feathered serpent deity.

Topiltzin Quetzalcoatl—the Man and the Myth

The conflation of a historical person called Ce Acatl Topiltzin Quetzalcoatl with the so-called cult of the feathered serpent poses a great challenge to a Western-style compartmentalized understanding of the phenomenon of Quetzalcoatl. I follow, as did Willey, the lead of Henry Nicholson, whose definitive work on TQ (1957, 2000, 2001) was based upon an exhaustive examination of early ethnohistoric Mesoamerican sources—a corpus of extremely rich and conflicting accounts. Nicholson concluded (2001, 259) that TQ had been an actual person whose persona was conflated (either during his life or posthumously) with the ancient creator deity and god of wind and rain, called Quetzalcoatl in Nahuatl, the language of the Aztecs, or Mexica. This conclusion clearly predisposed Professor Willey, a member of Nicholson's 1957 dissertation committee, to consider TQ in terms of historical events. Willey also could have been familiar with the publications of Mexican archaeologist Laurette Séjourné (1957, 158–59; 1962) in which the notion of Quetzalcoatl's transcendence and apotheosis had been discussed.

At any rate, neither Willey nor Nicholson cared to deal with the intersecting paths of TQ as culture hero and the abundant corpus of iconography and architecture representing a feathered serpent deity, the latter of which extends back to the time of Teotihuacan (Sugiyama 2000). Described by Nicholson as "one of the most striking icons ever developed in pre-Hispanic Mesoamerica" (2000, 145), the plumed serpent deity has enjoyed a longevity and popularity unmatched by other highland Mexican deities and even played a central role in a fictional account of a central Mexican nativistic movement written by D. H. Lawrence (1926). Academic literature relating to the iconography of Quetzalcoatl is as profoundly complex as the ethnohistoric accounts of the life of the putative Toltec ruler Topiltzin Quetzalcoatl. Moreover, the former material is decidedly recursive, as the question of the place and time (and metaphor or reality) of

Tollan or Tula (seat of power of TQ) is revisited by successive generations of Mesoamerican archaeologists and art historians as well as historians of religion.

For example, the straightforward historical exegesis of this culture hero/feathered serpent deity offered by Nicholson has been questioned by Susan Gillespie, who approaches the ruler-deity complex as a social construction of Colonial Highland Mesoamerica—one aided and abetted by both Spanish missionaries and Nahuatl scribes (Gillespie 1989). Other scholars have not shied away from integrating the person with the deity. Such seamlessness is displayed in the work of Davíd Carrasco, who approaches the Quetzalcoatl narrative as a grand Mesoamerican epic, a metaphor of urbanization and rulership (2000). To Carrasco, the great cities of Mesoamerica—from Teotihuacan to Mayapan—represent a recursive series of Tollans, each with a locally nuanced version of the Quetzalcoatl story. While Clemency Coggins disengages TQ, the alleged ruler of Tula, from the feathered serpent deity, she has proposed (2002) that the original Toltecs resided at Teotihuacan (the first Tollan) and that every Mesoamerican city thereafter defined itself in terms of that great metropolis, with its fearsome warriors, incomparable artisanship, and mercantile connections. Alfredo López Austin and Leonardo López Luján prefer to dissect this tightly woven bundle into three levels of analysis—myth, legend, and history (2000, 45)—and to speak somewhat abstractly of a Zuyuan ideology (materialized in post-Teotihuacan, multiethnic, militaristic regimes) and "sovereigns who embodied the force of the Feathered Serpent god" (2000, 68). By Terminal Classic times (A.D. 800–1000), feathered serpent iconography gained visibility across a wide array of venues in both the highlands and the lowlands of Mesoamerica. This fact has persuaded many scholars that the ideology behind feathered serpent representations transcended linguistic and ethnic boundaries to knit polities together into multiethnic confederations (see, e.g., López Austin and López Luján 2000, 22). The roles of militarism and mercantilism in one such confederation are discussed below.

Of great interest to both Gillespie and Carrasco are the ironic twists and contradictions within the story of TQ. For example, Topiltzin was renowned as a great and beloved ruler who disdained human sacrifice and warfare, and yet he lost control of his kingdom. To add insult to injury, TQ—as a deified ruler—then became associated with some of the most militaristic empires (heavily vested in human sacrifice) ever to exist in Mesoamerica. Willey, too, noted this twist of fate (1976, 209) and ascribed it to the processes of "containment" and "routinization," or the manner in which transcendent movements are normalized and co-opted by existing power structures. From Willey's perspective, the transcendent ethos of TQ did not culminate in a recognizable religious movement in the same manner as did the ethos of Buddhism or Jainism but rather was subverted and converted to an expansionistic political agenda. The persistent legend of TQ suggests that a self-conscious inner dialogue existed within Mesoamerican society—one that questioned the role of human sacrifice and war in societal governance—although Gillespie (1989, 184), following Litvak King (1972, 27), would attribute this "dialogue" to the textual input of Spanish friars.

Regardless of hermeneutical orientation, all scholars agree with Nicholson (2001, 191, 264) that Quetzalcoatl was the "dispenser of all legitimate political authority"; opinions diverge, however, on whether or not Quetzalcoatl was also a dynastic founder. Generalized scholarship on Quetzalcoatl by Davíd Carrasco and Enrique Florescano emphasize his authoritarian role as political legitimizer (Carrasco 2000, 106; Florescano 1999, 34), and ethnohistorical sources contain innumerable accounts of legitimizing rituals that transpired at the Postclassic Quetzalcoatl-dominated religious center of Cholula (or Chololan; see McCafferty 2000). The religious power to grant political authority is particularly intriguing in light of the supposed pacifist stance of Topiltzin Quetzalcoatl, suggesting that effective political leadership may not have been predicated solely upon success in warfare. Furthermore, Willey's observation (1976, 206) that transcendent movements tend to occur during times of civilizational crisis strikes a chord here. Cycles of civilizational crises occurred in Mesoamerica, with the events of 1521 constituting the final political crisis of indigenous highland societies that had survived and regrouped after the earlier crises of the fall of Tula and the decline of Teotihuacan. The post-Teotihuacan period in the highlands, in particular, can be characterized as a time of profound crisis. Within this stressful political climate, a new ethos of rulership seems to have been embraced—one that contained a mixture of paradoxical elements that justified a wide range of political actions. Increasingly, evidence is coming to the fore that suggests a similar series of events transpired in the Maya Lowlands at the close of the Classic period, less than two hundred years after the fall of Teotihuacan.

The Long Reach of the Feathered Serpent

Karl Taube has concerned himself with the geographic distribution of iconographic symbolism of Ehecatl-Quetzalcoatl (EQ), the wind deity (2001). In the Terminal Classic and Postclassic Maya Lowlands, Taube traces (2001, 102) materialization of the "breath of life" to feathered serpent representations, conch spirals, and circular structures found at Northern Lowland sites such as Uxmal, Chichén Itzá, and San Gervasio and at the Pasión River site of Seibal. Although images of celestial serpents are part of the standard repertoire of Classic Maya iconography (Schele and Freidel 1990, 415–17), rarely are they covered with plumage. Adorning an airborne reptile with precious quetzal feathers is a highland convention observed by A.D. 200 at the Feathered Serpent Pyramid of Teotihuacan (Sugiyama 2000, 125–26). In this guise, the wind deity is said to sweep the path for the rain god. By Terminal Classic times (A.D. 830–950), feathered serpent imagery is prominently displayed at northern Maya Lowland sites such as Uxmal (Nunnery Quadrangle, west building) and Chichén Itzá (El Castillo pyramid). The conch shell, often used as a trumpet, is a natural metaphor for the wind deity, and the highland culture hero Topiltzin Quetzalcoatl (as well as feathered serpent deity impersonators) is often shown with a conch spiral, the *ehecacozcatl* (wind jewel) (see fig. 10.1).

Perhaps because conch shells have circular cross sections or because powerful winds can create tight, circular flow patterns, round structures generally were dedicated to the feathered serpent deity (Taube 2001, 111–12). The circular shrine in the Templo Mayor district of Tenochtitlán is a notable, if more recent, example. In the Maya Lowlands during the Early Classic and Late Classic periods, circular structures were rarely constructed, although round platforms were built during Preclassic times (Aimers, Powis, and Awe 2000; Powis and Hohmann 1995; Ricketson 1937). From the Terminal Classic through the Postclassic, on the other hand, circular shrines were built at selected locations throughout the Maya Lowlands and generally are associated with conch shells. The exterior of a shrine (C1–1-a) located at the site of Caracol on Cozumel Island and thought to date to Postclassic times was decorated with a cupola studded with conch shells that trumpeted as the sea breeze passed through them (Freidel and Sabloff 1984, 59–61).

Taube shies away from discussing the power politics underlying the incorporation of such imagery into sacred Maya centers. In contrast,

Figure 10.1. Highland culture hero Ce Acatl Topiltzin Quetzalcoatl shown with his circular shield adorned with a conch spiral. Reproduced by permission from Sahagún 1982, 165.

William Ringle and his colleagues assert unabashedly that a political charter embraced by messianic militaristic traders—dubbed the "Quetzalcoatl cult"—provided the underpinnings of this local innovation in iconography and architecture (Ringle, Gallareta N., and Bey 1998, 183). Neither Taube nor Ringle and colleagues concern themselves with the paradoxical life and transcendent aspirations of Topiltzin Quetzalcoatl, yet their interpretations are linked to both the legacy of TQ and the timeless deity of creation and wind. If we accept the chains of inference proposed by Taube and by Ringle and colleagues, then we must admit that an "ethos of Quetzalcoatl" was embraced during the Terminal Classic period (A.D. 830–950) in selected parts of the Maya Lowlands.

Could this embrace have been caused by the "civilizational crisis" that had erupted in the Southern Lowlands? Given the recent finding that construction at Chichén Itzá started declining before A.D. 1000 (Andrews, Andrews, and Castellanos 2003, 152; Cobos Palma 2004), such a scenario cannot be dismissed. Even in northern Yucatán, the Terminal Classic is now perceived to have been a time of "growing stress. . . . when overpopulation, land shortages, ecological stress, and climatic change were testing the capacity of the existing political and economic frameworks" (Andrews, Andrews, and Castellanos 2003, 152). In the Southern Lowlands, capacity had already been exceeded, and judging from the abrupt ninth-century cessation of monumental construction and hieroglyphic inscriptions, statecraft modeled on divine dynastic rulership was in full dissolution. Civilizational crisis—in the sense that Gordon Willey envisioned—gripped the Maya Lowlands during the Terminal Classic period and thus opened the door to new, possibly transcendent, ideologies.

But the new ideology—materialized by feathered serpent imagery and circular shrines—was not draped uniformly over the final construction activities of Classic-period rulers. Rather, selected locales—strategic due to location or available resources—evince continued occupation or initial settlement, construction programs that feature circular shrines, and iconography of the feathered serpent represented in architecture, sculpture, and portable artifacts. Most explicitly and massively displayed at Chichén Itzá, this materialized ideology is thought to have been the guiding political philosophy of this northern capital, from which an expansive political economy of undocumented size was controlled. Field research along the Caribbean side of the Maya Lowlands has yielded information that expands the spatial limits of the feathered serpent ideological network. Specifically, in Belize circular shrines have been documented at Nohmul (Chase and Chase 1982), Ambergris Cay (Guderjan 1995), Caye Coco (Rosenswig and Masson 2002), and as far south as the Sibun River valley. Whether these Caribbean seaboard sites were linked with Chichén Itzá through mercantile transactions (Willey's "peaceful processes of penetration") or through vertical political linkages engendered by military conquest is profoundly difficult to determine.

The southernmost-known site of Terminal Classic round shrines occurs about 375 kilometers south of Chichén Itzá in the Sibun, or Xibun, Valley

Figure 10.2. Excavated portion of a circular shrine at the Samuel Oshon site, lower Sibun Valley, Belize. Photograph by Kimberly A. Berry.

of central Belize, the locale of a long-term, valleywide archaeological project (Thomas 2005; McAnany 2002; McAnany et al. 2002; McAnany and Thomas 2003; McAnany, Harrison-Buck, and Morandi 2004; McAnany et al. 2004). Three recorded sites—all located within thirty kilometers straight inland from the sea—have been found to contain circular shrines: the ancient Maya communities of Pechtun Ha, Samuel Oshon, and Augustine Obispo (Harrison and Acone 2002; Harrison 2003; Harrison-Buck 2004). Figure 10.2 shows one of these shrines.

Interestingly, the shrines were smoothly incorporated into Terminal Classic plaza plans rather than added, as an afterthought, to earlier plaza arrangements. Diminutive versions of the massive circular shrine (called Caracol) at Chichén Itzá, these structures measure only six to eight meters in diameter. Each contained a cluster of complete conch shells found immediately outside of the structure walls (see fig. 10.3), confirming a symbolic link with the feathered serpent. The sites within which these distinctive shrines were built are small communities that cover less than half of a square kilometer. Although Carrasco characterized Quetzalcoatl as an icon

Figure 10.3. Conch shells found outside the walls of a circular structure at the Augustine Obispo site, lower Sibun Valley, Belize. Photograph by author.

of the urban sacred center (2000, 106), the presence of circular Ehecatl-Quetzalcoatl-affiliated shrines at nonurban locales reinforces a recursive quality of Quetzalcoatl—*conceptual complexity and paradox.* The presence of diminutive shrines at small sites also suggests a flexibility to the feathered serpent ideology that rendered it attractive and operational both to rulers occupying regional seats of power and to local leaders coordinating labor and ritual practices at smaller communities.

Factors underlying the architectural manifestation of the circular shrine could have taken several forms. Possibilities include (1) a paradigmatic expression of legitimate authority (issuing from the north) in the face of political disintegration in the south (an ethos in line with Nicholson 2001 and Carrasco 2000, which stress the role of the feathered serpent deity as authority legitimizer), (2) messianic militarism (as per Ringle, Gallareta N., and Bey 1998), (3) peaceful trading (following Willey 1976), and (4) influx of a new population from the north. The ceramic evidence does not provide support for this final possibility. Architectural, mortuary, and botanical evidence from the Sibun Valley does support the importance of both militarism and trading but not necessarily authority legitimization. The largest site in the valley—located over sixty kilometers upriver—yielded Terminal Classic pottery but no evidence of a circular shrine. This pattern is contrary to what one would expect if the Sibun Valley seat of power had converted to the feathered serpent ideology in order to legitimate continued rulership through the Terminal Classic period.

Logically, if trading played a role in the local establishment of circular shrines, then these features should be found at resource-rich locations or strategic ports of trade. Cozumel Island, with its circular shrines, is a clear example of the latter. Within the Sibun Valley, cacao is grown currently, was cultivated during the Colonial period, and was likely grown as far back as the Classic period. The presence of circular shrines in the lower part of this valley probably relates to the cacao groves that flourished in the rich alluvial soils of the river terraces. In northern Yucatán, cacao could be grown only in point-specific edaphic locales—primarily collapsed *cenotes*, or limestone sinkholes—that retained the moisture necessary for pod formation (Gomez-Pompa, Flores, and Fernandez 1990; Kepecs and Boucher 1996; Perez Romero 1988). So, mercantile activities (or the extraction of resources through tribute) are implicated by the presence of circular shrines in this cacao-producing valley.

Regarding military activities, the time after the hegemony of Teotihuacan often is perceived as the period during which military sodalities, such as existed among Aztec warriors, coalesced. Iconographically linked with the feathered serpent deity, these military orders have been identified with various animals—particularly the jaguar, coyote, and eagle—that figure prominently in the iconography of Epiclassic seats of power such as Tula, Xochicalco, and Chichén Itzá. Although the nonurban sites of the Sibun Valley are not replete with architectural imagery, a Terminal Classic mortuary deposit found within the largest platform of a midvalley site called Pakal Na has yielded a human trophy mandible carved with bird and jaguar/coyote cartouches (see fig. 10.4). Placed near the primary interment—of a large adult male—were a conch shell whorl and pyriform redware pottery vessels that are Yucatecan in shape and finish. The carved human mandible is a strong indicator of martial activities.

Findings from this Caribbean valley point towards several conclusions. Although Lowland Maya imagery and architecture linked to the feathered serpent are often ascribed to the Postclassic period, they occur in

Figure 10.4. Bird and coyote/jaguar cartouches carved into a human mandible from a mortuary context at Pakal Na, Sibun Valley, Belize. Drawing by Kevin Acone.

unambiguously Terminal Classic contexts within the Sibun Valley. Although the nature of the ideology materialized in this manner is anything but self-evident, chronologically it appears either in tandem with or shortly after the "civilizational crisis" of divine rulership. Moreover, its appearance is not restricted to political capitals; rather, relevant imagery and architecture also have been found at resource-rich and strategic locales (regardless of site size). This finding leads to the suspicion that some factors other than, or in addition to, authority legitimization played a critical role in the expansion of this ideology throughout the Maya Lowlands. In the Sibun Valley, more readily apparent factors include mercantile and militaristic activities, both of which have been linked with the "cult" of the feathered serpent (Ringle et al. 1998). Finally, although this ideology may be characterized as a response to a civilizational crisis, this particular bundling of elements of Mesoamerica's most famous icon was relatively short-lived. In the Sibun Valley, the network of shrines and communities was abandoned by A.D. 1000, a date in line with evidence from other Southern Lowland sites that display a vibrant Terminal Classic occupation.

Discussion

Increased chronological precision and an enlarged regional perspective have enabled scholars to assess more accurately the impact of the feathered serpent ideology on the Mesoamerican world of post-Teotihuacan times. While the strength and the extent of the impact have been well documented, its exact nature is still open to conjecture. Efforts to discriminate between the culture hero and deified ruler, Topiltzin Quetzalcoatl, and the ideology of the feathered serpent have been relaxed, as have efforts to locate Tollan as a single point on a map. In effect, history, legend, and metaphor are now seen as constitutive elements of a complex bundle that forms the Mesoamerican past. Scholarship following the 1976 essay by Gordon Willey on the culture hero Topiltzin has tended to reiterate the importance of mercantile activities, while discussion of the philosophical transcendence of this ruler has been set aside in favor of a perspective stressing messianic militarism and the pan-ethnic nature of feathered serpent–inspired political units. Although a transcendent ideology certainly could have been at the heart of this effective and expansionistic program of governance, it was not the antiwar or anti–human sacrifice ethos discussed by Willey. Thus, one wonders whether the events that transpired during the ninth and tenth centuries in the Maya Lowlands were an incidence of transcendence or simply a changing of the guard as local dynastic rulers were replaced by new structures of authority that sought legitimacy through linkage to a pan-ethnic charter of rulership.

Regardless, Gordon Willey's notion that civilizational crises provide opportunities from which new ideas about governance and society come forth enjoys considerable support among Mesoamericanists. Building on the central role of ideology in civilizational change that Willey discussed in his 1976 article, recent perspectives on the feathered serpent phenomenon continue to place prime importance on ideology as a force in social transformation and to model it as occupying that fertile ground at the crossroads of economy and politics.

Conclusion

The 1976 essay by Gordon Willey indicated a path by which the study of ideas might be incorporated into an analysis of past events. While the essay did not aggressively challenge the modus operandi of processual archaeology, Willey did clearly state that the story of Mesoamerica was more than the remains of maize, mounds, and metates. As William Fash noted in a biographical article (2004), Willey did not reinvent himself in the 1970s so as to become a processualist, but he remained open to many points of view, and when postprocessualism came into vogue, he had already considered (and written about) many of its central tenets. More broadly, Willey's essay challenged historians of religion who had been accustomed to discussing "world religions" with no regard for the indigenous religions of the Americas. He expanded the horizons of scholars outside of anthropology by asking them to consider the fact that a Mesoamerican culture hero called Ce Acatl Topiltzin Quetzalcoatl may have represented an instance of ideological transcendence that rocked the foundations of the status quo. Whether or not this was the case, the sophistication of Willey's discussion revealed a deep ambivalence within ethnohistorical texts regarding the roles of human sacrifice and warfare. Thus, Willey problematized these two characteristics of Mesoamerican society that repeatedly have been stereotyped, even within academic discourse. The mythico-historical figure of Quetzalcoatl—replete with paradox and irony—has fascinated scholars for decades and, clearly, Professor Willey was not immune to his allure. We can perceive in Gordon Willey's treatment of the narrative of Topiltzin Quetzalcoatl a strong interest in the convergent trajectories of ideology, history, and culture process—recursive and dialectical themes in Mesoamerican archaeology.

Acknowledgments

Originally presented at the 2003 Society for American Archaeology symposium in honor of Gordon R. Willey, this essay has benefited from the insightful comments of Bill Fash, Jerry Sabloff, and an anonymous reviewer. I alone accept responsibility for introducing any additional confusion into the interpretation of this most influential but complex Mesoamerican icon—Quetzalcoatl.

Archaeological field research in the Sibun Valley was supported by the National Science Foundation (BCS grant number 0096603), the Ahau Foundation, and the Division of International Programs at Boston University. I wish to thank the many staff members, students, specialists, and volunteers, who over the course of four field seasons helped to bring the deep history of a hitherto little-known archaeological district into focus. Permission to conduct archaeological research in the Sibun Valley was granted by the Institute of Archaeology in Belmopan, Belize. I extend my gratitude to the institute's staff and directors, who graciously facilitated this research.

Although we were generations apart in term of theoretical orientation and fieldwork praxis, I will always treasure the memory of my luncheon dates with Professor Willey at the Harvard Faculty Club. Each time, he would lean over and confide/confess to me that he had never taken a woman into the field. What a sea change he witnessed during his lifetime, yet his intellectual contributions continue to provide a touchstone against which we measure our progress. But above and beyond his scholarship, we shall not see the likes of his collegiality anytime soon.

References

Aimers, James J., Terry Powis, and Jaime Awe. 2000. "Formative Period Round Structures of the Upper Belize Valley." *Latin American Antiquity* 11:71–86.

Andrews, Anthony P., E. Wyllys Andrews, and Fernando Robles Castellanos. 2003. "The Northern Maya Collapse and Its Aftermath." *Ancient Mesoamerica* 14 (1):151–56.

Binford, Lewis R. 1962. "Archaeology as Anthropology." *American Antiquity* 28 (2):217–25.

———. 1968. "Some Comments on Historical versus Processual Archaeology." *Southwestern Journal of Anthropology* 24:267–75.

Benson, Elizabeth P., ed. 1981. *Mesoamerican Sites and World-Views*. Washington, D.C.: Dumbarton Oaks.

Blanton, Richard E. 1976. "Anthropological Studies of Cities." *Annual Review of Anthropology* 5:249–64.

Carrasco, Davíd. 2000. *Quetzalcoatl and the Irony of Empire: Myths and Prophecies in the Aztec Tradition*. Boulder: University Press of Colorado.

Chase, Diane Z., and Arlen F. Chase. 1982. "Yucatec Influence in Terminal Classic Northern Belize." *American Antiquity* 47:596–614.

Cobos Palma, Rafael. 2004. "Chichén Itzá: Settlement and Hegemony during the Terminal Classic Period." In *The Terminal Classic Period in the Maya Lowlands: Collapse, Transition, and*

Transformation, ed. Arthur A. Demarest, Prudence M. Rice, and Don S. Rice, 517–44. Boulder: University Press of Colorado.

Coggins, Clemency. 1979. "A New Order and the Role of the Calendar: Some Characteristics of the Middle Classic Period at Tikal." In *Maya Archaeology and Ethnohistory*, ed. Norman Hammond and Gordon R. Willey, 38–50. Austin: University of Texas Press.

———. 2002. "Toltec." *RES* 42:34–85.

Conrad, Geoffrey W., and Arthur A. Demarest. 1984. *Religion and Empire: The Dynamics of Aztec and Inca Expansionism*. Cambridge: Cambridge University Press.

Fash, William L. 2004. "Sprinter, Wordsmith, Mentor, and Sage: The Life of Gordon Randolph Willey, 1913–2002." *Ancient Mesoamerica* 14 (2):169–77.

Flannery, Kent V., ed. 1976. *The Early Mesoamerican Village*. New York: Academic Press.

Florescano, Enrique. 1999. *The Myth of Quetzalcoatl*, trans. L. Hochroth. Baltimore: Johns Hopkins University Press.

Freidel, David A. 1986. "Maya Warfare: An Example of Peer Polity Interaction." In *Peer Polity Interaction and Socio-Political Change*, ed. Colin Renfrew and John F. Cherry, 93–108. Cambridge: Cambridge University Press.

Freidel, David A., and Jeremy A. Sabloff. 1984. *Cozumel: Late Maya Settlement Patterns*. New York: Academic Press.

Gillespie, Susan. 1989. *The Aztec Kings: The Construction of Rulership in Mexica History*. Tucson: University of Arizona Press.

Gomez-Pompa, Arturo, J. Salvador Flores, and Mario Aliphat Fernandez. 1990. "The Sacred Cacao Groves of the Maya." *Latin American Antiquity* 1:247–57.

Guderjan, Thomas H. 1995. "Maya Settlement and Trade on Ambergris Cay, Belize." *Ancient Mesoamerica* 6 (2):147–59.

Harrison, Eleanor. 2003. "A Circular Shrine and Repositioned Stelae at the Oshon Site (Operation 24)." In *Between the Gorge and the Estuary: Archaeological Investigations of the 2001 Season of the Xibun Archaeological Research Project*, ed. Patricia A. McAnany and Ben S. Thomas, 165–85. Boston: XARP. http://www.bu.edu/tricia/reports.shtml.

Harrison-Buck, Eleanor. 2004. "Circular Shrine at the Augustine Obispo Site (Operation 32)." In *Sibun Valley from Late Classic through Colonial Times: Investigations of the 2003 Season of the Xibun Archaeological Research Project*, ed. Patricia A. McAnany, Eleanor Harrison-Buck, and Steven Morandi, 19–39. Boston: XARP. http://www.bu.edu/tricia/reports.shtml.

Harrison, Eleanor, and Kevin Acone. 2002. "Further Investigations at Pechtun Ha: Feasting and Mass Importation of Cave Speleothems." In *Sacred Landscape and Settlement in the Sibun River Valley*, ed. Patricia A. McAnany and Ben S. Thomas, 123–40. SUNY Institute of Mesoamerican Studies Occasional Paper 8. Albany, New York: SUNY Institute of Mesoamerican Studies.

Hodder, Ian, ed. 1982. *Symbolic and Structural Archaeology*. Cambridge: Cambridge University Press.

Kepecs, Susan, and Silviane Boucher. 1996. "Pre-Hispanic Cultivation of *Rejolladas* and Stone-Lands: New Evidence from Northeast Yucatán." In *The Managed Mosaic: Ancient Maya Agriculture and Resource Use*, ed. Scott L. Fedick, 69–91. Salt Lake City: University of Utah Press.

Kluckhohn, Clyde. 1962. "The Conceptual Structure of Middle American Studies." In *The Maya and Their Neighbors*, ed. Clarence L. Hay, 41–51. New York: Appleton-Century. (Orig. pub. 1940.)

Lawrence, D. H. 1926. *The Plumed Serpent*. London: Heinemann.

Litvak King, Jaime. 1972. "La introducción posthispánica de elementos a las religiones prehispánicas: Un problema de aculturación retroactiva." In *Religión en Mesoamerica*, ed. Jaime Litvak King and Neomí Castillo Tejero, 25–29. Mexico City: Sociedad Mexicana de Antropología.

López Austin, Alfredo, and Leonardo López Luján. 2000. "The Myth and Reality of Zuyuá: The Feathered Serpent and Mesoamerican Transformations from the Classic to the Postclassic." In *Mesoamerica's Classic Heritage: From Teotihuacan to the Aztecs*, ed. Davíd Carrasco, Lindsay Jones, and Scott Sessions, 21–84. Boulder: University Press of Colorado.

MacLeod, Barbara, and Dennis Puleston. 1980. "Pathways into Darkness: The Search for the Road to Xibalba." In *Third Palenque Round Table, 1978, Part 1*, ed. Merle G. Robertson and D. C. Jeffers, 71–78. Monterrey, Mexico: Pre-Columbian Art Institute.

Marcus, Joyce. 1978. "Archaeology and Religion: A Comparison of Zapotec and Maya." *World Archaeology* 10 (2):172–91.

———. 1983. "Zapotec Religion." In *The Cloud People: Divergent Evolution of the Zapotec and Mixtec Civilizations*, ed. Kent V. Flannery and Joyce Marcus, 345–51. New York: Academic Press.

McAnany, Patricia A., ed. 2002. *Sacred Landscape and Settlement in the Sibun River Valley*. SUNY Institute of Mesoamerican Studies Occasional Paper 8. Albany, New York: SUNY Institute of Mesoamerican Studies.

McAnany, Patricia A., Eleanor Harrison, Polly A. Peterson, Steven Morandi, Satoru Murata, Ben S. Thomas, Sandra L. López Varela, Daniel Finamore, and David G. Buck. 2004. "The Deep History of the Sibun River Valley." In *Archaeological Investigations in the Eastern Maya Lowlands: Papers of the 2003 Belize Archaeology Symposium*, ed. Jaime Awe, John Morris, and Sherilyne Jones, 295–310. Research Reports in Belizean Archaeology, vol. 1. Belmopan, Belize: Institute of Archaeology, National Institute of Culture and History.

McAnany, Patricia A., Eleanor Harrison-Buck, and Steven Morandi, eds. 2004. *Sibun Valley from Late Classic through Colonial Times: Investigations of the 2003 Season of the Xibun Archaeological Research Project*. Boston: XARP. http://www.bu.edu/tricia/reports.shtml.

McAnany, Patricia A., and Ben S. Thomas, eds. 2003. *Between the Gorge and the Estuary: Archaeological Investigations of the 2001 Season of the Xibun Archaeological Research Project*. Boston: XARP. http://www.bu.edu/tricia/reports.shtml.

McAnany, Patricia A., Ben S. Thomas, Steven Morandi, Polly A. Peterson, and Eleanor Harrison. 2002. "Praise the Ahaw and Pass the Kakaw: Xibun Maya and the Political Economy of Cacao." In *Ancient Maya Political Economies*, ed. Marilyn A. Masson and David A. Freidel, 123–39. Walnut Creek, Calif.: AltaMira.

McCafferty, Geoffrey G. 2000. "Tollan Cholol008 and the Legacy of Legitimacy during the Classic-Postclassic Transition." In *Mesoamerica's Classic Heritage: From Teotihuacan to the Aztecs*, ed. Davíd Carrasco, Lindsay Jones, and Scott Sessions, 341–67. Boulder: University Press of Colorado.

Nicholson, Henry B. 1957. "Topiltzin Quetzalcoatl of Tollan: A Problem in Mesoamerican Ethnohistory." PhD diss., Department of Anthropology, Harvard University.

———. 2000. "The Iconography of the Feathered Serpent in Late Postclassic Central Mexico." In *Mesoamerica's Classic Heritage: From Teotihuacan to the Aztecs*, ed. Davíd Carrasco, Lindsay Jones, and Scott Sessions, 145–64. Boulder: University Press of Colorado.

———. 2001. *Topiltzin Quetzalcoatl: The Once and Future Lord of the Toltecs*. Boulder: University Press of Colorado.

Perez Romero, J. A. 1988. "Algunas consideraciones sobre cacao en el norte de la peninsula de Yucatán." Tesis de licenciatura en ciencias antropologicas, Universidad Autónoma de Yucatán, Merida.

Powis, Terry, and Bobbi Hohmann. 1995. "From Private Household to Public Ceremony: Middle Formative Occupation at the Tolok Group, Cahal Peck, Belize." In *Belize Valley Preclassic Maya Project: Report on the 1994 Field Season*, ed. Paul F. Healy and Jaime J. Awe, 45–94. Trent University, Department of Anthropology, Occasional Papers in Anthropology, no. 10. Peterborough, Ontario: Trent University Department of Anthropology.

Puleston, Dennis E. 1977. "The Art and Archaeology of Hydraulic Agriculture in the Maya Lowlands." In *Social Process in Maya Prehistory*, ed. Norman Hammond, 449–67. New York: Academic Press.

Ricketson, Oliver G., Jr. 1937. *Uaxactun, Guatemala Group E—1926–1931. Part I: The Excavations*. Carnegie Institution of Washington Publication 477. Washington, D.C.: Carnegie Institution of Washington.

Ringle, William M., Tomás Gallareta N., and George J. Bey III. 1998. "The Return of Quetzalcoatl: Evidence for the Spread of a World Religion during the Epiclassic Period." *Ancient Mesoamerica* 9:183–232.

Rosenswig, Robert M., and Marilyn A. Masson. 2002. "Transformation of the Terminal Classic to Postclassic Architectural Landscape at Caye Coco, Belize." *Ancient Mesoamerica* 13:213–35.

Sabloff, Jeremy A., and Gordon R. Willey. 1967. "The Collapse of Maya Civilization in the Southern Lowlands: A Consideration of History and Process." *Southwestern Journal of Anthropology* 23 (4):311–35.

Sahagún, Fray Bernardino de. 1982. *Historia general de las cosas de Nueva España*. Mexico City: Fomento Cultural Banamex.

Santley, Robert S. 1980. "Disembedded Capitals Reconsidered." *American Antiquity* 45 (1):132–45.

Schele, Linda, and David Freidel. 1990. *A Forest of Kings: The Untold Story of the Ancient Maya*. New York: William Morrow.

Schele, Linda, and Mary E. Miller. 1986. *The Blood of Kings: Dynasty and Ritual in Maya Art*. New York: George Braziller.

Schwartz, B. I. 1975. "The Age of Transcendence." *Daedalus*, Spring, 1–8.

Séjourné, Laurette. 1957. *Pensamiento y religión en el México antiguo*. Mexico City: Fondo de Cultura Económica.

———. 1962. *El universo de Quetzalcoatl*. Mexico City: Fondo de Cultura Económica.

Sugiyama, Saburo. 2000. "Teotihuacan as an Origin for Postclassic Feathered Serpent Symbolism." In *Mesoamerica's Classic Heritage: From Teotihuacan to the Aztecs*, ed. Davíd Carrasco, Lindsay Jones, and Scott Sessions, 117–43. Boulder: University Press of Colorado.

Taube, Karl. 2001. "The Breath of Life: The Symbolism of Wind in Mesoamerica and the American Southwest." In *The Road to Aztlan: Art from a Mythic Homeland*, ed. Virginia Fields and Victor Zamudio-Taylor, 102–23. Los Angeles: Los Angeles County Museum of Art.

Thomas, Ben S. 2005. *Maya Settlement and Political Hierarchy in the Sibun River Valley, Belize, Central America*. Ann Arbor, Mich.: University Microfilms.

Willey, Gordon R. 1962. "The Early Great Styles and the Rise of the Pre-Columbian Civilizations." *American Anthropologist* 64:1–14.

————. 1976. "Mesoamerican Civilization and the Idea of Transcendence." *Antiquity* 50:205–15.

Willey, Gordon R., and Jeremy A. Sabloff. 1993. *A History of American Archaeology*. 3rd ed. New York: W. H. Freeman.

Conclusion

Jeremy A. Sabloff

In assessing Gordon R. Willey's scholarly legacy, one of the first things you notice is how unbelievably prolific he was and how the large quantity is matched by the high quality. Gordon had that rare ability to produce something close to a final draft of a manuscript in one sitting at the typewriter. Using an exceedingly fast two-finger hunt-and-peck system, he made his typewriter sound like a machine gun (the computer did not produce the same effect!). He also was highly motivated and had great energy and terrific power of concentration. These skills might help explain the quantity of his scholarly output, but they do not explain the strength of his writings. Clearly, his intelligence, intellectual curiosity, voracious reading habits, and ability to draw together a large array of data had something to do with the importance of his scholarly contributions.

The second thing you notice is the incredible diversity of his writings. On the one hand, you have his speculative pieces, from "Growth Trends in New World Cultures" in 1950 (with its wonderful ending statement: "What is particularly interesting and important is that the molding and channeling forces . . . growing out of the interaction of technology and environment, give terrific impetus to the culture; and this impetus, mounting snowball

233

fashion, carries the society along in its momentum. Sooner or later historical forces concur to smash or disarrange these dynamic patterns. The result, cultural death, deflection, or a new integration, depends to a great extent on the rigidity and velocity with which the original culture growth has been molded and propelled toward its fate" [p. 242]) to "Mesoamerican Civilization and the Idea of Transcendence" (discussed by Patricia McAnany) in 1976 (with its wonderful closing line: "Topiltzin Quetzalcoatl who rose transcendent over the contemporary darkness with his millennial vision of a bright future" [p. 213]). You also have his mystery novels, such as *Selena* and several unpublished manuscripts, as well as the many plays he wrote for the Tavern Club in Boston.

On the other hand, you have the rich variety of Gordon's substantive publications. (The types of publications listed in the following paragraphs are obviously not mutually exclusive, as Gordon's writings usually had multiple goals.) First, there are his detailed monographs and articles reporting on basic archaeological data, such as surveys, excavations, ceramics, and nonceramic artifacts.

Second, there are Gordon's pattern recognition studies, ranging from survey data, as in his Virú Valley report (discussed by Michael Moseley), to artifact analyses, as in the Altar de Sacrificios and Seibal monographs (discussed by Norman Hammond and Gair Tourtellot).

Third, there are his numerous broader culture-historical syntheses, for which Gordon had no peer. He is perhaps most renowned for his monumental two-volume *An Introduction to American Archaeology* (as discussed by Jeffrey Quilter), but his synthetic pieces for the School of American Research advanced seminars on the Maya (one of which is discussed by Prudence Rice) also had a very significant impact on the field, as did his early article with James A. Ford, "An Interpretation of the Prehistory of the Eastern United States," and his overview of Floridian prehistory (discussed by Jerald Milanich).

Fourth, Gordon wrote about his uses of specific techniques, starting with his first published article, "Notes of Central Georgia Dendrochronology," in 1937, and published extensively on methods and methodology, as exemplified by his classic book with Philip Phillips, *Method and Theory in American Archaeology* (discussed by Richard Leventhal and Deborah Cornavaca), which in the 1950s and 1960s was probably read by every North American archaeologist.

Fifth, there are the many theoretical articles that Gordon produced throughout his career. Gordon liked to talk and write about what he termed the "big questions," just like his intellectual heroes Alfred L. Kroeber and Julian H. Steward (whose photographs were on the Peabody Museum office wall behind Gordon's desk). He was deeply interested in cultural evolution and optimistic that scholars would, over time, find general regularities in human development.

Amidst all the diversity of Gordon's prolific scholarly output, what is the most enduring aspect of his archaeological work? My answer not only reveals my own bias, but also reflects a pattern I have perceived in the chapters in this volume. This answer is his monographs: the baseline data and interpretations he published on his research throughout the Americas. Gordon loved mystery novels, and his broad archaeological view, I believe, is best seen in a statement by that great fictional detective Sherlock Holmes: "It is a capital mistake to theorize before one has the data" (in "A Scandal in Bohemia"). That is not to say that Gordon operated in a theoretical vacuum. He did not follow the dictates of another fictional detective, LAPD Sergeant Joe Friday—"Just the facts, ma'am"; rather, he had a great sense of problem in his work. So to Sherlock Holmes's quote, one could add a remark by the nineteenth-century historian and philosopher Hippolyte Taine: "After the collection of facts, the search for causes" (as noted in *The Macmillan Book of Social Science Quotations*, p. 227). Gordon was always interested in and concerned with causality—the big picture—but causality that was inferred from the archaeological data. In commenting on the argument that considerations of process should precede field attempts to build archaeological databases, Gordon—in the 1977 article "A Consideration of Archaeology," in *Daedalus*—stated, "There is something to be said for this position, but it is equally true that to ask the proper questions demands a certain foreknowledge of the prehistory of the region under examination. Fortunately, there is at least a practical answer. Any modern archaeologist should have the kind of awareness and vision that combines a data base recovery with a concern for process" (p. 91).

If you look at Gordon's writing career, which spanned sixty-five years, you immediately notice—besides its great volume—that he published more than a dozen major monographs on his archaeological research in North, Middle, Central, and South America. These monographs include the following: *Crooks Site: A Marksville Period Burial Mound in La Salle*

Parish, Louisiana (with James A. Ford); *A Supplement to the Pottery Sequence at Ancon, Peru*; *Archaeological Notes on the Central Coast of Peru* (with William Duncan Strong); *Archeology of the Florida Gulf Coast*; *Surface Survey of the Virú Valley, Peru* (with James A. Ford); *Prehistoric Settlement Patterns in the Virú Valley, Peru*; *Early Ancon and Early Supe Culture: Chavin Horizon Sites of the Central Peruvian Coast* (with J. M. Corbett); *The Monagrillo Culture of Panama* (with Charles R. McGimsey); *Prehistoric Settlement Patterns in the Belize Valley, British Honduras* (with William R. Bullard, Jr., John H. Glass, and James C. Gifford); *The Ruins of Altar de Sacrificios, Department of Peten, Guatemala* series (various authors, including Richard E. W. Adams, A. Ledyard Smith, and John A. Graham); *Excavations at Seibal, Department of Peten, Guatemala* series (various authors, including A. Ledyard Smith, Gair Tourtellot, and me); and *Ceramics and Artifacts from Excavations in the Copan Residential Zone* (with William L. Fash, Jr., Richard M. Leventhal, and Arthur Demarest).

With all of his superb contributions, many of which are discussed so well in this volume, I would argue that these substantive monographs form the heart of Gordon's awesome scholarly legacy. As Jerry Milanich notes in his chapter—and I think he hits the nail on the head—Gordon was highly skilled in collecting data, ordering and organizing them, interpreting them, and publishing the results with unmatched speed! When coupled with his great optimism that archaeology had contributed and would continue to contribute to understandings of cultural change through time and space—the big questions—these skills produced the publications that remain so influential today.

To conclude, let me reiterate a comment that I made at Gordon's memorial service in Cambridge. In the end, I suspect that as much as his former students and colleagues will miss his archaeological reports, insights, and ideas, many will miss, even more, the warm person—who, as I oft remember, would take my elbow, steer me into a Chinese restaurant, and enthusiastically say, "Wait 'til you taste the egg drop soup here, my boy, it's terrific!"

It was a privilege and a joy to have known Gordon Randolph Willey.

Contributors

Jeremy A. Sabloff is the Christopher H. Browne Distinguished Professor of Anthropology at the University of Pennsylvania and the Curator of Mesoamerican Archaeology at the University of Pennsylvania Museum. He is a former President of the Society for American Archaeology and is a member of the National Academy of Sciences, the American Academy of Arts and Sciences, and the American Philosophical Society. Among his many books are *A History of American Archaeology* (with Gordon R. Willey), *Cities of Ancient Mexico*, and *The New Archaeology and the Ancient Maya*.

William L. Fash is the William and Muriel Seabury Howells Director at the Peabody Museum of Archaeology and Ethnology, Harvard University, and Charles P. Bowditch Professor of Central American and Mexican Archaeology and Ethnology in the Department of Anthropology, Harvard University. He has directed a series of multidisciplinary research projects at the ancient Maya city of Copán, Honduras, and directed or codirected projects in Teotihuacan and Cuauhtinchan, Mexico. He was awarded the Order of José Cecilio del Valle by the Government of Honduras in 1994 for his contributions to the study and conservation of the cultural patrimony of the Copan Valley. His most recent publications are *The Ancient American World* with Mary E. Lyons (Oxford University Press, 2005) and *Copan: The History of an Ancient Maya Kingdom* coeditor with E. Wyllys Andrews (School of American Research Press, 2005).

Wendy Ashmore is Professor of Anthropology at the University of California, Riverside. She has conducted field research in Guatemala (Quiriguá), Honduras (Gualjoquito and Copán), and most recently, Belize (Xunantunich). Her publications include *Lowland Maya Settlement Patterns* (editor, 1981), *Archaeologies of Landscape: Contemporary Perspectives* (coedited with A. Bernard Knapp, 1999), "'Decisions and Dispositions': Socializing Spatial Archaeology," (*American Anthropologist*, 2002), "Social Archaeology of Landscapes" (in *A Companion to Social Archaeology*, 2004), "Xunantunich in a Belize Valley Context" (with Richard M. Leventhal, in *The Ancient Maya of the Belize Valley: Half a Century of Archaeological Research*, 2004), and "The Idea of a Maya Town" (in *Structure and Meaning in Human Settlement*, 2005).

Deborah Erdman Cornavaca, a recent PhD from the University of California at Los Angeles, focuses her research onindigenous cultures of Mesoamerica and Central America. Her doctoral work examined the contact between Spanish and indigenous groups at Leon Viejo, the first Spanish capital of modern Nicaragua. Modeling social identity and interaction are the driving theoretical interests guiding her research and writing.

Héctor L. Escobedo is Professor of Archaeology at San Carlos University in Guatemala City. He holds a doctoral degree from Vanderbilt University. Since 2003 he has been codirecting a research project at the Classic Maya city of El Perú, Petén, in collaboration with David Freidel from Southern Methodist University. He has published four books and sixty-three articles, and coedited eighteen books and nine technical reports. His latest book is *Ciudades Milenarias* (2006), about the eleven most important ancient Maya sites in Guatemala.

David Freidel is University Distinguished Professor in the Department of Anthropology, Southern Methodist University. He has directed research at Cerros in Belize, Yaxuna in Yucatan, and is currently codirector of the El Peru-Waka' Archaeological Project in Peten.

Stanley Paul Guenter received his BA degree from the Department of Archaeology, Calgary, in 1999. He received his MA from La Trobe University in 2002. His thesis, "Under A Falling Star: The Hiatus at Tikal," deals directly with the topic of the article in this volume. He is a graduate student in the Department of Anthropology, Southern Methodist University and is researching the monumental inscriptions of El Perú-Waka' and the contexts of carved stone monuments as empirical bases for his dissertation on the ancient history of northwestern Peten. He is the staff epigrapher of the Mirador Basin project as well as the epigrapher of the El Perú-Waka' project and the La Corona project in Laguna del Tigre National Park, northwestern Peten.

Norman Hammond is Chairman of the Department of Archaeology and Professor of Archaeology at Boston University, and also Associate in Maya Archaeology of the Peabody Museum, Harvard University. He has directed excavations and surveys on Maya sites in Belize, including Lubaantun, Nohmul, Cuyello, and La Milpa, and is the author of numerous books, monographs, and papers on Maya and other archaeology, including *Ancient Maya Civilization* (1982) *Cuello: an Early Maya Community in Belize* (1991) and *Lubaantun: a Classic Maya Realm* (1975). He has also directed projects in Afghanistan, Ecuador, Libya and Tunisia, and edited *The Archaeology of Afghanistan* (1978).

Richard M. Leventhal is the Williams Director of the University of Pennsylvania Museum of Archaeology and Anthropology and a Professor in the University of Pennsylvania Department of Anthropology. He received his BA in 1974 and his PhD in Anthropology in 1979, both from Harvard. He has done extensive field research in Belize and other parts of Central America for over twenty-five years.

Patricia A. McAnany, Professor of Archaeology at Boston University, has directed archaeological research in the Maya Lowlands since 1990. Her current project, the Xibun Archaeological Research Project, is focused on political, ritual, and economic transformations of Terminal Classic Maya society. Significant publications include *K'axob: Ritual, Work, and Family in an Ancient Maya Village* (Cotsen Institute of Archaeology at UCLA, 2004), *Living with the Ancestors: Kinship and Kingship in Ancient Maya Society* (University of Texas Press, 1995), *Sacred Landscape and Settlement in the Sibun River Valley* (Institute of Mesoamerican Studies, 2002), and *Prehistoric Maya Economies of Belize* (JAI Press, 1989).

Joyce Marcus is the Robert L. Carneiro Distinguished Professor of Anthropology and the Curator of Latin American Archaeology at the University of Michigan. She is a member of the National Academy of Sciences and the American Academy of Arts and Sciences. Among her books are *Mesoamerican Writing Systems, Zapotec Civilization* (with Kent V. Flannery), *Emblem and State in the Classic Maya Lowlands*, and *Women's Ritual in Formative Oaxaca: Figurine-making, Divination, Death and the Ancestors.*

Jerald T. Milanich is curator in archaeology at the Florida Museum of Natural History in Gainesville. He is the author or editor of twenty books describing the Indian societies of the Americas and their interactions with Europeans during the colonial and postcolonial periods. His latest book is *Frolicking Bears, Wet Vultures, and Other Oddities: A New York City Journalist in Nineteenth-Century Florida.*

Michael E. Moseley, with forty years of active field research in the central Andes, is a Distinguished Professor at the University of Florida and a Member of the National Academy of Sciences. He studies human adaptations from Paleo-Indian through Spanish Colonial time frames. His current research addresses both ancient political ceremonies and recurrent natural disasters.

Jeffrey Quilter is Deputy Director for Curatorial Affairs and Curator of Intermediate Area Archaeology at the Peabody Museum of Archaeology and Ethnology, Harvard University. His most recent publications are *Treasures of the Andes* (Duncan Baird, 2005) and *Cobble Circles and Standing Stones: Archaeology at the Rivas Site Costa Rica* (University of Iowa Press, 2004).

Prudence M. Rice is currently Associate Vice Chancellor for Research and Director of the Office of Research Development and Administration at Southern Illinois University Carbondale, where she is also Professor and Distinguished Scholar in the Department of Anthropology. She received her PhD in Anthropology from Pennsylvania State University and taught at the University of Florida before moving to SIUC. Her research interests include pottery analysis, Maya calendrics, and the Spanish Colonial wine industry. Former president of the Society for American Archaeology and founding editor of *Latin American Antiquity*, Rice is author of *Pottery Analysis, A Sourcebook* (2005) and *Maya Political Science* (2004), and coeditor (with Arthur A. Demarest and Don S. Rice) of *The Terminal Classic in the Maya Lowlands* (2004).

Gair Tourtellot is a Research Fellow in the Department of Archaeology at Boston University. He is codirector of the La Milpa Archaeological Project, primarily concerned with settlement mapping whose long transects discovered a "cosmological" design 7.5 km across. Previously he codirected a project at Sayil, Yucatán, México, and learned his trade under Gordon Willey at Seibal, Petén, Guatemala.

Index

References to illustrations are in italic type.

Adams, Richard E. W., 10, 128, 131, 133, 149, 236

Adaptive Radiations in Prehistoric Panama (Linares and Ranere), 121

Aguateca, 134, 190

Aguateca Stela 2, 165

Aldana, Gerardo, 164

Altar de Sacrificios, 6, 9, 126, 127, 128, 131, 133, 135, 136, 234; collapse of Maya civilization and, 149, 150; Willey's hiatus model and, 190

Altun Ha, 204

Ambergris Cay, 220

American Academy of Arts and Sciences, 12

American Anthropological Association (AAA), 6–7, 8, 12, 64

American Anthropologist, 7, 18, 61, 63, 64, 211, 212, *213*, 214

American Antiquity, 20, 21, 29, 211, 212, *213*

American Ethnologist, 211, 212, *213*

American Formative cultures, 113

Americanist archaeology, 64, 66, 67, 69, 210

American Museum of Natural History (New York), 26

American Philosophical Society, 12

Ancient Civilizations of Mexico and Central America (Spinden), 146

Ancón Bay, 28, 29

Andean archaeology, 5, 9, 75, 105, 112; *See also* Peru

Andes, 118, 119–20; art styles and, 7, 72, 74, 81–83, 89; Bennett on, 112; *Introduction to American Archaeology* (Willey) and, 115; Willey and McGimsey article in *Archaeology* magazine and, 107; Willey's paper at Thirty-Third International Congress of Americanists and, 109

Andrews, Will, V, 128

Angas, George, 96

Angel, Lawrence, *17*

Anthropological Society of Washington, 108–9

Antiquity, 8, 11, 209, 211–12
"Archaeological Classification of Culture Contact Situations, An" (Willey), 30
Archaeological Notes on the Central Coast of Peru (Willey and Strong), 236
Archaeological research: model for, 68; Modern Period in, 210
Archaeological Researches in Retrospect (Willey), 6
Archaeology magazine, 107–8
Archeology of the Florida Gulf Coast (Willey), 15, 22–23, 236
Armillas, Pedro, 83
Art, 8, 30, 121, 214; Huari and Tiwanaku, 29; Intermediate Area and, 110–11; Manabí, 110; in Mesoamerica/Andes, 6–7; in South America, 111; Waka' and, 197; *See also* Chavín art; Early Horizon art style; Olmec art
Artificial stratigraphic units, 27
Ashmore, Wendy, 5–6, *52*, 237–38
Atwood, Caleb, 33
Augustine Obispo, 221, *222*
Austin, Alfredo López, 216
Australia, 195
Authority, 91, 97, 98–99, 223, 225
A. V. Kidder Medal, 12
Aztecs, 112, 117, 145, 163, 215, 223

Baja Verapaz, 128
B'aktun 9, 149
Balaj Chan K'awiil, 204
Ball games, 152, 164, 166–67, 174, 175, 176
Barton Ramie, 43, *45*, 46, 48, 49, 53, 126
Baudez, Claude, 113, 116
Bayal, 134, 135
Bay Islands, 112
Becan battlements, 190
Belize, 135, 144, 220, 221, *221, 222, 224*
Belize River valley, 126
Belize Valley, 6, 9, 41–54; general archaeology and, 51–53; map, *44*; Maya archaeology and, 47–51; photo of Willey at Barton Ramie in, *42*; settlement patterns and, 43, 46–47, 48, 50, 51, 53, 54; *See also* Barton Ramie
Bennett, Wendell, 26, 33, 111–13, 117
Benson, Elizabeth, 214

Berkeley, 28
Binford, Lewis, 54, 67
Bird, Junius, 27, 33, 109
Birdsell, Joseph, *17*
Bishop, Ronald, 130, 135
Blanton, Richard, 54, 214
Bloodletting, 164
Blood of Kings, The (Schele and Miller), 214
Blue jade "stiletto" bloodletter, *132*
Boas, Franz, 62–63
Bolivia, 28, 29
Bonampak, 163, 168
Braidwood, Robert, 6
British Honduras, 43, 109
Buddhism, 209, 217
Bullard, William R., Jr., 43, 49, 50, 127, 236
Bullen, Ripley P., 21
Bureau of American Ethnology (BAE), 21, 22, 106
Burger, Richard, 74, 83

Calakmul, 171, 172, 173, 174, 187, 191, 203, 204, 206
Cambridge University, 12
Campeche, 149, 168, 187
Cancuén, 134, 203, 205
Caracol, 153, 172, 173, 174, 203, 205
Carnegie Institution, 9, 47, 48
Carneiro, Robert, 75
Carrasco, Davíd, 216, 217, 221–22
Casma Valley, 75, 81
Cauca Valley, 75
Caye Coco, 220
Central America, 4, 7, 46, 73, 106, 108, 117, 121; *Civilizations of Ancient America* and, 112; Ford and, 113; Intermediate Area and, 117; pottery and, 113; Stirling (Matthew) and, 107; Willey and McGimsey article in *Archaeology* magazine and, 107; Willey monographs on research in, 235–36; Willey's fieldwork in, 113; Willey's paper at Thirty-Third International Congress of Americanists and Lower, 109
Ceramics, 4, 8, 33, 222; Belize Valley research and, 47, 50–51; Chavín art style and, 86; "Chronological Outline for the Northwest Florida Coast" (Willey and Woodbury) and, 20; Fine Paste, 127, 128,

134, 135; Florida and, 19, 23; Mesoamerica and, 76, 80; Mexico and, 84, 85; Monagrillo mound and, 107; Peru and, 28; pre-Olmec styles of, 76; Seibal project and, 130, 131; Swift Creek, 18; Willey's hiatus model and, 189; *See also* Pottery
Ceramics and Artifacts from Excavations in the Copan Residential Zone (Willey, Fash, Jr., Leventhal, and Demarest), 236
Cerro Mangote, 107
Cerro Sechín, 75, 81, *82*, 86
Chaa Creek, 155
Chacchob, 155
Chak Tok Ich'ak, 173
Chancay Valley, 21, 27
Chan Chan, 35, 36
Chase, Arlen, 153
Chase, Diane, 153
Chavín, 29, 30, 31, 117
Chavín art, 72–73, 74, 81–83, 85–91, *87–90*, 93, 98, 99; Intermediate Area and, 110; San Agustín and, 111
Chavín de Huántar, 27–28, 30, 74, 83, 85–86, *88*, 89; Old Temple, 90, *90*, 96
Chavinoid, 30, 83
Cherry, John, 73, 74
Chiapas coast, 76
Chibcha, 112
Chichén Itzá, 148–49, 155, 171, 218, 220, 221, 223
Chiefdoms: Andes and, 83; authority and, 91, 97, 98–99; Chavín, 85–91; great art styles and, 74–75, 76, 83–84; *See also* Coclé, of Panama; Maori, of New Zealand
Chilam b'alam, books of the, 168
Childe, V. Gordon, 73
Chimor, 35
Chimu, 35, 37
Chiriquí, 108
Chixoy river, 127
Cholula, 217
"Chronological Outline for the Northwest Florida Coast, A" (Willey and Woodbury), 20, 21
Chunchucmil, 155
Circular shrines, *122*, 221, *222*, 223
Civilian Conservation Corps (CCC), 16

Civilizations of Ancient America, The, 112
Classic Maya Collapse, The, 141, 142, 151
"Classic Maya Hiatus: A Rehearsal for the Collapse?, The" (Willey), 189
Classic period, 195, 206, 217; collapse of Maya civilization and, 166, 172, 174, 175, 177n3; core-buffer zone model and, 191, 192; Kan kingdom of, 203; Willey's hiatus model and, 189
Classificatory-Historical Period, 113
Cobá, 155
Coclé, of Panama, 83, 91–93
Coe, Michael, 113, 116
Coggins, Clemency, 191, 214, 216
Colha, 155
Collier, Donald, 33
Colombia, 75, *94*, 112, 116, 117, 118
Columbia University, 4, 18, 20, 26, 27, 113
Committee on Un-American Activities, 62
Communism, 62–63
Competition, 152–55, 174, 190
"Conceptual Structure in Middle American Studies, The" (Kluckhohn), 64
Conch shells, 218, 221, *222*, 223
Conjunctive approach, Taylor's, 53, 54, 64, 66
Conrad, Geoffrey, 211
"Consideration of Archaeology, A" (Willey), 235
Copán, 51–52, 146, 153, 154, 192, 196, 199, 200, *202*, 202, 203
Corbett, John M., 27, 236
Cordillera, 29, 32, 35, 38
Core-buffer zone model, 189, 191–92
Cornavaca, Deborah, 6, 234, 238
Corpus of Maya Hieroglyphic Inscriptions field drawings, 193, 197, 199
Cortés, Hernán, 210
Costa Rica, *92*, 106, 109, 110, 113, 118, 119, 195; Bennett and, 112; *Introduction to American Archaeology* (Willey) and, 116; Middle America and, 109
Covarrubias, Miguel, 74
Cowgill, George, 143, 148
Cozumel Island, 223
Crooks Site: A Marksville Period Burial Mound in La Salle Paris, Louisiana (Willey and Ford), 235–36

Crooks site (in Louisiana), 21
Cruciform causeway system, 134
Crystal River site (in Citrus County), 22
Cuca, 155
Culbert, T. Patrick, 150
Cultural evolutionary models, 62–64, 67,
    69–70
Cultura madre, 74
Cultura matriz, 74
Culturas hermanas, 74
Cummings, Byron, 6, 11
Cuzco, 28

Daedalus, 235
Daniel, Glyn, 210
Darien, 108
Davis, George, 33
Day, Kent, 128
Demarest, Arthur, 74, 121, 134, 154, 190,
    204, 205, 211, 236
Dendrochronology, 16, 21
Depopulation, collapse of Maya civilization
    and, 146–47, 150, 170, 174
Diego de Landa, Bishop, 167
Diffusion, 109, 111, 112, 113, 121
Disciplinary matrix, 68
Doornbos, Martin, 99
Doran, Edward, 18
Dos Pilas, 134, 135, 154, 155, 165, 204
Drennan, Dick, 119
Dual processual theory, 54
Dumbarton Oaks (DO), 106, 117–20, 214
Dzibanché, 191, 192, 203, 204
Dzibilchaltun, 50

Earle, Timothy, 75
*Early Ancon and Early Supe Culture: Chavin
    Horizon Sites of the Central Peruvian Coast*
    (Willey and Corbett), 236
Early Classic period, 136, 196, 197, 199,
    200, 201, 202, 204; collapse of Maya civi-
    lization and, 151, 155, 163, 172; core-
    buffer zone model and, 191; Seibal
    project and, 133; tombs of Río Azul, 203;
    Willey's hiatus model and, 189
"Early Great Styles and the Rise of the Pre-
    Columbian Civilizations, The" (Willey),
    7–8, 72, 99, 214

Early Horizon art style, 76–80, 83–85, 93, 99
Early Mesoamerican Village (Flannery), 210
East, James N., 107
Ecuador, 112, 116, 117, 118
Edmonson, Munro, 168, 169
Edzná, 168, 170
Ehecatl-Quetzalcoatl (EQ), 218, 222
Ek'Balam, 155
El Mirador, 192, 203
El Perú, 187, 192, 193
El Salvador, 117, 121
El Zodz, 195
Epi-Olmec La Mojarra Stela, 163
Escobedo, Héctor L., 10, 187, 238
Estrada, Emilio, 116
Eta-Aquarids, 165–66
Ethnography, 66, 119
Ethnohistory, 66
Ethnohistory, 211, 212, *213*
Evans, Clifford, 33, 116
Evolutionary theory, 113
*Excavations at Seibal, Department of Peten,
    Guatemala* series, 236
Excavations in Southeast Florida (Willey), 22
Excavations in the Chancay Valley (Willey), 27

Fahsen, Federico, 204
Fairbanks, Charles H., 17, 24n2
Fash, Barbara, *202*
Fash, William L., Jr., 3, 153, 154, 226, 236,
    237
Feathered serpent, 210–11, 215, 216, 218–25
Feathered Serpent Pyramid of Teotihuacan,
    218
Feldman, Lawrence, 130
Feng, H. Y., *17*
Field archaeology, 4, 9, 11, 13, 105, 107
Fiske, Timothy, 128
Flannery, Kent, 74, 210
Florescano, Enrique, 217
Florida, 4, 15–24, 26, 105, 234
Ford, James A., 4, 5, 17, 18, 21, 26, 33, 34,
    113–14, 234, 236; cultural evolutionary
    models and, 63, 64; Virú Valley and, 21
Fort Walton, 23
Freidel, David A., 10, 165, 187, 190, *198*,
    200, 214, 238
Friday, Sergeant Joe, 235

Games. *See* Ball games
Gann, Thomas, 146
Georgia, 19, 20, 21, 26; *See also* Ocmulgee
  site (Macon, Georgia)
Gifford, James C., 51, 236
Gillespie, Susan, 216, 217
Glass, John H., 236
Goggin, John M., 21
"Gold and Power in Ancient Costa Rica,
  Panama, and Columbia," 120
Graham, Ian, 128, 130, 197
Graham, John A., 128, 130, 236
Graham, Mark Miller, 119
Gran Chibcha, 118, 119
"Gran Chibcha as a Culture Area(?): Hori-
  zon Styles, Cultural Traditions, and
  Temporal Depth at the Center of the
  Pre-Columbian World, The," 118
Greater Nicoya, 117
Griffin, James B., 18
Griffin, John W., 21
Grijalva Depression, 76
Grove, David, 74
"Growth Trends in New World Cultures"
  (Willey), 233–34
Grube, Nikolai, 163, 164, 191, 193
Guatemala: "Interrelated Rise of the Native
  Cultures of Middle and South America"
  (Willey) and, 109; Kaminaljuyú, 9; Kroe-
  ber and, 109; Maya languages in, 145;
  Maya Lowland Ceramic Conference in
  Guatemala City, 143; Middle America
  and, 109; Order of the Quetzal from, 12;
  Willey and McGimsey article in *Archaeol-
  ogy* magazine and, 108; *See also* Petén;
  Seibal project
Guenter, Stanley Paul, 10, 187, 192–93,
  195, 200, 238
Gulf Coast, 76, 79, 80, 83, 84, *132*, 168;
  Florida, 4, 15–24
Gulf of Mexico, 135

Haas, Jonathan, 152
Haberland, Wolfgang, 116
Hammond, Norman, 9, 48, 126, 128, 234,
  238
Handbook of South American Indians (Willey
  and Sabloff), 4–5, 21, 33, 113

Hartman, Carl V., 116
Harvard Faculty Club, 12
Harvard Peabody Museum, 6, 12, 16, 19,
  22, 116, 120, 121, 235
Harvard University, 11, 30, 42, 64, 128
Hassig, Ross, 152
Haury, Emil, 112
Haviland, William, 48
Hay, Clarence L., 65
Healy, Paul, 121
Herrera, 91
Herrera y Todesillas, Antonio de, 167
History of American Archaeology, A (Willey),
  6, 113
Hodder, Ian, 211
Holactún, 168
Holder, Preston, 18
Holmburg, Alan, 33
Holmes, Sherlock, 235
Holmes, William Henry, 114
Honduras, 6, 109, 112, 117, 118
Hoopes, John, 118, 119, 120, 121
Horizon markers, 121
Horizon styles, 29, 30, 31, 33, 35, 38, 120
Households/communities, study of ancient,
  51, 52
Houston, Stephen, 134, 190
Huaca Prieta, 109
Huari, 29, 31, 32
Huari-Tiahuanaco, 117
Human agency, 11
"Hunting Prehistory in Panama Jungles:
  Tracing Lost Indian Civilizations, an
  Archeologist and His Wife Narrowly
  Escape Disaster on the Isthmus' Wild
  North Coast" (Stirling), 107
Huxley, Aldous, 66
Huxley Medal, 12
Hybridization, 73

Ica Valley, 31
Ichmul de Morley, 155
Ideology, study of, 8, 11, 209–26; as a
  courageous enterprise, 211–15; discus-
  sion/conclusion, 225–26; feathered ser-
  pent and, 210–11, 215, 218–25;
  Quetzalcoatl and, 209, 215–17
Incas, 27, 28, 29, 30, 31, 35, 112, 117

Inomata, Takeshi, 134, 190
Institute of Andean Research (IAR), 26, 27
Intermediate Area, 105–22; Bennett and, 111–13; Dumbarton Oaks (DO) and, 117–20; fieldwork in Central America and, 113; Ford and, 113–14; "Interrelated Rise of the Native Cultures of Middle and South America" (Willey) and, 108–9; *Introduction to American Archaeology* (Willey) and, 114–16; School of American Research (SAR) seminar and, 116–17; Willey and McGimsey article in *Archaeology* magazine and, 107–8; Willey's paper at Thirty-Third International Congress of Americanists and, 109–11
International Style, 120
"Interpretation of the Prehistory of the Eastern United States, An" (Willey and Ford), 18, 63, 234
Interregional interaction, 73–74, 75
"Interrelated Rise of the Native Cultures of Middle and South America, The" (Willey), 108–9
Introduction to American Archaeology, An (Willey), 8–9, 114, 234
Introgression, 73
Invasion hypothesis, 135–36
Irrigation systems, 34, 35–37
ISI Web of Knowledge search engine, 211, 212
Isthmus of Tehuantepec, 76
Itzá, 168, 170, 173
Itzán, 134
Ixkun, 171

Jadeite celts, *132*
Jaguar, Dragon, 199
Jaguar Paw dynasty, 173, 174
Jaina, 168
Jainism, 209, 217
Jama Coaque, 111
Jasaw Chan K'awiil, 204
Jasaw Kan K'awil, 169, 172
Jijón y Caamaño Jacinto, 116
Jimba, 127, 128, 136
Johnson, Allen, 75
Johnston, Kevin, 134

Jones, Katherine Burton, 16
Journal of American Folklore, 211, 212, *213*
Journal of Field Archaeology, 211, *213*
JSTOR search engine, 211, 212
Judaism, 209
Junco phase, 135
Justeson, John, 164

Kabah, 155
K'ab'il, Lady, 204
Kai Tangata (Eat Man), 96
Kan, 191, 192, 203, 205
Karwa, 89
K'atuns, 155, 167–74, 177n3, 177n4
Kelley, Arthur R., 16, 18–19
Kennings, 86
Kidder, Alfred, II, 27
King, Arden, 18
King, Litvak, 217
K'inich B'alam, 193, 194, 195, 199, 204
K'inich B'alam Chan Ahk, 199
K'inich Yax K'uk Mo', 200
K'inich Waaw, 205
Kirchoff, Paul, 109
Kluckhohn, Clyde, 64, 65, 67, 69
Knapp, A. Bernard, 53
Kosok, Paul, 34
Kroeber, Alfred L., 26, 27, 28, 29, 73, 109, 110–11, 235
Kuhn, Thomas, 68, 69
k'ul ajaw, 175
Kuylen, Rudi, 130

Labná, 155
Ladd, John, 116
Laguna Petexbatún (at Dos Pilas), 134
La Libertad, 128
Landscape archaeology, 52–53, 54
Lange, Frederick W., 115, 116, 118
Las Monjas, 155
Late Classic period, 137, 204; collapse of Maya civilization and, 145, 151, 153–54, 155, 156, 163, 166, 168, 169, 171, 176; Willey's hiatus model and, 189
Late Classic Tepeu 2, 133
Late Preclassic Period, 155, 163
Lathrap, Donald, 30, 87

Latin American research, 26
La Venta, 80, 84
Lawrence, D. H., 215
Lehmann, Henri, *130*
Leone, Mark, 128
Leonids, 165–66
Leventhal, Richard M., 6, 46, 51, *52*, 61, 63, 234, 236, 239
Linares, Olga (de Sapir), 91, 116, 121
Linné, Sigvald, 116
Linton, Ralph L., 65
Littmann, Edwin, 130
Los Santos, 91
Lothrop, Samuel K., 26, 65, 116
Louisiana, 18, 19, 21, 26
Louisiana State University, 18
Lower Mississippi Valley, 18, 20
Luján, Leonardo López, 216
Lyon, Edwin, 16
Lyrids, 165

MacLeod, Barbara, 214
Macmillan Book of Social Science Quotations, The, 235
Maler, Teobert, 127, 128, *129*
Man, 211, 212, *213*
Manabí art, 110, 111
Manabí-Esmeraldas, 111
Maori, of New Zealand, 83, 90, 93–98, *95, 97*
Marañon River, 89
Marcus, Joyce, 8, 72, 191, 214, 239
Mariana Mesa, 107
Marin, David Mora, 195
Martin, Simon, 163, 164, 191, 193, 196
Marxism, 62, 63
Masul, 200
Mathews, Peter, 130, 134
May, 167–74
Maya and Their Neighbors: Essays on Middle American Anthropology and Archaeology, The (Hay, Linton, Lothrop, Shapiro, and Vaillant, ed.), 65
Maya archaeology, 7, 8, 10, 11, 105, 106, 107, 114, 119, 121, 214, 218, 234; Belize Valley research and, 42–43, 47–51, 54; Kluckhohn and, 65–66; Maya communi-

ties and circular shrines, 221; settlement patterns and, 43, 46; study of ancient households/communities and, 52; *See also* Guatemala; Maya civilization, collapse of; Maya Lowlands; Seibal project
Maya civilization, collapse of, 141–76; depopulation and, 146–47, 150, 170, 174; introduction/ideas about, 142–45; Maya art and, 150; warfare/militarism and, 141–42, 145–76, *157—62*, 177n2, 190, 193; Willey's hiatus model and, 189–96; *See also* Maya archaeology
Maya Lowland Ceramic Conference (Guatemala City), 143
Maya Lowlands, 6, 9–10, 47, 187–88, 189, 205, 211, 217, 218, 220, 223; Belize Valley research and, 48, 49, 50, 51; ideology and, 224, 225; landscape archaeology and, 53; Teotihuacancos and, 202; Willey's hiatus model and, 190, 191
Mayapán, 155, 216
McAnany, Patricia A., 11, 209, 234, 239
McBride, Webster, 33
McCarthy, Joseph, 62–63
McGimsey, Charles R., 107, 115, 236
Meggers, Betty J., 116
Melgar y Serrano, José María, 72
Mesoamerica, 5–6, 9, 11, 65, 105, 117, 118, 119, 120, 210, 211; art styles and, 7, 72, 74–80, 110; ball game and, 166; Bennett on, 112; chiefdoms and, 75; ideology and, 226; "Interrelated Rise of the Native Cultures of Middle and South America" (Willey) and, 108, 109; *Introduction to American Archaeology* (Willey) and, 114, 115; Mesoamerican archaeology, 214; Mesoamerican literature, 214; Quetzalcoatl and, 216, 216–17; research of the "high cultures" of, 8; warfare/meteors and, 177n2; Willey's paper at Thirty-Third International Congress of Americanists and, 110
"Mesoamerican Civilization and the Idea of Transcendence" (Willey), 8, 11, 209, 226, 234
Mesoamerican Sites and World-Views (Benson, ed.), 214

Meteor showers, 165–66, 177n2
Method and Theory in American Archaeology (Willey and Phillips), 6, 61–70, 114, 234
Mexico, 195, 196, 204, 205, 211, 215; collapse of Maya civilization and, 150, 151, 173, 174; great art styles and, 76, 77, *78*, *79*, 80, 83, 83–85, 93, 99; interacting chiefdoms and, 74; "Interrelated Rise of the Native Cultures of Middle and South America" (Willey) and, 109; Kroeber and, 109; Maya languages in, 145; Mexican invasion theory and collapse of Maya civilization, 148–49; Mexico City, 106, 148; Middle America and, 109; Willey and McGimsey article in *Archaeology* magazine and, 107, 108; Willey's hiatus model and, 193
Middle America, 105, 109, 112, 114
Middle Classic period, 189
Middle Formative period, 80
Middle Preclassic temple mound, 131
Milanich, Jerald T., 4, 15, 234, 236, 239
Miller, Arthur, 128
Miller, Mary, 214
Mirror-back, 195
Moche, 31, 32, 34
Mochica, 111
Monagrillo ceramic complex, 113
Monagrillo Culture of Panama, The (Willey and McGimsey), 114, 236
Monagrillo mound, 107, 108, 110
Monte Albán, 214
Moore, Clarence B., 19, 22–23, 24n3
Moquegua, 32
Morelos, 80, 85
Morley, Sylvanus G., 128, 146, 147, 189
Moseley, Michael E., 5, 26, 234, 239
Mosna Valley, 86
Motagua Valley (of southern Guatemala), *132*
Mound C/Funeral Mound, 16–17
Moxeke, 74–75, 81
Mulloy, William, 18
Murra, John, 32

Naachtun, 200
Nahuatl scribes, 216
Nahua tribes, 147

Nakoms, 167
Naranjo, 156, 168, 172
National Academy of Sciences, 12
National Park Service, 16, 18
National Science Foundation, 47
Neitzel, Robert S., 18
Nepeña Valley, 75, 81
New Mexico, 107, 116
New World archaeology, 29
New Zealand. *See* Maori, of New Zealand
Nicaragua, 109, 110, 112, 113, 116
Nicholson, Henry, 215, 216, 217
Nohmul, 220
North America, 4, 7, 105, 114, 235–36
Norweb, Albert, 113
"Notes of Central Georgia Dendrochronology," 234
Nuclear America, 113

Oaxaca, 80, 85, 168, 214
Ocmulgee site (Macon, Georgia), 16–17, *17*, 24n2
Oliveros, José Antonio, 128
Olmec, 117, *132*
Olmec art, 72–76, 81, 84, 85, 98, 110
Olmec jade bloodletter, 131
Olmecoid, 83
Olson, Stanley, 130
Order of the Quetzal (from Guatemala), 12
Origins of Maya Civilization, The (Adams, ed.), 10–11
Owens, Jesse, 14
Oxkintok, 155, 170, 202

Pachacamac, 27, 28
Pa' Chan (Split Sky) kingdom, 195
Pakal Na, 223, *224*
Palenque, 146, 168, 195–96, 202–3
Pampas, 33
Panama, 6, 8, 42, *94*, 105, 106, 107, 119, 120, 122; Intermediate Area and, 112; *Introduction to American Archaeology* (Willey) and, 115, 116; pottery and, 113; Sitio Conte, *92*, *94*; Willey and McGimsey article in *Archaeology* magazine and, 107–8; *See also* Coclé, of Panama
Panama City, 18
Paracas, 28

Paracas Peninsula, 89
Paradigms, 68–69, 70, 121
Parallel evolution, 73
Parita Bay, 107, 108
Pars pro toto, principle of, 84
Pasión River (Rio Pasión), 127, 128, 133–36, 148, 149, 192, 204, 218
Pastmasters: Eleven Modern Pioneers of Archaeology, The, 4
Pattern recognition studies, 234
Pechtun Ha, 221
Peer-polity interaction, 73–74
Peru, 26–38, 105, 117; Cerro Sechín in, *82*; Chancay Valley in, 21; culture contact and, 27–33; great art styles and, 83, 110; interacting chiefdoms and, 74; "Interrelated Rise of the Native Cultures of Middle and South America" (Willey) and, 109; *Introduction to American Archaeology* (Willey) and, 114, 115; Kroeber and, 109; Lima, 27; Mochica of, 111; Nepeña Valley in, 81; research in coastal, 5; research of the "high cultures" of, 8; settlement patterns and, 33–38; Willey and McGimsey article in *Archaeology* magazine and, 108; Willey's paper at Thirty-Third International Congress of Americanists and, 109; *See also* Chavín de Huántar; Virú Valley
Petén, 49, 126, 127, 128, 134, 135, 148, 149, 154, 165, 173, 187, *188*, 196, 197, 200
Petexbatún project, 204
Petexbatún region, 144, 154, 155, 190, 205
Phillips, Philip, 6, 17, 61–70, 234
Piedras Negras, 147, 168, 204
Piedras Negras Stela 35, 165
Pohl, Mary, 130
Pollock, Harry, 126
Polo, José, 72
Popol Vuh, 166
Portraits in American Archaeology: Remembrances of Some Distinguished Americanists (Willey), 4, 12, 18
Postclassic period, 192, 206, 218, 223; collapse of Maya civilization and, 144, 145, 155, 168, 169, 172, 174, 175
Pottery, 108, 113, 223; Bayal, 134; Chavín art and, 81; Coclé, of Panama and, 91;

Early Classic, 128; "Interrelated Rise of the Native Cultures of Middle and South America" (Willey) and, 108; Mesoamerican, 74, 76, *78*; Seibal project and, 135; Willey's paper at Thirty-Third International Congress of Americanists and, 110; *See also* Ceramics
Pre-Columbian Man Finds Central America: The Archaeological Bridge (Stone), 116, 121
Pre-Columbian Man in Costa Rica (Stone), 121
Prehistoric Settlement Patterns in the Belize Valley (Wiley, Bullard, Glass, and Gifford), 236
Prehistoric Settlement Patterns in the Viru Valley, Peru (Willey), 34, 236
Processual archaeology, 67, 70, 106, 210, 211, 214
Proskouriakoff, Tatiana, 127, 135, 189
Proyecto Arqueológico Waka', 201, 203
Puebla, 80
Puerto Supe, 28
pujb', 195
Puleston, Dennis, 131, 214
Puleston, Olga, 131
Punkurí, 75, 81
Putun, 149
Puuc area, 148, 155, 168

Quilter, Jeffrey, 8–9, 105, 234, 239
Quimby, George, 18
Quintana Roo, 192
Quiriguá, 153

Rands, Robert, 130, 190
Rangihaeata, 96
Rathje, William, 189, 191, 191–92
Rayborn, J. S., 19
Real complex, 131
Real Xe, 131, *132*
Red Scare, 62–63
Reichel-Dolmatoff, Gerardo, 116
Religion and Empire (Conrad and Demarest), 211
Renfrew, Colin, 73, 74
Rice, Prudence M., 9, 141, 234, 239–40
Ringle, William, 155, 156, 219
Rio Azul, 196, 202

Rio Hondo, 196
Río Moquegua sierra, 31–32
Río Pasión. *See* Pasión River (Rio Pasión)
Río Pesquero, Veracruz, 77
Rise and Fall of Maya Civilization, The
  (Thompson), 147–48
Riverine model, 131
Rose, Richard, 128
Rouse, Irving, 21, 22
Rowe, John, 30, 31, 86
Ruins of Altar de Sacrificios, Department of
  Peten, Guatemala, The series, 236

Sabloff, Jeremy A., 11, 233, 236, 237; Clas-
  sificatory-Historical Period and, 113; col-
  lapse of Maya civilization and, 148, 149;
  History of American Archaeology, 6; Seibal
  project and, 128, *130*, 130, 131, 135; on
  settlement pattern studies, 51, 53
Sacbeob, 128
Sacul, 171
Safety Harbor, 23
Sage, Sarah, *198*
Salvador, 109
Samuel Oshon, *221*, 221
San Agustín, 110, 111
San Gervasio, 218
San José Mogote, 76
San Juan River, 187
San Lorenzo, 76, 80, 85
San Pedro Mártir, 187
San Pedro River, 205
Santa Elena Balancán, 195
Saul, Frank, 130
Sayaxché, 127
Sayil, 155
"Scandal in Bohemia, A" (Holmes), 235
Schele, Linda, 165, 214
School of American Research (SAR), 10, 48,
  116–17, 190, 234; seminar on collapse of
  Maya civilization, 141, 142, 149, 150, 175
Schuyler, Bob, 128
Seibal, 149, 218
Seibal project, 6, 9, 126–37, *129*, *130*, *131*,
  132, 234; collapse of Maya civilization
  and, 148, 150; invasion hypothesis,
  135–36
Séjourné, Laurette, 215

Selena (Willey), 12–13, 234
Serendipity, 126, 136
Settlement pattern studies, 5, 8, 10, 105,
  126, 127, 187; Belize Valley and, 6, 41, 43,
  46–48, 50, 51, 53, 54; Cauca Valley and,
  75; Florida Gulf Coast and, 23; Maya
  archaeology and, 9; Peru and, 33–38;
  Seibal project and, 128; Willey on, 41
Shapiro, Harry L., 65
Sharer, Robert, 13, 176n1
Shimkin, Demitri B., 9, 141, 142, 145, 150,
  175, 176, 190
Sibun River valley, 211, 220
Sibun Valley, 220, *221*, *222*, 223, *224*,
  224, 225
Sidrys, Raymond, 130
Site units, 30, 31, 32
Siyaj Chan Ahk, 195
Siyaj K'ak', 193, 194, 195, 196, 199, 200,
  201
Smith, A. Ledyard, 127, 128, *130*, 133,
  190, 236
Smith, Hale G., 21
Smith, Robert E., 189
Smithsonian Institution, 5, 15, 17, 21, 22,
  33, 106
Socialism, 62–63
Social Science Citation Index, 211
Society for American Archaeology, 12, 105
South America, 4, 7, 105, 106, 108, 111,
  112, 114, 115, 235–36
Southeastern archaeology, 18, 21, 22
Southern Illinois University Press, 64
Southwestern archaeology, 16
Space-time synthesis, 113, 114
Space-time systematics, 4, 8
Spearthrower Owl, 193, 196
Spinden, Herbert J., 109, 116, 146
Split representations, 87, 89
Squier, Ephraim, 33
Sri Lanka, 126
St. Andrew Bay, 18
Stelae, 16, 89, 163, 165, 193, *194*, 194, 196,
  197, *198*, 199, 200, *201*, 204
Steward, Julian H., 4, 5, 21, 33, 43, 109, 235
Stirling, Marion, 107, 116
Stirling, Matthew, 17, 18, 21, 22, 106–7, 116
Stone, Doris, 116, 121

Stratigraphic excavations, 19
Strong, William Duncan, 4, 11–12, 18, 27, 28, 33, 109, 236
Structure of Scientific Revolutions, The (Kuhn), 68
Stuart, David, 156, 177n2, 193
"Study of Archaeology: A Dialectic, Practical and Critical Discussion with Special Reference to American Archaeology and the Conjunctive Approach, A" (Taylor), 64
Study of Archaeology, A (Taylor), 66–67
Supe, 29
Supplement to the Pottery Sequence at Ancon, Peru, A (Willey), 236
Surface Survey of the Virú Valley, Peru (Willey and Ford), 236
Swift Creek, 18, 23
Synthesis, 4, 8, 22, 26, 33, 42, 54, 105, 113, 114, 234

Tabasco, 149
Taine, Hippolyte, 235
Tamarindito, 155
Taube, Karl, 177n2, 199, *202*, 218, 219
Tavern Club (Boston), 234
Taylor, Walter, *17*, 53, 54, 64, 66–67, 69
Tedlock, Barbara, 177n2
Tello, Julio C., 26, 27, 28, 29, 74, 81, 86
Tello Obelisk, 86–87, *89*, 89
Teotihuacan (Mexican metropolis of), 9–10, 117, 127, 128, 133, 163, 172, 173, 197, 199, 200, 202, 205, 210, 211, 223; core-buffer zone model and, 191; Feathered Serpent Pyramid of, 218; legacy in hegemonic states, 202–5; Quetzalcoatl and, 215, 216, 217; style fire darts, *202*; Willey's hiatus model and, 192–96
Tepejilote, 133, 134
Terminal Classic period, 9, 127, *129*, 135–36, 197, 205, 211, 216, 218, 220, 220–21, 223, 224; collapse of Maya civilization and, 142–43, 144, 145, 153, 170, 172, 175, 176, 176n1
Terminal Late Classic period, 128
Thirty-Third International Congress of Americanists, paper delivered by Willey at, 109–11
Thompson, J. Eric, 146–48, 149

"Three Princes of Serendip, The," 126
Tiahuanaco, 111
Tikal, 50, 126, 133, 153, 169, 171, 172, 173, 174, 194–97, 200, 202–6; core-buffer zone model and, 191; Willey's hiatus model and, 189, 193
Timmerman, Evelyn Adams, 24n2
Tiwanaku (Bolivian center of), 28, 29, 30, 31, 35
Tlapacoya, 76
Tollan, 225
Tollans, 216
Toltec, 117, 127, 215
Topiltzin Quetzalcoatl (TQ), 209, 210, 214–17, 218, *219*, 219–20, 221–22, 225, 226, 234
Tortuguero, 156
Tourtellot, Gair, 9, 126, 128, 234, 236, 240
Tozzer, Alfred Marston, 6, 42, 65, 167
Trait units, 30, 32
Tres Islas, 203
Triadan, Daniela, 134
Tula, 216, 217, 223
Tz'i, Chak Chay, 195

Uaxactun, 127, 190, 195
Ucanal, 135
Uhle, Max, 27–28, 29, 30, 31
Une Balam K'awil, 193
"Unity and Heterogeneity within the Chavin Horizon" (Burger), 83
University of Arizona, 6, 12, 16, 26
University of Michigan, 17, 18
University of New Mexico, 12
University of Pennsylvania project, 126
University of Southern California, 27
Upper Temple of the Jaguars, 155
Usumacinta (river), 127, 142, 149, 168, 187, *188*
Uxmal, 155, 168, 170, 218

Vaillant, George C., 65
Valdez, Juan Antonio, 190
Vanderbilt research, 190, 203
Venus, 163–66, 169, 172
Veracruz-Tabasco lowlands, 76
Veraguas, 91, 108
Viking Medal, 12

Virú Valley, 21, 33, 33–34, 35–38, 42, 105, 234; aerial photo in background, 5; landscape archaeology and, 53; settlement patterns and, 5, 41, 43, 47
Vogt, Evon, 46

Wa-Bird kingdom, 195
Wagley, Charles, 17
Waka', 10, 187, 188, 189, 192–205
Walpole, Horace, 126
Warfare/militarism, 9, 93, 94, 95, 97, 97, 202, 203, 205, 206, 214, 222–23; collapse of Maya civilization and, 141–42, 145–76, 157—62, 177n2, 190, 193; great art styles/rise of complex societies and, 75, 85; ideology and, 225, 226; Quetzalcoatl and, 216–17; Venus and, 163–66; war/warfare defined, 152; Willey's hiatus model and, 190, 192, 193
Waring, Antonio J., Jr., 22
W. C. McKern cultural classification system, 16
"Wealth and Hierarchy in the Intermediate Area," 118
Webster, David, 152, 154, 190
Weeden Island, 16, 18, 23
Wilk, Richard, 130
Willey, Gordon Randolph: Bowditch Chair at Harvard, 105, 107; description of, 12; education of, 4, 6, 16, 18, 26, 33; leadership/awards of, 12; mystery novels, 12–13, 234, 235; photo of fieldwork in Florida, 19; photos of, 5, 13, 17, 42, 52, 137; retirement years of, 12–13; on running with Jesse Owens, 14; Sabloff on writings of, 233–36; on settlement pattern studies, 41, 46; summary of Origins of Maya Civilization, 10–11; as teacher/mentor, 11–12; wife of, 12, 17, 24n2, 27; See also names of individual articles/books/monographs of Willey
Willey, Katharine (nee Whaley), 12, 17, 24n2, 27
Wite' Naah structures, 199
Woodbury, Richard B., 19, 19, 19, 20, 22
Works Progress Administration (WPA), 16, 18
World Archaeology, 211, 213
Wright, Sewall, 74

Xe complex, 131
Xiu, 170
Xiw, 168, 172, 173
Xochicalco, 223
Xochiltepec White pottery, 76
Xunantunich, 144

Yale University Publications in Anthropology series, 22
Yauya Stela, 89
Yax Nuun Ayiin, 193, 197
Yaxchilán, 156, 166, 168, 195
Yaxhá, 196
Yaxuna project, 190
Yik'in Chan K'awiil, 204
Yoffee, Norman, 143
Yucatán, 146, 148, 156, 167, 169, 171, 173, 190, 220, 223
Yuknoom Ch'een the Great, 187, 203
Yura-yako, 86, 88

Zapotec religion, 214
Zender, Marc, 195
Zuyuan ideology, 216